The AMBIVALENCE *of* ABORTION

The AMBIVALENCE *of* ABORTION

Linda Bird Francke

Random House New York

For Andrew, Caitlin, and Tapp

Grateful acknowledgment is made to the following for permission to reprint previously published material:
The New York Times: "There Just Wasn't Room in Our Lives Now for Another Baby" by Jane Doe, of May 14, 1976. (Op-Ed). Copyright © 1976 by the New York Times Company.

Library of Congress Cataloging in Publication Data
Francke, Linda Bird.
   The ambivalence of abortion.
    1. Abortion—United States—Case studies. 2. Abortion—Psychological aspects—Case studies. I. Title.
HQ767.5.U5F7   301   77–90257
ISBN 0–394–41080–7

Manufactured in the United States of America
9 8 7 6 5 4 3 2
First Edition

We recognize the right of the individual, married or single, to be free from unwarranted governmental intrusion into matters so fundamentally affecting a person as the decision whether to bear or beget a child. That right necessarily includes the right of a woman to decide whether or not to terminate her pregnancy.

—United States Supreme Court,
January 22, 1973

There is probably no psychologically painless way to cope with an unwanted pregnancy whether it is voluntarily interrupted or carried to term . . .

—National Academy of Sciences,
1975

Acknowledgments

There were many people who helped me in the concept, research and writing of this book, and I appreciate this opportunity to thank them publicly. There is Kelsey Maréchal, who presented the idea to Anne Freedgood, my editor, who bought it and supported me throughout the writing; Elaine Ewing, Cathy FitzSimmons and Ann Freeberg, who typed the manuscript flawlessly against deadline, in spite of the spring thunderstorms that interrupted the electrical power and their typewriters; Robin Elliott at Planned Parenthood, who checked and rechecked facts for the book, and my good friend Jane O'Reilly, who read the manuscript and offered valuable criticism; Ed Kosner and Lynn Young, my editors at *Newsweek,* who granted me a leave of absence and therefore the time to spend on the book, and Cheryl Hedges, who coped with my children and the household to make that time realistic. A special thanks should go to my agent Lynn Nesbit, who believed in the book from the beginning, Albert Francke, who gave me the space to work it out, and to the men and women on the clinic staffs who gave freely of their time and thought. But lastly, and most importantly, credit must be totally given to the people who shared their abortion experiences and indeed, their lives, with me, and now with you.

—Sagaponack, New York
July 1977

Contents

The AMBIVALENCE *of* ABORTION

Introduction

"Jane Doe," thirty-eight, had an abortion in New York City in 1973. The mother of three children, then three, five, and eleven, Jane had just started a full-time job in publishing. She and her husband, an investment banker, decided together that another baby would add an almost unbearable strain to their lives, which were already overfull. What Jane had not anticipated was the guilt and sadness that followed the abortion. She wrote about the experience shortly thereafter and filed the story away. Three years later she reread it and decided it might be helpful to other women who experience the ambivalence of abortion. The *New York Times* ran it on their Op-Ed page in May 1976. This is what she wrote:

We were sitting in a bar on Lexington Avenue when I told my husband I was pregnant. It is not a memory I like to dwell on. Instead of the champagne and hope which had heralded the impending births of the first, second and third child, the news of this one was greeted with shocked silence and Scotch. "Jesus," my husband kept saying to himself, stirring the ice cubes around and around. "Oh, Jesus."

Oh, how we tried to rationalize it that night as the starting time for the movie came and went. My husband talked about his plans for a career change in the next year, to stem the staleness that fourteen years with the same investment-banking firm had brought him. A new baby would preclude that option.

The timing wasn't right for me either. Having juggled pregnancies and child care with what freelance jobs I could fit in between feedings, I had just taken on a full-time job. A new baby would put me right back in the nursery just when our youngest child was finally school age. It was time for *us,* we tried to rationalize. There just wasn't room in our lives now for another baby. We both agreed. And agreed. And agreed.

How very considerate they are at the Women's Services, known formally as the Center for Reproductive and Sexual Health. Yes, indeed, I could have an abortion that very Saturday morning and be out in time to drive to the country that afternoon. Bring a first morning urine specimen, a sanitary belt and napkins, a money order or $125 cash—and a friend.

My friend turned out to be my husband, standing awkwardly and ill at ease as men always do in places that are exclusively for women, as I checked in at nine A.M. Other men hovered around just as anxiously, knowing they had to be there, wishing they weren't. No one spoke to each other. When I would be cycled out of there four hours later, the same men would be slumped in their same seats, locked downcast in their cells of embarrassment.

The Saturday morning women's group was more dispirited than the men in the waiting room. There were around fifteen of us, a mixture of races, ages and backgrounds. Three didn't speak English at all and a fourth, a pregnant Puerto Rican girl around eighteen, translated for them.

There were six black women and a hodge-podge of whites, among them a T-shirted teenager who kept leaving the room to throw up and a puzzled middle-aged woman from Queens with three grown children.

"What form of birth control were you using?" the volunteer asked each one of us. The answer was inevitably "none." She then went on to describe the various forms of birth control available at the clinic, and offered them to each of us.

The youngest Puerto Rican girl was asked through the interpreter which she'd like to use: the loop, diaphragm, or pill. She shook her head "no" three times. "You don't want to come back here again, do you?" the volunteer pressed. The girl's head was so

4

low her chin rested on her breastbone. "*Sí,*" she whispered.

We had been there two hours by that time, filling out endless forms, giving blood and urine, receiving lectures. But unlike any other group of women I've been in, we didn't talk. Our common denominator, the one which usually floods across language and economic barriers into familiarity, today was one of shame. We were losing life that day, not giving it.

The group kept getting cut back to smaller, more workable units, and finally I was put in a small waiting room with just two other women. We changed into paper bathrobes and paper slippers, and we rustled whenever we moved. One of the women in my room was shivering and an aide brought her a blanket.

"What's the matter?" the aide asked her. "I'm scared," the woman said. "How much will it hurt?" The aide smiled. "Oh, nothing worse than a couple of bad cramps," she said. "This afternoon you'll be dancing a jig."

I began to panic. Suddenly the rhetoric, the abortion marches I'd walked in, the telegrams sent to Albany to counteract the Friends of the Fetus, the Zero Population Growth buttons I'd worn, peeled away, and I was all alone with my microscopic baby. There were just the two of us there, and soon, because it was more convenient for me and my husband, there would be one again.

How could it be that I, who am so neurotic about life that I step over bugs rather than on them, who spend hours planting flowers and vegetables in the spring even though we rent out the house and never see them, who make sure the children are vaccinated and inoculated and filled with vitamin C, could so arbitrarily decide that this life shouldn't be?

"It's not a life," my husband had argued, more to convince himself than me. "It's a bunch of cells smaller than my fingernail."

But any woman who has had children knows that certain feeling in her taut, swollen breasts, and the slight but constant ache in her uterus that signals the arrival of a life. Though I would march myself into blisters for a woman's right to exercise the option of motherhood, I discovered there in the waiting room that I was not the modern woman I thought I was.

When my name was called, my body felt so heavy the nurse had

5

to help me into the examining room. I waited for my husband to burst through the door and yell "stop," but of course he didn't. I concentrated on three black spots in the acoustic ceiling until they grew in size to the shape of saucers, while the doctor swabbed my insides with antiseptic.

"You're going to feel a burning sensation now," he said, injecting Novocaine into the neck of the womb. The pain was swift and severe, and I twisted to get away from him. He was hurting my baby, I reasoned, and the black saucers quivered in the air. "Stop," I cried. "Please stop." He shook his head, busy with his equipment. "It's too late to stop now," he said. "It'll just take a few more seconds."

What good sports we women are. And how obedient. Physically the pain passed even before the hum of the machine signaled that the vacuuming of my uterus was completed, my baby sucked up like ashes after a cocktail party. Ten minutes start to finish. And I was back on the arm of the nurse.

There were twelve beds in the recovery room. Each one had a gaily flowered draw sheet and a soft green or blue thermal blanket. It was all very feminine. Lying on these beds for an hour or more were the shocked victims of their sex, their full wombs now stripped clean, their futures less encumbered.

It was very quiet in that room. The only voice was that of the nurse, locating the new women who had just come in so she could monitor their blood pressure, and checking out the recovered women who were free to leave.

Juice was being passed about, and I found myself sipping a Dixie cup of Hawaiian Punch. An older woman with tightly curled bleached hair was just getting up from the next bed, "That was no goddamn snap," she said, resting before putting on her miniskirt and high white boots. Other women came and went, some walking out as dazed as they had entered, others with a bounce that signaled they were going right back to Bloomingdale's.

Finally then, it was time for me to leave. I checked out, making an appointment to return in two weeks for an IUD insertion. My husband was slumped in the waiting room, clutch-

6

ing a single yellow rose wrapped in a wet paper towel and stuffed into a baggie.

We didn't talk the whole way home, but just held hands very tightly. At home there were more yellow roses and a tray in bed for me and the children's curiosity to divert.

It had certainly been a successful operation. I didn't bleed at all for two days just as they had predicted, and then I bled only moderately for another four days. Within a week my breasts had subsided and the tenderness vanished, and my body felt mine again instead of the eggshell it becomes when it's protecting someone else.

My husband and I are back to planning our summer vacation and his career switch.

And it certainly does make more sense not to be having a baby right now—we say that to each other all the time. But I have this ghost now. A very little ghost that only appears when I'm seeing something beautiful, like the full moon on the ocean last weekend. And the baby waves at me. And I wave at the baby. "Of course, we have room," I cry to the ghost. "Of course, we do."

I am "Jane Doe." Using a pseudonym was not the act of cowardice some have said it was, but rather an act of sympathy for the feelings of my family. My daughters were too young then to understand what an abortion was, and my twelve-year-old son (my husband's stepson) reacted angrily when I even broached the subject of abortion to him. Andrew was deeply moralistic, as many children are at that age, and still young enough to feel threatened by the actions of adults; his replies to my "suppose I had an abortion" queries were devastating. "I think abortion is okay if the boy and girl aren't married, and they just made a mistake," he said. "But if you had an abortion, that would be different. You're married, and there is no reason for you not to have another baby. How could you just kill something—no matter how little it is—that's going to grow and have legs and wiggle its fingers?

"I would be furious with you if you had an abortion. I'd lose all respect for you for being so selfish. I'd make you suffer and remind

7

you of it all the time. I would think of ways to be mean. Maybe I'd give you the silent treatment or something.

"If God had meant women to have abortions, He would have put buttons on their stomachs."

I decided to wait until he was older before we discussed it again.

There were other considerations as well. My husband and I had chosen not to tell our parents about the abortion. My mother was very ill at the time and not up to a barrage of phone calls from her friends about "what Linda had written in the newspaper." And there were my parents-in-law, who had always hoped for a male grand-child to carry on the family name. So I avoided the confessional and simply wrote what I thought would be a helpful piece for other women who might have shared my experience.

The result was almost great enough to be recorded on a seismo-graph. Interpreting the piece as anti-abortion grist, the Right-to-Lifers reproduced it by the thousands and sent it to everyone on their mailing lists. In one Catholic mailing, two sentences were deleted from the article: one that said I was planning to return to the clinic for an IUD insertion, and the other the quote from a middle-aged woman, "That was no goddamn snap." Papers around the country and in Canada ran it, culminating in its appearance in the Canadian edition of the *Reader's Digest,* whose staff took it upon their editorial selves to delete the last paragraph about the "little ghost" because they considered it "mawkish." They also changed the title from "There Just Wasn't Room in Our Lives for Another Baby" to "A Successful Operation" in the hopes that it would change their maga-zine's pro-abortion image.

Hundreds of letters poured into the *New York Times,* some from Right-to-Lifers, who predictably called me a "murderer," and others from pro-choice zealots who had decided the article was a "plant" and might even have been written by a man. Women wrote about their own abortions, some of which had been positive experiences and some disastrous. One woman even wrote that she wished her own mother had had an abortion instead of subjecting her to a childhood that was "brutal and crushing." Many of the respondents criticized me, quite rightly, for not using birth control in the first

8

place. I was stunned, and so was the *New York Times.* A few weeks later they ran a sampling of the letters and my reply, which follows:

The varied reactions to my abortion article do not surprise me at all. They are all right. And they are all wrong. There is no issue so fundamental as the giving of life, or the cessation of it. These decisions are the most personal one can ever make and each person facing them reacts in her own way. It is not black-and-white as the laws governing abortion are forced to be. Rather it is the gray area whose core touches our definition of ourselves that produces "little ghosts" in some, and a sense of relief in others.

I admire the woman who chose not to bear her fourth child because she and her husband could not afford to give that child the future they felt necessary. I admire the women who were outraged that I had failed to use any form of contraception. And I ache for the woman whose mother had given birth to her even though she was not wanted, and thus spent an empty, lonely childhood. It takes courage to take the life of someone else in your own hands, and even more courage to assume responsibility for your own.

I had my abortion over two years ago. And I wrote about it shortly thereafter. It was only recently, however, that I decided to publish it. I felt it was important to share how one person's abortion had affected her, rather than just sit by while the pro and con groups haggled over legislation.

The effect has indeed been profound. Though my husband was very supportive of me, and I, I think, of him, our relationship slowly faltered. As our children are girls, my husband anguished at the possibility that I had been carrying a son. Just a case of male macho, many would argue. But still, that's the way he feels, and it is important. I hope we can get back on a loving track again.

Needless to say, I have an IUD now, instead of the diaphragm that is too easily forgotten. I do not begrudge my husband his lack of contraception. Condoms are awkward. Neither do I feel he should have a vasectomy. It is profoundly difficult for him to face the possibility that he might never have that son. Nor do I regret

9

having the abortion. I am just as much an avid supporter of children by choice as I ever was.

My only regret is the sheer irresponsibility on my part to become pregnant in the first place. I pray to God that it will never happen again. But if it does, I will be equally thankful that the law provides women the dignity to choose whether to bring a new life into the world or not.

I had obviously and unintentionally touched a national nerve. With abortion becoming an everyday occurrence since the Supreme Court ruling in 1973, which overturned the right of individual states to intervene in a woman's decision to abort in the first trimester (twelve weeks) of pregnancy and to intervene in the second trimester (twenty-four weeks) only to ensure medical practices "reasonably related to maternal health," American women of all ages, races, and backgrounds were facing the same sort of dilemma I had. So I set out to discover not only how some of these women felt about their own decisions to terminate their pregnancies, but also how their husbands or boyfriends and their families felt about it. More importantly, I wanted to know how their abortions had affected their lives after the fact. I was not after the more bizarre abortion patients or women who were undergoing therapeutic abortions for medical reasons, but rather "everyday" women who for reasons known only to them had chosen not to continue their pregnancies.

My research took me to Harlem Hospital and to various Planned Parenthood clinics in New York, to Preterm and Planned Parenthood in Cleveland and Cincinnati, to the Atlanta Center for Reproductive Health and Grady Hospital in Atlanta, to the Feminist Women's Health Center in Los Angeles, to Planned Parenthood in San Francisco, and to the Special Care Center in Oakland, California. I interviewed single women, married women, teenagers, couples, doctors, clinic staffs, the men in the waiting rooms, and the parents. I talked to some women before their abortions, some just afterwards, some a few years afterwards, others fifty years after the fact. Everywhere I went—to dinner parties, to business meetings, during rides in taxis and airplanes—I would bring up the subject of abortion, and inevitably, more interviews would follow. While discussing the book with older women, contemporaries of my parents, I faced a spate of abortion stories, until it seemed as though every woman I met had had at least one.

What follows are some of those stories. Again, as in the story of my own abortion, I hope that women who are suffering from guilt will feel comforted that others have suffered like them, and that women who feel guilty because they *don't* feel guilty will also find comfort in the stories of others who have no regrets. I hope that teenagers will learn how arbitrarily many of their peers deal with their sex lives, counting on abortion rather than birth control, and that couples will learn what irreversible stresses abortion can put on their relationships, unless these stresses are dealt with promptly. Men in particular should know that after an abortion not only may a woman feel anger and hostility toward them, but that they may suffer from the same emotions to such an extent that they become temporarily impotent. And everyone should know that, in spite of the rhetoric from the right, claiming that women who abort are murderers, and from the left, claiming that abortion is an instant panacea for an unwanted pregnancy, the abortion experience is actually a period of great stress for every person involved. There is indecision; there is pain. There is regret, and there is relief. And all persons entering or leaving the abortion experience without recognizing the probability of these emotions are simply fooling themselves.

The strains and pressures on abortion-providers, and indeed the whole state of abortion in America today, are also important issues to consider. So much has happened in the short time since abortion was legalized that only now is there an opportunity to draw breath and begin to evaluate what the 1973 Supreme Court decision has wrought, and what repercussions the 1977 Supreme Court decision upholding states' rights to withhold abortion funding for the poor will have. Abortion is not new by any means. But confronting the fact of it without furtiveness and danger is. The quantum leap from women's age-old need and desire to control their reproductive lives to their sanctioned ability finally to do so has raised questions of ethics and morality that have yet to be answered. Perhaps they never will be.

1

Abortion: Then and Now

Women have been seeking ways to control their pregnancies since the correlation between intercourse and childbearing was made. Over 5,000 years ago in China, women drank quicksilver fired in oil or swallowed fourteen live tadpoles three days after they had missed a menstrual period in the hope of bringing it on. Egyptian women in 1500 B.C. used various techniques for both contraception and abortion: an inserted plug made of crocodile dung and paste, a douche brewed from honey and salt. In more modern times, Russian women attempted to abort themselves by squatting over pots of boiling onions, while members of certain Indian tribes climbed up and down coconut palms, striking their stomachs against the trunks.

To this very day women have continued to try their own internal home remedies for aborting, many just slightly less bizarre than the ancient "paste of mashed ants, foam from camel's mouths and tail hairs of the blacktail deer dissolved in bear fat" recorded in Linda Gordon's book *Woman's Body, Woman's Right: A Social History of Birth Control in America.* Women have made brews of turpentine, castor oil, quinine water, and even water in which a rusty nail has been soaked. Such hot herbs as horseradish, ginger, and mustard are still wrongly thought of as effective abortifacients, and women sometimes poison themselves with ammonia and laundry bluing in their desperate attempts to rid themselves of an unwanted fetus. These deadly potions have sometimes worked—by injuring the woman's body so severely that it spontaneously rejected the fetus.

The body often became too injured to survive at all. Self-induced abortions in which panicked women douched themselves with lye or inserted knitting needles, coat hangers, or chicken bones into their uteruses to try and dislodge the fetus resulted all too often in perforation, leaving the women to die of internal hemorrhaging or infection. As the blood vessels in the uterus and cervix dilate greatly during pregnancy, any scraping or probing easily leads to bleeding and possible infection. But prior to the legalization of abortion many women who were admitted to hospitals with just such an abortion-induced infection refused to admit the cause of it. "I remember a teacher from Brooklyn College who came into the hospital. I could smell that she'd had a septic abortion," recalls Joyce Craigg, a surgical nurse who is now director of Planned Parenthood's Borough Hall clinic in Brooklyn, New York, "but they insisted on doing a spinal tap and believing the woman. When I came back on duty the next day, she was dead."

Such barbaric attitudes toward abortion did not always exist. Indeed, it is only within the past hundred years that abortion was decreed illegal in the United States and deemed a mortal sin by the Roman Catholic church. Prior to that time, abortion under certain circumstances was accepted and condoned by both church and state. In terms of canon law, for centuries the Catholic church accepted abortion in a woman until the "quickening" of the fetus—that time when the woman first feels it moving in her womb. It was then, the church reasoned, that the "animate soul" entered the fetus, changing it from an "inanimate soul" to a person. Though the quickening usually occurs between the sixteenth and eighteenth weeks of gestation, the Catholic church moved the date up to forty days. The Catholic version of the time of quickening dated from ancient Greek and Roman times when Aristotle, in an extraordinary act of sexism, decided that the male quickened at forty days, while the female took over twice as long, not acquiring a soul for eighty days. Hippocrates, at least, was less discriminating. After studying miscarried fetuses to determine when male genitalia were first visible, Hippocrates settled upon thirty days for males, forty-two for females. How a woman could determine which sex she was carrying was not recorded, and the church adopted the compromise date of forty days.

13

As medical knowledge increased, however, the church became increasingly uncomfortable with its arbitrary stance on abortion. The living properties of sperm in the male were discovered by a Dutch microscopist in the seventeenth century, and in 1827 the existence of eggs in the female was also medically documented. It was not until 1875, however, that the joint action of sperm and egg was medically proven to be the cause for conception, but the handwriting was already on the human-reproduction wall, and six years before it became downright embarrassing to pinpoint just when body and soul began, Pope Pius IX banned abortion altogether. From then on, the canon law, which lists the reasons for excommunication, was changed, and the phrase "ensouled fetus" was deleted. From 1869 on, the Catholic church deemed abortion not just a sin but, indeed, homicide.

There were also social reasons that made abortion unacceptable to the church. Recent wars in western European countries had depleted the numbers of Catholics, and many in the hierarchy were concerned about this. At the same time, abortion was receiving high acceptance as the only effective form of reproduction regulation and was being practiced with increasing frequency throughout Europe and America. The movement was capped off by a highly popular book by the Marquis de Sade published in 1795, which not only attacked the restrictions the church put on abortion, but actually extolled the values of abortion. According to John T. Noonan, Jr., a religious historian and author of *The Morality of Abortion: Legal and Historical Perspectives,* the de Sade treatise was more than the Pope could bear and contributed greatly to his decision that the church could no longer tolerate abortion at any gestational age. In the 1869 law, however, the biological mother of the fetus was not subject to excommunication; she was believed to be the innocent party until 1917, when the word "mother" was included among those sinners who participated in any abortion. That canon law still stands today.

At the same time that the Catholic church was anguishing about abortion in Rome, abortion was being questioned in this country by the medical establishment, legislators, and industrialists. Until the nineteenth century, American law had gone along with English common law, under which abortion was legal unless the woman died.

14

Only then had a crime been committed, and it was not the woman who had committed it, but the abortionist, who was charged with a felony. Infanticide was still common in nineteenth-century America, and women convicted of it—most of whom were poor and single— were hanged. Abortion, on the other hand, while painful and risky, carried no such charges and was widely sought after. Its very popularity was its undoing.

In a ground swell of Puritanism, abortion began to be decried from the nation's pulpits, and the words of Martin Luther became grist for the anti-abortionist mill: "If a woman grows weary and at last dies from childbearing, it matters not," the fifteenth-century zealot had written. "Let her only die from bearing, she's in there to do it." The carnage of the Civil War during the 1860's was also a great factor in the increasing resistance to abortion, which was then a primary rather than a back-up method of birth control. More and more states passed legislation banning or severely restricting abortion. This movement was given further impetus by pressure from business and farming communities, whose economic future depended on an expanding population. Women were considered an asset as breeders. Much has been written about the breeding of slaves prior to the Civil War, but it should not be forgotten that white women were expected to breed as well. Farm and factory hands were not that easy to come by.

The medical establishment played its part in the anti-abortion movement as well. With health standards being raised both in the nation and throughout the world because of discoveries in the health-care field, deaths or injuries resulting from abortion became less and less acceptable. There was still high risk in any kind of surgery in the nineteenth century, and many doctors felt the ends did not justify the risk involved in abortion. There was also a move away from midwives to the male-dominated medical profession, and many doctors were far less sympathetic than midwives to the wishes of women who wanted to terminate unwanted pregnancies. Though sympathizers, quacks, and money-hungry doctors continued to perform abortions even after anti-abortion legislation was passed, by the end of the 1870's virtually every state had a law restricting abortion to those women whose lives were endangered by the fact of their pregnancies.

15

At this point, abortion on demand went underground, where it remained until Colorado in 1967, and New York, Alaska, Hawaii, and Washington in 1970, and finally the Supreme Court in 1973, returned the right of controlling reproduction to the women who were actually doing the reproducing. The result has been what some people call the "abortion epidemic."

For every three live births in America today, there is approximately one abortion. The number is approximate because no one is really sure how many abortions are performed. The Center for Disease Control (CDC) in Atlanta, Georgia, whose Abortion Surveillance Branch is the official tabulator of abortions nationwide, reported 875,000 abortions in 1975, as opposed to 1,100,000 reported by the Alan Guttmacher Institute in New York and Washington, D.C. The discrepancy in numbers results from the fact that the CDC receives its abortion data from state health departments, many of whom have not established complete or indeed any reporting systems since the legalization of abortion in 1973. The Alan Guttmacher Institute, on the other hand, seeks out abortion statistics from the actual providers of abortion, and the CDC generally accepts those statistics as more accurate. "Go with the Guttmacher figures," said Willard Cates, Jr., chief of the Abortion Surveillance Branch. "Some states require the reporting of fetal deaths due to abortion. Others don't. We think we're pretty lucky to have 85 percent of them recorded."

Officially and unofficially, then, 1,100,000 abortions are performed annually in the United States.

Worldwide, the numbers swell to between 40,000,000 and 55,-000,000 abortions per year, a startling increase in the last decade. During the past ten years some thirty-three countries have liberalized their abortion laws, and according to a recent study conducted by the United Nations, twelve nations now permit abortion on demand during the first three months of pregnancy. "Few social changes have ever swept the world so rapidly," the authors of the study concluded. These changes are not likely to be reversed, either. No democratic nation that has made abortion more available, the study points out, has ever retreated to more restrictive conditions. Indeed, only four countries—Romania, Bulgaria, Czechoslovakia

16

and Hungary—have adopted more restrictive legislation regarding abortion. In those Eastern European countries, national concern about low birth rates has prompted the more restrictive legislation.

In countries where birth control is readily available, however, abortion does not have as devastating an effect on birth rates as might be expected. In a report by Christopher Tietze, senior consultant with the Population Council in New York and probably the most respected statistician on abortion in the country, legalized abortion counts for only one-fifth of the spiraling decline in the birth rate in America (1.8 children per family in 1975, as opposed to 3.7 in 1957). Nor does increased use of birth control make up the other four-fifths. It is Tietze's opinion, and that of many others, that 70 percent of the legal abortions now performed in this country have merely replaced the illegal abortions that historically have been readily available in many parts of the country for those who could afford to pay for them.

Abortion is now cheaper (ranging from $120 to $200 for first-trimester abortion, $350 to $800 for second-trimester abortion), safer (fourteen times safer than giving birth, five times safer than a tonsillectomy during the first trimester), and as accessible in many areas as the abortion-clinic listings in the yellow pages. But there is risk in any surgical procedure, and abortion is no exception. Timing is critical; the risk in abortion increases dramatically with every week of pregnancy until, during the sixteenth to twentieth weeks of pregnancy, the risk is greater than the risk for normal maternal delivery (17 maternal deaths per 100,000 abortions, as compared to 14 maternal deaths per 100,000 live vaginal deliveries).

There is also some discomfort both during and after the abortion procedure, the discomfort increasing with the length of the pregnancy. Abortion hurts. It is not unbearable pain, nor anything like the pain of childbirth (except in second-trimester abortions), but everyone suffers somewhat. After the abortion, many women experience cramps, which can be mild or so heavy that they necessitate pain medication. There is also the risk of hemorrhage or infection. Post-abortion women are instructed to monitor themselves carefully to make sure their menstrual bleeding does not exceed twice that of a normal period, that their temperatures do not rise above 100.5, and that any cramping does not become severe or go on and on. Women

17

are advised not to take tub baths or to have intercourse for at least two weeks after the procedure and to be sure to return to the clinics for a post-abortion checkup two weeks afterward. Yet many women either balk at the aftercare or are astonished there is any discomfort at all. "They assume abortion is as easy as one, two, three," says P. J. Viles, director of nursing at the Atlanta Center for Reproductive Health, where most abortions are performed under a general anesthesia. "Even though they've been told that there will be some discomfort, they wake up from the anesthetic crying because of cramping. They can't believe it's going to hurt."

Emotionally there is almost always a feeling of relief after an abortion, followed by a period of depression aptly named the "post-abortion blues." No one really knows what causes it; it may be as simple as the hormonal change the female body undergoes as it passes from being pregnant to not being pregnant, very much like the postpartum blues. The depression may be more severe in women who have been ambivalent about making the decision to abort, a situation that can be greatly alleviated by counseling both before and after the abortion. But for most women, any depression or regret fades somewhere between two weeks to six months after the procedure. The important thing to bear in mind is that having an abortion is not as simple as some of its advocates have led women to believe. It is a shock to the system, the womb in particular. The Greek word for the uterus is *hystera,* which is also the word "hysteria" is derived from. A woman's womb is her emotional core, and during an abortion, it is tampered with.

For all the consciousness-raising that modern women have been through and the greater interest women are taking in their own health care, the ignorance surrounding the actual mechanics of the abortion procedure is surprising. Many who just want to "get it over with" and "have it done" have little or no knowledge of what "it" is. Similarly, parents and men accompanying women to their abortion appointments nervously prowl the waiting rooms of the clinics and hospitals, having no idea what is being "done." Actually, what is being done, especially during the first trimester, is very simple. These are the most usual methods of abortion:

Menstrual regulation or menses extraction. Performed very early

18

on in pregnancy, often before a pregnancy can even be confirmed, this procedure was developed by two women from the Feminist Women's Health Center in Los Angeles, not necessarily to perform abortions but to eliminate the nuisance of monthly bleeding and cramps. In this procedure, usually performed between five and seventeen days after a missed period, one end of a small, flexible tube is inserted into the uterus; the other end is attached to a suction pump. The lining of the uterus (the endometrium) is then gently sucked out, and if the woman happens to be pregnant, the tiny bit of fetal tissue is presumably sucked out with it.

The problem with this method is that the fetus is so small at this point that lab technicians cannot be certain that it has been removed, and there is the risk that the woman will still be pregnant. At one clinic in Georgia, the method has been discontinued altogether, as the doctors do not feel the risk of infection is warranted when pregnancy is merely suspected but not confirmed. Even when the doctors did perform menses extractions, the clinic suggested that the women return within two weeks for another pregnancy test to make sure the abortion had occurred. This procedure is inexpensive, ranging in cost from $60 to $90.

Vacuum aspiration. The most common form of abortion procedure, vacuum aspiration or suction abortion is performed between six and twelve weeks of pregnancy—that is, during the first trimester. A local anesthetic, usually a shot of Novocaine or a similar numbing drug, is injected into the cervix. The doctor then dilates the cervical canal by inserting larger and larger metal rods into it until the last rod, about the size of a finger, has opened the canal enough for the doctor to insert plastic tubing about one-third of an inch wide into the uterus. The dilation process can be painful for women who are very nervous or those who have not had children, but it is usually no more painful than menstrual-like cramps. The doctor then turns on the suction pump, and the vacuum pressure breaks up the fetal tissue and sucks it through the tube in about twenty to forty seconds. To make sure all the fetus and the placenta have been removed, the doctor usually then gently scrapes the uterine wall with a small spoonlike instrument called a curette. The whole process takes about ten minutes and costs between $120 and $200.

19

For younger teenagers and very apprehensive women, a general anesthetic is used. This makes it easier for the doctor because the patient doesn't squirm or move suddenly, and it is of course painless for the woman. There is always risk in the administration of a general anesthetic, however, and the procedure takes much longer to recover from. Most women experience dizziness and nausea coming out of the anesthetic, and there is still the probability of cramping after the procedure.

Dilation and curettage (D and C). This method is often employed between the twelfth and sixteenth weeks of pregnancy, an interim period that is thought by some to be too late for suction and too early for later methods. Performed during the period of illegal abortions without any anesthetic, D and C's are now done only with general anesthetic and almost always in a hospital. As in the vacuum aspiration abortion, the doctor dilates the cervical canal, then scrapes the inside of the uterus with a spoon-shaped curette. The patient is required to spend the night at least in the hospital, so the procedure is more expensive, from $285 up.

Hypertonic saline abortion. The most commonly used second-trimester abortion method, salines are performed on women who are sixteen to twenty-three weeks pregnant. It is a very unpleasant experience for both the woman and the medical staff attending her, and luckily, with the growing accessibility of first-trimester clinics and patient knowledge of abortion, the numbers of second-trimester abortions have been steadily decreasing. The theory behind saline abortions is that when a fetus dies *in utero,* the uterus will automatically contract and force the fetus out. The fetus can be killed by injecting a concentrated salt solution into the uterus, and spontaneous abortion takes place.

The doctor first numbs a small area around two inches below the navel, then inserts a long needle into the amniotic sac to withdraw about two fluid ounces of the amniotic fluid before injecting 200 milligrams of the saline solution into the amniotic sac. Labor usually begins from six to forty-eight hours later. The mean time for the abortion to occur is 29.2 hours, and as the woman often retains the afterbirth, the placenta has to be removed by D and C. Almost always performed in hospitals, salines are made more harrowing

20

because the patients undergoing them are often housed on the same floor as women giving normal birth and attended by nursing staffs who are apt to be less understanding than abortion-clinic personnel. The cost is high, from $350 up.

Intraamniotic prostaglandin abortion. Another second-trimester abortion method, this involves injection of prostaglandin chemicals instead of saline solution into the uterus, causing the body to go into labor and expel the fetus. Prostaglandins, which are present in the body anyway, increase normally at the end of a full-term pregnancy and cause the contractions that precede a normal birth. Considered safer than saline abortion in the early seventies, this procedure proved to be otherwise, causing more of such complications as fever, endometritis, hemorrhage, and incomplete abortion than the saline. Another complication was equally disturbing. Because prostaglandins do not kill the fetus as saline does, more prostaglandin fetuses were born alive, though very few were developed enough to live for more than a few hours. The cost is $350 up.

Dilation and evacuation (D and E). This is an increasingly popular abortion method for second-trimester patients. Decreed by the Center for Disease Control as the safest of the three late-pregnancy abortion techniques, D and E's are also being heralded by women's groups as being far less traumatic to the patient than the birth process caused by both saline and prostaglandin infusions.

D and E's are a combination of medical procedures. First the cervical canal is dilated, as with early abortions. Then, using larger tubing to account for the increased size of the fetus, the contents of the uterus are sucked out, and forceps are used if necessary. Afterwards the uterine wall is scraped to make sure all the tissue has been removed. Since the uterine walls become increasingly spongy and thin as pregnancy advances, many doctors are reluctant to use the suction method in advanced pregnancies. But according to the CDC, despite the risk of cervical injury and uterine perforation, a D and E performed between the thirteenth and twentieth weeks of pregnancy has a risk factor 2.6 times lower than the saline procedure. And the patient endures far less trauma.

Hysterotomy and hysterectomy. In complicated pregnancies and in cases where saline infusion has not resulted in abortion, there are two types of major surgery to fall back on. A hysterotomy, or mini-Caesarean, is performed by making one incision in the abdominal wall just above the pubic bone and another in the uterine wall itself. The fetus and the placenta are then removed. Because this operation leaves a scar on the uterus, the probability of normal delivery for subsequent births is greatly reduced, and Caesarean sections will probably be required. In a hysterectomy, the entire uterus is removed, obviously making it impossible for the woman ever to conceive or bear another child. A hysterectomy is not considered an abortion process but is sometimes performed as a result of a botched abortion in which the uterine wall has been badly damaged or intense and uncontrollable infection has set in. The cost is $1,000 or more.

There are two other procedures a woman facing abortion may have to go through, though they are not in themselves abortions. With medical technology taking giant steps toward understanding and controlling more and more of the reproductive process, these techniques are used as much for women wanting to carry a baby to term as they are for women who have chosen to abort, especially in the second trimester.

Sonogram. In late pregnancies, the position and size of the fetus in the uterus used to be determined by X-ray, but doctors have been increasingly cautious about using X-rays because of the dangers of radiation. In late abortions, the patient was X-rayed to determine the size of the fetus so as to make as certain as possible that the fetus was under 500 grams, the lowest possible weight to sustain life after birth.

Now the size, weight, and position of the fetus and its gestational age can be more safely and accurately determined by performing a sonogram. Sound waves are "bounced" off the fetus and make a picture easily read by technicians; thus the fetus can be clearly "seen" and evaluated. In abortions that border on the twenty-four-week cutoff (though few doctors perform abortions after the twentieth week), sonograms are regularly administered to make sure the fetus is still too undeveloped to survive on its own.

Amniocentesis. It was not too long ago that one of the only legal reasons for abortion was if the mother had German measles during the first three months of pregnancy, which often resulted in the baby being born blind and deformed. Now there is a prenatal test that can pinpoint any of seventy disorders that may be affecting the development of the fetus. Between the fourteenth and sixteenth weeks of pregnancy, fluid is withdrawn from the amniotic sac surrounding the fetus; this fluid contains cells sloughed off its body. The cells are then grown in cultures to determine what, if any, abnormalities the fetus has. The problem is that the cultures take another two to four weeks to diagnose, and if any abnormalities are found, the woman is faced with a second-trimester abortion.

For pregnant women over thirty, many doctors now consider amniocentesis a must. The probability of Down's syndrome (mongolism) increases dramatically with age, whether there is a history of the disorder in the family or not. When a woman is between thirty and thirty-four, her chances of bearing a mongoloid child are 1 in 750. When she is between thirty-five and thirty-nine, the chances jump to 1 in 300, and for women over age forty, the risk increases to 1 in 40. In contrast, the odds are only 1 in 1,500 for women under thirty years old. Amniocentesis takes the agonizing guesswork out of pregnancies occurring late in life; it is also invaluable in the case of couples in which either spouse has a hereditary defect in his or her family history. The abortion decision is no less agonizing, however, and can cause severe feelings of guilt, especially in the case of women who have had previous abortions and consider the damaged fetus to be some kind of punishment.

Amniocentesis has also opened a new area of ethics in abortion. Not only are metabolic and developmental disorders pinpointed, but so also is the sex of the fetus. In a most disturbing trend, some women are having the test done solely to determine the sex of the fetus, and are opting to abort if it is a girl. It is a macabre twist of irony that although it was women who spearheaded the movement to legalize abortion, the sex that some are choosing to abort is female.

And it is getting easier to obtain and diagnose fetal cells. A Chinese scientific team has developed a technique for taking a cervical smear as early as the seventh week of pregnancy, and the results of the tests they do are 80 to 90 percent accurate. In another test under development, the fetus's white blood cells are located in the mother's bloodstream and isolated for testing. Both these procedures are ex-

23

pected to be available in the United States during the next few years, which will undoubtedly increase the numbers of therapeutic abortions for genetic disorders—and for the sex of your choice.

The legalization of abortion has brought with it the development of an abortion industry that is at the same time both profitable to its members and supportive and safe for the women seeking its services. Far from the dingy back-alley abortion mills of not so long ago, over 370 free-standing (nonhospital) first-trimester abortion clinics have sprung up around the country. Airy, painted in bright colors, and dotted with green plants, these clinics in 1975 performed over 60 percent of all the abortions in the United States, and the numbers of clinics continue to climb. The atmosphere in most of these clinics is warm and friendly, and their staff members are politically and personally sympathetic to abortion. Abortion patients are counseled before the procedure about their decision to have an abortion and what methods of contraception will best suit them to avoid further unwanted pregnancies. The abortion technique is explained, aftercare instructions are given, and the abortion itself is performed, all in a three-to-five-hour time period. The women are asked to return to the clinic two weeks after the procedure for a check-up and additional contraceptive counseling.

Because of the burgeoning number of clinics, the competition between them is keen. The *Atlanta Constitution,* a daily paper in Atlanta, Georgia, for example, carries advertisements for no fewer than eight different clinics, listing all the extras the clinics throw in to land the business of the woman in need. "Make no mistake about it. This is a highly competitive business," says Helen Ford, director of the Atlanta Center for Reproductive Health. "We were the first to offer free pregnancy tests in Atlanta. Now they all do. Then we started doing vasectomies, and the rest followed. Now we're the first with the new pregnancy test which is reliable ten days after conception. You watch. They'll all pick it up."

Like the Atlanta Center for Reproductive Health, most clinics offer a smorgasbord of reproductive services. At Planned Parenthood's San Francisco Guttmacher Clinic, contraception classes include breast and pelvic exams, a Pap test for cervical cancer, and prescriptions for contraceptives. Other offerings include the "Teen Scene," during which teenagers sit on floor pillows, drink Cokes, and "rap" about birth control; pregnancy testing and counseling for infertility, sterilization, and sexuality; vasectomy counseling and procedure at a nearby center; suction abortion for those up to nine weeks pregnant; and for those who choose to continue their pregnancies, a course in the Lamaze method of natural childbirth.

At the Feminist Women's Health Center in Los Angeles, and its affiliates in Detroit, Michigan; Tallahassee, Florida; Atlanta, Georgia; Cambridge, Massachusetts; and Santa Ana, San Diego, and Chico in other parts of California, the services go beyond first-trimester abortion to self-help clinics where women learn to give themselves gynecological examinations with the help of speculums to open their own cervical canals and well-placed mirrors for a good view. For second-trimester abortions, staff members of the Feminist Women's Health Center act as patient advocates and guide their abortion patients through every step of the procedure in the hospital, even to watchdogging the actual abortion itself in the operating room. "We are looking for respect for the woman, basically," says Lynn Heidelberg, one of the feminist patient advocates. "Women can hear what people are saying through the anesthetic, for example. We make the doctors keep the conversation about the abortion rather than last Saturday night's date. We cut into their good time."

The feminists even keep their eyes on the instruments the doctors employ in the operating room, insisting on those that are best for the patient rather than those that make it easiest for the doctor. "We make sure he uses the smallest tube possible so there will be less trauma to the cervix," says Heidelberg. "We also make sure the doctor uses a plastic speculum instead of a weighted metal one, which can pull on the vagina and cervix and affects how the woman feels afterwards." Though some hospitals and almost all clinics have counselors for abortion patients, the Feminist Women's Health Center goes a ten-league step farther.

"Counselors are just to give the appearance of help," says Roberta Massy, another patient advocate in Los Angeles. "But counselors think of themselves as company for the woman rather than as advocates. They don't argue with the doctors or nurses

25

who are dehumanizing the patients. That's what we do."

Other clinics, although not as politically active as the feminist confederation, have personalities of their own. In Cleveland, Ohio, for example, Preterm goes out of its way to make an abortion as natural as possible by letting the patients go through the whole procedure in street clothes rather than in hospital gowns. For added support, each of their thirty-one part-time counselors accompanies a patient through the process on a one-to-one basis, even to the point of holding her hand when she is on the operating table. At the Guttmacher Clinic in San Francisco, women coming in for abortions are urged to bring a friend and/or boyfriend or husband with them for company through the whole procedure, including the abortion itself. "Getting pregnant is a couple act, and the abortion should be a couple procedure," says Linda DuBrow, coordinator of surgical services. "Most couples do come together and go through it together. The man sits at the head of the operating table and holds her hand. She'd rather hold his hand than one of the medical staff's."

Other clinics do not agree with abortion togetherness and the informality of piped-in rock music and jeans. At the Special Care Center in Oakland, California, the clinic resembles a mini-hospital. The abortion patient is wheeled in and out of the operating room on a gurney (a bed-high stretcher) and recuperates after the procedure on a hospital bed in a semi-private room, unlike the communal twenty-daybed recovery room common in other clinics. At the Atlanta Center for Reproductive Health, the clinic also goes out of its way to create as professional an atmosphere as possible. Again, friends or parents are encouraged to bring the patients to the clinic, but they are not allowed beyond the waiting room, and the music is Muzak, not rock. "Kids don't want to think they're in some sort of playground and sit around on the floor on pillows," says Helen Ford, the center's executive director. "They want to see a clean, crisp place like the sort of place their mothers would go to. This atmosphere gives them confidence."

Abortion does vary geographically, not in the procedures themselves but in the regional attitudes toward the whole issue. In Ohio, for example, patients at Preterm in Cleveland wear name tags with just their first name on them in an effort to preserve anonymity. "No one I've ever seen here wants anyone else to find out who they are," says counselor Betty Orr. "There's still a stigma about abortion in the Midwest. It's much harder to come to an abortion decision here." To protect their patients, the clinic fields phone calls from angry husbands, boyfriends, and even parents who demand to know whether their wives, girlfriends, or daughters have come into the clinic. In each case, the clinic says it has no idea whether the woman in question is there or not. To add another layer of protection, many women in the Midwest give fictitious names when making their appointments. "We don't care," says Orr. The desire for anonymity sometimes reaches *Mary Hartman, Mary Hartman* levels. One woman who was involved in a custody suit with her ex-husband came in for an abortion and saw her husband's lawyer's girlfriend in the waiting room. The woman fled in panic.

The atmosphere in the South is no less secretive. No names are used at all at the Atlanta Center for Reproductive Health, for example, and the patients are called by number from the waiting room and are not referred to by name until they are safely in the interior of the clinic. "Abortion is not accepted here," says Helen Ford. "We're still working on it."

Besides lobbying for more second-trimester facilities, which now consist of one doctor in the entire state who works at one hospital and charges a whopping $1,450, the clinic is sometimes forced to fight for the acceptance of abortion on a one-to-one basis. Ford recalls the morning a red-faced father burst into the clinic and demanded to know if his daughter was there, which indeed she was. A counselor asked him to step into a counseling room with her and spent the next hour wagging a finger at him and telling him to stop thinking about himself and to start thinking about his daughter. Sobered by the lecture, the father emerged from the counseling room, and upon confronting his terrified daughter, took her in his arms and hugged her.

"It was a lovely moment," says Ford. "I wish we had more of them."

Abortion and family planning are even more complex in the South, where some blacks consider reproduction control a form of genocide being launched against them by whites. Such charges were

27

leveled against the Atlanta Center for Reproductive Health when it opened five years ago. "The Panthers were saying that the whites were just trying to get rid of black babies," recalls Helen Ford. "We retaliated by advertising on black radio stations, hiring black help at the clinic, and inviting the members of a black TV talk show over to the clinic. You could feel them bristle when they walked in, but after we had talked for a while and I had explained what we were trying to do here, the head of the show invited us on his program. He ended up giving us the whole hour."

Because of the preoccupation with genocide among blacks in the South, black counselors and social workers have far greater credibility in disseminating information. Mellonée Houston Willis, now director of community affairs at the Atlanta center, has become almost a reproductive-health celebrity locally because she has been on so many radio and television talk shows. "What you hear all the time about abortion and birth control is 'This is what the white man says I should think,' " says Willis, a vibrantly attractive black woman. "Then I say, well, it is the white man who also taught us to go to the bathroom inside. Now if you want to be tee-totally black, go back to Africa. But be consistent. Do you use deodorant? Well, leave it behind because in Africa, the muskier you are, the sexier you are. Get it on. You live in Atlanta in 1977. You may think abortion is genocide, but it's not. You must make an individual decision about your own situation. It's you, not them."

The problem is not just one of race, Willis insists, but also one of lack of information and education. Monthly bags of prophylactics, for example, are available free at Grady Hospital in Atlanta, but few of the men who use them realize they can't be worn more than once. Willis points this out all the time to groups she talks to. "You can't assume anything," she says. " 'Assume' makes an ass out of you and me. That's where that verb came from." Though she believes that progress is being made, Willis still endures bouts of frustration that leave her with a literal case of the hives. The problem, she says, is not so much with black women but with black men. "They have been indoctrinated to think of themselves as breeders," she says. "It goes all the way back to slave times when that's what they were used for, and it's going to take longer than our lifetime to change.

And that's not just in the South. That's universal."

In New York, where abortion has been legal since 1970, and in California, where less restrictive laws have been in force since as early as 1967, abortion is far more matter-of-fact. Though abortion is still not quite a subject for dinner-party chatter, virtually no social shame is attached to single or married women who have chosen to abort. Indeed, there is almost a social obligation to have an abortion if the conditions for carrying a baby to term are not perfect. "It's gotten to the point in some metropolitan communities that if you get pregnant, then you have an abortion," says Carol Downer, director of the Feminist Women's Health Center in Los Angeles. "It's that simple. And if you don't have the abortion, then there must be something wrong with you. You must really have some sort of complex. And so most women go ahead and have them."

The lifting of shame and guilt about abortion has had physical as well as emotional effects on abortion patients. The Feminist Women's Health Center in Los Angeles has always had a couple of daybeds available for women who felt faint or nauseated after their abortions and wanted to rest for a while. Now, says Downer, these daybeds are hardly used at all. "Before, the minute the doctor would turn off the machine or the counselor would say, 'It's over,' the woman would at that point begin to tremble and have nausea. Now it's just not something we see. The vast majority of our patients get right up and go about their business within an hour at the most. They are impatient to leave. Women just don't have that overall total emotional body response to the situation the way they used to." Younger patients are apt to be the least disturbed. "They are tired and a little misty mentally," says counselor Norma Eidelman, at Planned Parenthood's Borough Hall clinic in Brooklyn. "But they bounce right back. We make them rest for an hour, but all they want to do is order in pizza or go right out to Burger King."

Such easygoing attitudes about abortion have caused some concern that the way women go about arranging for an abortion is perhaps too cavalier. Women in cities where there are more than one clinic now shop around, picking the clinic whose abortion schedule and fee best suits them, regardless of the reputation of the clinic. Others delay having an abortion because of work schedules or vacation plans, often putting themselves at far more risk physically. That early abortions are safer than later ones is irrefutable, but many women do not consider the fact that there is any risk at all.

The relatively new accessibility of abortion has also given rise to a new set of emotional problems. Prior to the 1973 decision legalizing abortion, women with unwanted pregnancies underwent severe stress trying to locate abortion facilities. Men and women active in the abortion movement helped these women find people who would perform abortions; the emphasis, however, was not on the decision-making process that led these women to the point of abortion in the first place but on the expediting of the abortion itself. Pregnancy counseling then was always supportive and reassuring. "Before, all you could offer to a woman who was really in a state of panic and fear was straightforward emotional support," says Frances Kissling, director of the National Abortion Council. "You were dealing with someone who was in a crisis, and all you had time to deal with was that overt manifestation. The counseling was more of an assurance process."

The accessibility of abortion has changed that picture dramatically. Where once there was almost always third-party intervention in the form of pregnancy counseling—women's groups or even the clergy provided situations in which doubts and fears could at least be aired—it is not uncommon now for a woman to call an abortion clinic directly, set up an appointment, come in for a pregnancy test, go through half an hour of counseling, have her abortion, and go home, all in the same day. This direct abortion dial has put stress on the abortion clinics, which were originally set up not to be forums for the decision-making process but simply to offer the abortion procedure in a surgically safe setting. In a rush to get the abortion over with, women can arrive at the clinics now with doubts about their decision unresolved. "We had one woman who got all the way to the operating room and burst into tears," says Helen Ford in Atlanta. "The doctor told her to get off the table, get dressed, and to come back when she firmly knew what she wanted to do."

The new ambivalence has caught many abortion activists by surprise and has spawned areas of debate and experimentation. "There was a short period after the Supreme Court decision when we all

30

thought there would be less of a need for counseling because we had the feeling that a lot of the counseling we'd done was based on the fact that abortion was illegal," says Frances Kissling of the National Abortion Council. "We thought that by moving from an era of something that had been considered both morally and legally wrong the need for counseling would diminish. But we haven't seen that. We haven't seen an increase in the need, either. What we've seen is the need for differences in our approach to counseling."

The shift in emphasis from helping women in their search for abortion facilities to studying what effect an abortion will have on their lives is changing the whole thrust of counseling. Michael Bracken, a research associate in the Department of Epidemiology at Yale, has been involved in family planning for nine years and has witnessed the shift. "When I first got into the whole area of pregnancy and abortion, clinic personnel were quite rightly into consciousness-raising, helping the political movement to get the laws changed, and trying to convince women that abortion wasn't such a bad thing after all," says Bracken. "I think the public has bought the fact of abortion so well that the clinics have in fact oversold it. Clinic personnel now are reacting the other way, saying, 'Hold on, wait a minute. It's not that easy.' " The point now, Bracken argues, is to sharpen up the decision-making process. "There is a great concern among clinic personnel who see young girls coming in to abort that though their decision is probably the right decision, the process they've gone through to reach it is very sort of shruggy-shoulders, and they're not really learning from the experience. The decision-making has not been a period of growth for them. They've not learned anything from it. This is especially true among repeat abortions."

In most clinics now, counseling is still more reassuring than challenging. The abortion technique is explained, the physical effects of abortion are spelled out, contraception is discussed and agreed-upon methods prescribed, and the patient's attitude toward her abortion is questioned, if not probed. Different counselors use different techniques to find out what a woman is really feeling. In Atlanta, counselor Marlene Rose talks to an average of five patients a day after they've heard the results of their pregnancy tests. She starts out by

31

saying, "I've got the results of your test," then watches their reaction. If the test is positive and the woman instantly says, "How much does the abortion cost?" or, "When can I come in for an appointment?" Rose knows the woman has already reached her decision. If the response is "Oh, shit," or complete silence, Rose interprets it as ambivalence. Many women remain silent. "They've repressed the idea that they might be pregnant," says Rose. "Denial is very common." Another clue to a woman's feelings is her body language, regardless of what she may say. "If they hug themselves, it means they feel insecure and undecided," Rose continues. "If they sit on the edge of their chairs and lean toward me, it means they are looking for support and encouragement." If the woman appears to be at all undecided, Rose says, "You seem to be feeling angry." "That opens the door," says Rose. "Then we can begin to talk."

Other counselors look for different clues. A common phrase many women use in describing their dilemma is "I want an abortion even though I know it's murder." To Martha Mueller, a counselor at a Planned Parenthood Clinic in Brooklyn, that phrase is a definite sign of ambivalence. "I tell them you can only have the abortion for yourself," says Mueller. "I want them to realize their thoughts are ambivalent and to work them out, so that when the procedure is done, they can take responsibility for it."

Some think that the legalization of abortion has opened a Pandora's box of faulty decision-making. When abortion was illegal, there was a common enemy in the form of the law. Now that abortion is primarily a matter of choice, the decision rests squarely on the shoulders of the woman, a decision many would rather not take the responsibility for. Some blame their husbands or boyfriends for "forcing" them to have the abortion. Others point the finger at their parents, who have insisted on the abortion or who, the patients maintain, would be furious if they found out their daughter was pregnant. Often it's the doctor who takes the "blame" for the abortion. "He did it to me" is a phrase heard often in clinic or hospital corridors when the doctor walks by. "That's just moving the responsibility," says Mueller. "Women are very good at that."

Another danger signal is the reference to the fetus as a "baby." After aborting, many women and often the men who have accompanied them to the clinic ask the clinic personnel what they've done with the "baby" (the fetal tissue is in fact sent to a lab where it is checked to make sure all of it is there and none has been retained in the uterus) and what sex the "child" was. "If they want to know what sex it was and still think it's a baby, then they should have had more counseling," says P. J. Viles in Atlanta. In one study conducted in Sydney, Australia, however, the author concluded that 60 percent of women thought life commenced at conception or during the first trimester, while only 36 percent of men did. This obviously can create a difficulty in communication between a woman and her doctor (if he is male).

For both second-trimester abortion patients and hospital personnel, it is increasingly difficult not to think of the fetus as a baby. In another study on late abortions, the author categorized first-trimester abortions as being "narcissistic," while after the quickening, the focus of the pregnancy shifts to the independent existence of the fetus. Some second-trimester patients in this study had fantasies of "killing the baby" that persisted for over a year. Counseling for late aborters obviously takes on a different significance, and many feel that medical staffs dealing with second-trimester abortions need counseling, too. Joyce Craigg, director of a Brooklyn clinic of Planned Parenthood, worked in surgery assisting in late abortions for two months, then quit. "The doctors would remove the fetus while performing hysterotomies and lay it on the table, where it would squirm until it died. One Catholic doctor would call for sterile water every time he performed a hysterotomy and baptize them then and there. They all had perfect forms and shapes. I couldn't take it. No nurse could," recalls Craigg.

Some medical staff members were haunted by second-trimester experiences long after they had quit doing them. "I used to have nightmares," says one nurse in New York who now works only with early-abortion patients. "I would open a door and there would be a giant fetus in it. It just didn't make sense. At one point I had a patient in one room who was going through her fifth miscarriage even though the doctors had sewed her cervix shut to try to retain it, while in the room across the hall I was taking care of four women having salines. It freaked me out. We had one saline born alive. I raced to the nursery with it and put it in an incubator. I called the pediatrician to come right down, and he refused. He said, 'That's not a baby. That's an abortion.' "

Women undergoing second-trimester abortions have cause to be disturbed. In many hospitals, for example, the fetus is expelled (the medical jargon is "slipped") and left lying on the bed until the afterbirth is also expelled. There is a natural curiosity for the women to look at the fetus, a curiosity the nurses try to squelch. "We tried to avoid the women seeing them," says Norma Eidelman, who worked for a short time with second-trimester patients. "They always wanted to know the sex, but we lied and said it was too early to tell. It was better for the women to think of the fetus as an 'it.' Then we'd scoop up the fetuses and put them in a bucket of formaldehyde, just like Kentucky Fried Chicken. I couldn't take it any longer, and I quit."

Problems with contraceptive side effects, contraceptive failure, or complete nonuse of contraceptives have given rise to a number of repeat abortions, and it is not uncommon now to find women coming back for their second, third, or even fourth. In 1974, for example, repeat abortions in New York City rose to 21.5 percent of all abortions, almost double the number of repeats in 1973. The increase was in fact greater than the relative increase in women seeking their first abortions. A profile of the repeater in New York City found that the highest incidence occurred in married women between the ages of thirty and thirty-five who already had children. Blacks accounted for 54 percent of the repeats, whites made up 32 percent, while Puerto Ricans comprised the remaining 14 percent.

The increase in repeats has occasioned charges of immorality and irresponsibility against the women who seek them, but a 1976 study from Sweden failed to turn up any deep pathological reasons for women returning for more than one abortion. The Swedish study, which involved 45 repeat aborters, 92 first-timers, and 118 women carrying to term, found that the repeaters were of a higher professional status, had more children, had had more sexual partners, had had greater experience with different kinds of contraceptives, and had had more trouble with their pregnancies. A good job, a full family, more sexual partners along the way for greater risk of pregnancy, and greater incapacities caused by pregnancy would seem more than logical reasons for seeking abortion. But perhaps most important is the search by the repeaters and, indeed, by all sexually active people for a safe and effective form of birth control.

Presently, except for abstention from sex altogether, there is none. The pill, which is 99 percent effective if taken regularly, carries a sobering legacy of side effects: blood clots and a greater risk of heart attack, especially in women who smoke, who have high blood pressure, high cholesterol levels, obesity, and diabetes, or who are over forty. Under guidelines issued by the Food and Drug Administration, a pamphlet accompanying each packet of pills warns that pill users may develop benign tumors or gall-bladder disease, and that preexisting migraine, epilepsy, kidney and heart disease, mental depression, jaundice, and high blood pressure may be aggravated by use of the pill. The pamphlet further cautions women wishing to conceive to discontinue pill use for three months and switch to an alternate form of birth control. Women who continue to take the pill while pregnant are warned that the pill "may cause limb and heart defects in the fetus and may increase the risk of vaginal and cervical cancer in female offspring." In spite of the risks, an estimated 10.4 million American women still take the pill. Its popularity appears to be waning, however. Whereas 80 percent of Planned Parenthood's contraceptive patients used the pill in 1973, 1974, and 1975, the percentage dropped to 74 percent in 1976.

The IUD, which is presently being used by an estimated 2.3 million women, is slightly less effective than the pill but does not rely on the user's daily habits and memory, as it is permanently placed in the uterus. Some IUDs release minute amounts of copper or progesterone into the uterus, forming an environment hostile to conception, while others, just by their presence, prevent conception. There are problems, however. Some women cannot tolerate an IUD at all; the uterus expels it. Other women suffer medical complications, which result in their doctors' having to remove the IUD. Heavy bleeding, especially among IUD users who have had children, is a common complaint. In one study done of 750 women before and after insertion of copper IUDs, the mean increase in menstrual blood loss after one year of IUD use among women who had never had children was 65 percent, while the increase was 91 percent in women who had had children. (The increase was not enough to cause a significant increase in anemia, however.) Bleeding usually becomes less heavy as the uterus becomes accustomed to the device.

The possibility of perforation of the uterine wall also exists, although it varies greatly with the shape of the device and the technique of insertion. In a 1975 assessment of IUDs published in *Family Planning Perspectives,* the perforation rate went from 1 in 376 insertions for the Copper 7 down to 1 in 1,000 insertions for the Lippes loop. Post-insertion, there is still risk of perforation if the IUD rotates in the uterus and withdraws into the abdominal cavity. In such cases, the IUD is removed. There is also risk if one becomes pregnant with the IUD in place. Although the IUD is 98 percent effective in preventing normal conception, it is only 90 percent effective in preventing tubal pregnancy, leaving an IUD-protected woman with a 1-in-20 chance of having an ectopic (outside of womb) pregnancy. If the pregnancy is intrauterine, however, and the woman wishes to continue it, the chance of a spontaneous abortion occurring rises to between 30 and 50 percent.

It is still not known exactly how the IUD works. It is thought that the presence of a foreign object in the uterus causes a sterile inflammation, which kills incoming sperm. In rabbits, however, an IUD does not prevent conception but rather discourages the implanting of the fertilized egg in the lining of the uterus. If that is the case, then IUD users may be experiencing a series of mini-abortions without knowing it. In terms of maternal mortality, however, the IUD is safer than the pill and far safer than birth.

The diaphragm, a round, molded piece of rubber that covers the cervical opening of the uterus, is theoretically 98 percent effective, but a 1970 National Fertility Study found it to be only 88 percent. Totally safe to the user and with no side effects, the diaphragm should be the answer to contraceptive dreams. But it is not. The woman must anticipate sex, spread the surface of the diaphragm with a sperm-killing contraceptive cream or jelly not more than two hours before intercourse, and insert the diaphragm into her vaginal canal in the proper position, where it has to remain in place for six hours after intercourse to make sure no sperm left alive slip by in the act of removing it. Only then can the woman take it out, wash and dry and dust it with cornstarch, and store it until she needs it the next time.

Beyond the loss of spontaneity in foreplay culminating in intercourse, the diaphragm can become dislodged in woman-superior positions, allowing sperm to get around it, and orgasm, weight gain or loss, childbirth, or any surgical operation can cause the size of the cervical opening to change and the diaphragm to become ineffective. Despite these risks, the diaphragm is very useful for women who have intercourse infrequently and don't want to run the risk of taking the pill daily or of having an IUD insertion. Though the diaphragm has dropped rapidly in popularity among married couples (only 3.9 percent used the diaphragm in 1975), it is thought to be gaining acceptance among young unmarried women.

Other contraceptive methods become increasingly ineffective, not so much because they fail, but because they are not used every time. There are vaginal jellies, creams, and foams which, when used in conjunction with a condom worn by the man, are almost as effective as the pill. But again, there is reluctance on the part of many couples to treat sex so clinically. The rhythm method, in which couples abstain from intercourse during the fertile days in the woman's menstrual cycle, is filled with pitfalls and surprise pregnancies, and douching with cold water after intercourse, a common practice among teenagers, whose sex lives are sporadic, also has a high rate of failure. So does coitus interruptus, which requires the man to remove his penis from the woman's vagina just before ejaculation. The most dedicated man can forget his dedication as he gets involved, and if he does withdraw in time, the smallest amount of semen, even on the outside of the vagina, can work its way up and into the uterus.

It is not surprising, therefore, that an increasing number of married couples in this country have undergone contraceptive sterilization. The fourth National Fertility Study released in 1977 indicated that an estimated 6.8 million married couples of childbearing age had chosen contraceptive sterilization over all other methods as their form of birth control, an increase from 16.3 percent in 1970 to 31.3 percent in 1975. Indeed, among couples married ten years or longer

37

or couples who have had as many children as they want, sterilization has become more popular than the pill. Using a statistical sample of 3,403 married white people, the study found that even among couples married only five to nine years the sterilization rate had risen dramatically from 8 percent in 1970 to 22 percent in 1975. On the whole, women were more apt to be sterilized than their husbands, but the numbers were close—16.3 percent to 15 percent.

Though the authors of the study, Dr. Charles Westoff, director of the Office of Population Research at Princeton University, and his research associate Elise Jones, found the trend to be an "extraordinary development," it seems less extraordinary considering the highly publicized risks in currently available forms of temporary contraception. If a woman has completed her family or is over thirty-five, sterilization would seem to be preferable to fifteen to twenty more years of facing the risks of birth control or being in need of one or more abortions.

Beyond the possibility of contraceptive failure, there is the irrevocable fact of patient failure. In a study conducted at a clinic in New York in 1974, among 160 women having their first abortions, 160 having their second, and 122 having third or fourth abortions, over 70 percent admitted to not using any form of birth control at the time of conception. Pill users had discontinued taking them because of side effects or fear of side effects. IUD users had either expelled the IUDs or had had them removed. Women who used the diaphragm had simply not worn it at the time of conception. But none of them had considered any other form of birth control to replace the one they had given up. This has given rise to the theory that contraception is method-specific. "A woman commits herself to use one method only, and if it doesn't work, she takes her chances," suggests a report by Jerry Cahn, senior program research analyst at Planned Parenthood of New York City. "Birth-control providers should help the woman commit herself to a system of contraception where, if one method is no longer used, then other methods can become temporary back-ups until an alternate method is chosen."

Many women are not about to commit themselves to any ongoing form of birth control, however. In *Taking Chances: Abortion and the Decision Not to Contracept,* Kristin Luker suggests that some women view conception risk-taking like other risks in life, such as "failing to fasten safety belts in cars, cigarette smoking and risk-taking in sports." Citing the costs of contraception as a further factor, Luker also points to the pain of admitting planned sexual activity, especially among Catholics, the embarrassment and inconvenience of buying either prescription or nonprescription methods of birth control, the reliance on male cooperation for nonprescription methods, and the side effects of all forms of contraception. Some women, then, still consider abortion a primary form of birth control, and when this attitude predominates, repeat abortions become inevitable.

During the day-to-day life of abortion clinics, many of the staff members become frustrated and impatient with the patients' lack of contraception information and use. Ignorance and misinformation abound. "A lot of women find foam disgusting and the IUD terrifying," says Norma Eidelman, a registered nurse and counselor at Planned Parenthood in Brooklyn. "They think the IUD will cause infection or cramps, or even get out of their uteruses and wander around their bodies. They're afraid of having an abortion because they're convinced it will cause birth defects later on. But they won't use a diaphragm either. People are lazy. Someone has got to come up with more effective birth control."

To other battle-weary staff members, saying no appears to be the only assured form of birth control. "We see failures on every level of birth control here," says Betty Orr, a part-time counselor at Preterm in Cleveland. "The number of IUDs that are still in place before we do a suction abortion is just amazing. Every time I see that, I go home and sleep in the guest room for a week."

There is endless debate as to whether contraceptive failure or patient failure in not using whatever form of contraception properly is the cause of pregnancy, but occasionally the debate topples in the face of complete absurdity. "We had one woman come in here last week insisting she couldn't be pregnant because her boyfriend had had a vasectomy and showed her the scar to prove it," recalls Orr. "We asked her where the scar was, and she lifted her arm. 'Here,' she said, pointing to her armpit."

Doctors also grow weary of seeing the same women—and hearing the same stories—time after time. "The staff gets awfully tired of the

39

abortion line-up," says Edward Eichner, director of medicine at Preterm in Cleveland, where he has trouble keeping a permanent staff of doctors to perform suction abortions. "They get very angry and have to sit on themselves to do the job without blowing up. They've heard the same excuses over and over again: 'I forgot to take the pill' or 'John doesn't like to use a rubber.' Sometimes the doctors want to kick them in the fanny." Such frustration has led to a sort of abortion gallows humor. In one hospital in New York, someone had hung up a huge hand-lettered poster reading: "You rape them. We scrape them. No fetus can beat us."

Medical staffs are further depressed by the tedium of performing suction abortions, a simple procedure that only gynecologists are legally allowed to perform. "No doctor for ethical, moral or honest reasons wants to do nothing but abortions," says Eichner. "They are merely willing to fit them in here and there. It's like ordinary shop-work. How many engineers want to do just punch press work? The work is rote and repetitious. Suction abortion is just not stimulating from the point of view of medicine." It is equally difficult to persuade women gynecologists to perform abortions regularly. "Women don't like to do abortions over and over for moral reasons," says Eichner. "Sometimes our women doctors become pregnant themselves, which upsets the patients. At the same time, if a woman is carrying a baby, she doesn't like to abort someone else's. We have much more trouble keeping women doctors on the staff than men."

There is also rising concern among members of the medical profession that abortion, and especially multiple abortions, may damage a woman's reproductive organs and curtail or even preclude her having children at a later date. Because so little time has passed since abortion became legal in this country, the various studies that have been initiated to document the physical effects abortion has are still in their infancy. Many studies have been done in European and Asian countries where abortion has been legal longer, but they are a mishmash of conflicting conclusions. A 1972 British study found that women who had had an abortion suffered bleeding during ensuing pregnancies; a 1973 survey done in Poland found increased evidence of premature delivery and fetal death; a 1972 study done in Greece suggested a tenfold increase in the likelihood of an ectopic pregnancy; a 1974 Japanese study found no effect at all on women who had had an abortion.

There is a school of thought that holds that the voluntary interruption of any pregnancy permanently affects a woman's nervous and hormonal systems, and that abortion may damage the lining of the womb and weaken the cervix to the point where it cannot stand the stress of a full-term pregnancy. No conclusions have yet been drawn in regard to the American abortion experience, however. "These reports are confusing," says Kenneth J. Ryan, chairman of the Harvard Medical School's Department of Gynecology and Obstetrics, who is directing a five-year study on the effects of abortion. "No two investigators have accounted for all the same factors, such as maternal age, state of health, reasons for seeking abortion, history of childbearing and miscarriage, abortion methods used and specific abnormalities involved in later problem pregnancies."

The long-term emotional effects of abortion are equally difficult to enumerate, as most of the existing studies stem from the experiences of women who underwent therapeutic abortions prior to the '73 decision. As instability of mental health was often the reason for a legal abortion, one cannot generalize from the women in these studies to the presumably mentally healthy women who are now undergoing abortion on demand. However, in several studies, it was found that women with severe psychiatric problems who qualified for abortion under the previous stringent laws did not become more disturbed after the abortion; many in fact improved. Women who were turned down in their quest for abortion approval and who were presumably healthier mentally fared considerably worse after delivery than the women who had an abortion.

In a study conducted by sociologists at a hospital affiliated with the State University of New York in Buffalo prior to the liberalization of the abortion law, 116 women were interviewed following their abortions. Few had regrets, and the ones who did had gotten over them by the time of an eight-month follow-up. In a second study done by sociologists at the same hospital, normal maternity patients and abortion patients were administered the Minnesota Multiphasic Personality Inventory test both before and six months after their deliveries or abortions. Preoperatively, according to the test criteria the abortion group seemed considerably more disturbed than did the maternity patients. But in the six-month follow-up, the abortion group had improved to a far greater extent than had the maternity group. In another study, this one at a medical center in Santa Clara, California, comparisons were drawn between women having therapeutic abortions, women having normal deliveries, and those undergoing deliveries resulting in adoption. All the groups had some psychological problems during their pregnancies, the abortion and adoption groups suffering the most. But in the six-month to three-year follow-up, 25 percent of the abortion group reported they felt better adjusted, while 20 percent of the adoption group and almost none of the abortion group reported they actually felt less well adjusted.

Post-abortion depression can take many forms. In a 1972 study on the psychosocial aspects of induced abortion conducted at the New South Wales Institute of Psychiatry in Sydney, Australia, post-abortion depression was thought to stem from a sense of failure felt by the woman involved, who was not allowed to carry out one of the tasks of her feminine role—that is to say, carrying a pregnancy to term. "The feeling of feminine inadequacy may flow over into other aspects of her womanly functioning," writes the author, "so that she becomes more concerned with her sexuality, her attractiveness to men, her ability to care for other children, or her capacity to ever reproduce again."

These reactions obviously have to be weighed against the results of carrying the unwanted pregnancy to term. "There is probably no psychologically painless way to cope with an unwanted pregnancy, whether it is voluntarily interrupted or carried to term," states a 1975 report from the National Academy of Sciences in Washington, D.C. "While an abortion may elicit feelings of guilt, regret, or loss, such alternatives as entering a forced marriage, bearing an out-of-wedlock child, giving up a child for adoption, or adding an unwanted child to a family may also be accompanied by psychological problems for the woman, the child, and the family."

In the interviews that follow, the women, their partners, and their parents all weighed the alternatives to unwanted pregnancies and opted for abortion. Whether the women were married or single, whether they were victims of contraceptive failure or failures themselves in contraceptive use, the result was the same. They were pregnant, and they did not want to be. For the married woman whose family was already large enough, another child would add stress to an already stress filled situation. For single women, the birth of a child would force changes that many were not willing or able to cope with. Childbearing for teenagers is more than just dangerous in terms of the health of the child and the mother; it also snips off a teenager's future before it has even begun. The lucky ones had the support of their partners and their parents. The less lucky had only themselves.

The interviews are raw and they ramble, with the inconsistencies that make up human communication and thought. This was not laziness on my part, but a conscious decision to allow the stories to tumble at their own pace. Abortion is so volatile an issue, and so personal to each circumstance, that I felt it would be an injustice to both subjects and readers to isolate the points that I felt were relevant. In fact, I could have used these interviews to prove that abortion is good for you or bad, that abortion causes all relationships to break up or brings people together, that abortion results in impotence and frigidity, or that it frees partners to have more fulfilling sex lives. The point is that an unwanted pregnancy and subsequent abortion affect each individual differently, and these differences deserve to be heard.

2

Single Women

Two-thirds of all the women receiving abortions are single. Indeed, in seventeen out of the twenty-nine states which reported abortion statistics to the Center for Disease Control in 1974, more unmarried women had abortions than had live births, a total of 1,675 abortions per 1,000 live births for single women as compared to 95 abortions per 1,000 live births for married women. With these numbers, the aggregate abortion ratio for unmarried women becomes eighteen times higher than that of married women.

For the vast majority of single women, the decision to abort is relatively simple to reach. Socially, the stigma of becoming an unwed mother still prevails, especially in middle-class communities. Before the legalization of abortion, single pregnant women were either shipped off to homes for unwed mothers until their babies were born and put up for adoption, or sent off on mysterious long trips, which whetted the appetites of neighborhood gossips. Or they endured the danger of illegal abortion. Though social mores have loosened considerably, the middle-class attitude toward birth has not. It is only within our lifetime that divorce has been considered acceptable behavior, and divorced mothers still face a subtle overload of guilt in many parts of the country. So one must still be almost a revolutionary single woman to willfully and positively carry a pregnancy to term and keep the child.

Financially, the future of a single pregnant woman is also perilous. Her options are extremely limited. To support her child, she must go out and work, but the support system for child care in this country is almost nil. What few day-care centers there are have long waiting lists, and if the mother is lucky enough to land a job that pays her a salary over the poverty level, she loses her eligibility for day care. The social and financial pressure to terminate her pregnancy by abortion, therefore, becomes so great as to make it almost mandatory.

Life styles have also changed considerably. Where once accidental pregnancy in an unwed couple generally resulted in a forced or "shotgun" marriage, both men and women now are resisting such unions. With the advent of the Women's Movement, women are staying single longer, pursuing a life more centered around their own achievements than around the needs of a family. Abortion, then, is the most obvious answer to an unwanted pregnancy.

Though these reasons for abortion are considered selfish and primarily a matter of convenience by anti-abortion proponents, the fate of unwanted children would tend to negate that accusation. *Legalized Abortion and the Public Health*, a 1975 compendium of abortion studies put together by the Institute of Medicine in Washington, D.C., found that children who were not wanted suffered for it. A twenty-year study in Sweden followed the lives of 120 children born to women who had been denied abortion matched up with a control group of "wanted" children; the results of the study indicate that children from the former group "were registered more often with psychiatric services, had engaged in more antisocial and criminal behavior and had received more public assistance." Another earlier study done in Czechoslovakia charted the first seven to nine years of life of 200 children whose mothers had also been denied abortion; this study suggested that "unwanted" boys in particular had fared less well than their "wanted" counterparts. The "unwanted" boys had a greater incidence of illness, poorer grades in school, and more difficulty with peer-group relationships, and they were "at seemingly greater risk for future delinquency." Abortion, then, does not necessarily strike such a note of selfishness on the part of a woman with an unwanted pregnancy, but indeed a more selfless attitude in that she does not want to subject a child to a situation in which he or she is less apt to thrive.

45

Abortion, for selfish or selfless reasons, is not such an obvious answer to women in lower socioeconomic classes, however, where it is still acceptable for single women to bear children out of wedlock. In black communities, extended families still exist, and there is usually an aunt, grandmother, or older sister who will undertake the care of a child born to one of the members. But as aspirations rise, the fact of a child being not only a financial burden but also a hindrance to the potential of a single woman is causing more and more poverty-level women to choose abortion. According to Yale's Michael Bracken, certain differences in approach to abortion occur in the different socioeconomic groups. Middle-class white women tend to abort their first pregnancies and to deliver later ones, while women of lesser financial and educational means tend to deliver their first pregnancies and to abort subsequent ones. "It's not that obvious to some black women that abortion is the right decision," says Bracken. "It's only later on that poor or black women realize they don't want more children tying them down. They need more pressure to abort."

The decision to abort is further complicated among black women by the attitude of some black men. Instead of avoiding conception, some black men appear to welcome it. In black communities in New York, a black man is said to have "bigged" a girl when she becomes pregnant, and rather than a cause for shame, it is cause for swagger. "It makes the guys proud," says a black counselor for Planned Parenthood. "Many of the single black women coming in here for abortions haven't told their boyfriends they were pregnant because they know the guys would encourage them to have the baby. It's a macho thing."

Parental relationships and reactions also play a role in a single woman's decision to abort, be she black or white, well off or poor. Among the black women I interviewed, some had abortions in spite of their mothers' willingness to take the child. Others had abortions because their mothers wouldn't agree to raise the baby. Among the white women, the role of the parent was more abstract. Over and over again single women of all ages would admit that they didn't want their parents ever to know about their abortion for fear it would hurt them, although they agreed that the alternative, having the child, would hurt them more. These women didn't give their parents the option to support or reject them. Isolating themselves, the white middle-class single women made their decision alone. "They wouldn't understand" was a recurring phrase. "They don't ever need to know" was another. Instead, these women turned to their peers for support and invariably found it.

The most critical factor in the decision to abort, however, is the relationship with the male partner. If the pregnancy is a result of a one-night stand or a meaningless relationship, the decision is easier. But when it is a result of an ongoing relationship, the emotional issues become myriad. The relationship suddenly reaches a crisis point and can seesaw wildly. Some women are stunned when their partners bolt and run in panic. Others are resentful that their partners support the abortion decision, feeling this represents a lack of commitment. Forced to evaluate the quality of their relationship, other couples split up because the fact of pregnancy and abortion is too weighty for them to handle. Many couples, on the other hand, become closer in facing such an agonizing decision together.

All these worries and doubts come to a head in the light of a confirmed pregnancy and at a time when a woman is feeling the most vulnerable. Her body is changing. Her emotions wobble. Often she is nauseated and unable to keep up the activities that are the fabric of her independence as a single woman. And she is very much alone. For no matter how close her relationship is to the people around her, it is she alone who is bearing the result of a shared sex life. It can be a lovely or a lonely time, depending on the circumstances. And for the woman deciding on abortion, opting for relief rather than more problems, opting for an unencumbered future rather than a forced commitment, the circumstances are never right.

Though abortion is an immediate solution, followed almost always by a feeling of relief, there are subtle disturbances that don't show up on statistical charts. In my research, almost every relationship between single people broke up either before or after the abortion. What had been pleasure became pain. What had been frivolous became heavy. Sex, which had brought intimacy and relief, brought memories of pain and guilt. Some women became man-haters. Others became promiscuous. More frequently, women went through a period of celibacy and resumed their sex lives not with the original partner but with somebody else. To all extents and purposes, they were not "clinically" disturbed enough to need hospitalization or to commit suicide, standards by which statisticians gauge reaction, but their lives did not continue without a ripple. Still other women, the lucky ones, became closer to their partners because of their abortion experiences, and went on to enjoy deeper relationships, and in some cases, marriage.

But the aftershock of abortion sometimes doesn't show up for years. Several women I talked to who eventually went on to marry and have children experienced grief and guilt as long as ten years after their abortions when, faced with children they wanted and loved in a family context that allowed it, they mourned the fetuses they had aborted. During her first wanted pregnancy, one woman had recurring nightmares that she had killed someone, a nightmare so vivid that she became an insomniac. She finally confided in a friend, who told her she was merely reliving the abortion she'd had as a young single woman. The nightmare never came back, and the woman has just had her second child—nightmare free.

What follows here are the stories of six single women who had legal abortions, how they became pregnant, how they felt about it, how they made their decision to abort, how they felt about the abortion itself, and what effect it had on their lives and relationships. In terms of timing, the women were interviewed at points from a week before a scheduled abortion to seven years after the fact. All the names have been changed.

After 1973

===============

Jessica Woodruff has masses of curly black hair which she doesn't attempt to push away from her face. Now twenty-seven, Jessica had an abortion four years ago in New York because abortion was still illegal in her home state of Ohio. Still bitter, Jessica has

48

decided never to have children of her own, though she works as a volunteer in the children's ward of a mental hospital.

"I was just breaking up with this guy four years ago. I was using foam and he was using a rubber, but half way through it, he ripped it off in anger. If men could think of their whole sexual selves rather than their one little appendage, life could be a whole lot better.

"I knew I was going to get pregnant. I asked him to stop, but he wouldn't and just kept slamming into me until he came. I had a premonition right away that I was pregnant, and sure enough, when I went off to get a urinalysis, it turned out positive. Then I went for a pelvic and the doctor told me I wasn't pregnant. He told me the reason I wasn't was that my breasts were small. But they've always been small. I felt offended. Goddamn men. And I was pregnant.

"When I told the guy I was pregnant, he accused me of it being someone else's kid. I felt really shitty and alone. He had taken up with his old girlfriend again and told me we were finished for good. It was horrible. There I was pregnant and being shafted. I felt very angry and alone.

"I was booking rock bands then, and I worked my ass off to book enough dates to get the money for my abortion. But the club wouldn't pay me. I finally went to the head of one of the bands and confessed what I needed the money for. I was crying and felt like shit. His wife overheard and got furious. She said her woman's group would raise the money for the abortion and the air fare. And they did. It was the first good thing that happened.

"The second good thing that happened was that my best friend came to visit me, and she seemed so unbelievably sympathetic and understanding about my situation that she finally confessed she was pregnant, too, so we went together to New York.

"The whole time I had a fantasy of keeping the baby. I wrote a few poems with earthy words in them like 'seed,' 'bloom,' and 'blossom,' but it was cynical. This seed? Let this seed grow? No way.

"My friend and I were terrified our families and friends back home would find out why we went to New York. Though we were adult women, we were still under parental pressure. Families are very

49

important here in Ohio. And sure enough, we ran into one of our friends at the airport and confessed what we were doing. She was shocked and made us feel worse than we already did. It really matters here what people think of you. You know you'll see them again. It was one of our terrors coming true.

"I was so nervous I fainted in the group counseling session at the abortion clinic. I'd had no food and a lot of cigarettes, and I had a great fear of having a shot in my cervix. I used to babysit for a kid who butted me once in the pubic bone and that really hurt. Where was the shot going to be?

"I wanted to smoke a joint, but the counselor said no. Instead of dope the counselor suggested we masturbate to relax and said that it helped to get rid of menstrual cramps, too.

"I never thought about the fetus. I had a pre-political feeling of what was inside me and my rights. It was something that didn't belong there and had no place in my life at that time. I'd hated it before the abortion, but mostly I hated the man. During the procedure I didn't think about it at all. I was practicing yoga breathing and was really mellowed out. I experienced no pain.

"I felt so relieved in recovery. I just wanted to get back to my life. My friend and I both felt great. We stuffed on ginger ale and cookies, then took the bus back to the airport. That night we went to hear one of the bands I had booked. We didn't dance, but we had a great time. What an incredible feeling of relief.

"My sex life didn't pick up though. The whole time I was pregnant, which ran almost ten weeks, I had felt very cold, whereas before I had been very sexual and orgasmic. Six months after the abortion I finally felt turned on by a guy who happened to be a doctor. It was the first time in a long time, and I was really excited to feel something. We went to bed where he was a very interesting lover and teased me for a long, long time. But when he went inside of me, he started to smash into me again and again. It really hurt and was so different from the foreplay that I thought I'd been deceived. I really freaked out. Instead of getting an orgasm, I got pain. I pushed him away, and he stopped. I thought all men had deceived me, and I was really upset. I've run into him from time to time after that, but that was it. What really pissed me off was that he was a medical person. If anyone could have helped me bridge the gap, it would have been someone like him.

"That turned me off altogether. For five months afterwards I didn't sleep with anyone. I thought maybe I was a lesbian, but I didn't feel anything sexual about women. Mostly I felt dead a lot of the time. I was afraid. Then I started again, but it wasn't like it used to be. And it never has been again. I'm still angry at men. In fact, probably more now than before. Or maybe it's more identifiable. In any event, the abortion catapulted me into the women's movement.

"I live with a guy now and it's basically all right, I guess."

———

Vanessa Truth, a New York photographer and actress, has run the gamut of abortion emotion. Now thirty-six, Vanessa had her first abortion three years ago; it was very positive and made her feel in control of her life. Her second abortion depressed her, as she felt there was a spirit somewhere trying to express itself through her. Her third abortion a year ago, which she didn't tell the man about, meant little to her.

"I had my love-child, a wanted child, a child that was lusted after, twelve years ago. My husband and I got divorced when she was six and we were living in the Orient. I went to Hollywood where I was convinced I was going to become a star. That was a real bomb. I hated every second of it. I picked up my daughter and moved to New York in 1969 right to this loft, and now I'm doing what I definitely want to do, have wanted to do since I was five years old.

"I started living with someone ten years younger than I was. I was twenty-eight and he was eighteen. It was very strange. It was the last thing I ever thought would happen. I had been going out with men in their thirties and forties for a long time. It was very odd. This fellow was helping me build my loft, and I let him stay there rent-free in return for his carpentry. He had his own life and his friends, and it all worked out. He lived here for eight months before anything happened. I don't know if it occurred to him long before, or if it ever

51

occurred to either one of us—I don't really know. But we got into this thing, and we ended up living together three years. A very intense and heavy relationship. He was so much younger than I was. I was already so far ahead of him. I had already been married and divorced and raised a daughter, and he didn't really know anything, though he thought he knew everything. But our relationship was very passionate and loving, a very heavy thing.

"I wasn't using any birth control. I didn't use anything all the time Larry and I were together, and we made love constantly—constantly. An eighteen-year-old guy and a twenty-eight-year-old woman—it was fantastic. I never got pregnant until we started having trouble. He kept agitating around saying he had to get out on his own, get his own apartment and see the world, and I would get threatened and freaked out. Finally he decided to seek his fortune in London, and by that time I was tired of the whole thing and I thought, great. So he went off, and there I was pregnant. I told him, but I didn't make much out of it. I didn't want him to stay or anything. I really didn't. I really wanted him to go.

"The day after he left, I had the abortion. The pregnancy was a nuisance. It was very inconvenient. You have all the little frustrations in your day-to-day life and some big ones, but then something like this comes along, and you think, no way. It's utterly inconvenient. I was teaching a two-day seminar at the time to eighty-five Episcopal women, my boyfriend had left, and there I was getting an abortion, too. It was grim.

"I cannot even remember where I had the abortion. It was some clinic outside the city. We had to drive a ways, I remember. The abortion was nothing. We drove back into the city afterwards, and I felt just incredible. I have never felt so in control of my destiny or my life. I could really make that decision. It felt fantastic. I never had a bad moment.

"The second time I had an abortion, he decided to come back from London. He arrived and said he couldn't live without me, that he'd been on his own for three months and he really hated it and that now he really did love me. I said all right, okay, and we got it back together again, and that first night, the very first night, I got pregnant. I still wasn't using any birth control because I didn't even know he was going to show up that day, and I hadn't slept with any guy since he'd left. It seemed like there was this baby that was trying to get born. I thought, uh-oh, this is very strange. We had slept together constantly for three years with no birth control, and I had been told that my uterus was very severely tipped so I couldn't get pregnant, and I never did get pregnant for three years, and I tell you we made love at least every day. I never had such a relationship with any man. He's twenty-six now. He's probably over his prime.

"This time I went to a clinic in New York. I couldn't believe it. I was very torn. It was awful because we really did love each other, but I would never consider having a child with him because he was just too young and irresponsible. When I had had my first child, I had picked very wisely and picked a fantastic father. I give him five stars as a father. He's much closer to her now than most fathers are to the kids they live with. I was also afraid that if I did some crazy thing like going and having an illegitimate child my husband would try to take my daughter away from me because he'd already tried once. He's very puritanical. He would have made fireworks out of it. So I had to protect my own child by not having this child.

"The guy, on the other hand, harbored deep resentment about it. There was this funny little edge in everything he did, and I thought he thought that the sooner I had the abortion the better. We never really discussed it. It was just understood that I'd have an abortion. He was just kind of a little cruel to me. I have never considered myself an emotionally mature person, and to me it was a rejection thing. It never occurred to me that he was upset that I was having this abortion. It never, never occurred to me. I didn't find out until a year and a half later that he had been very, very upset. He felt rejected and felt that I would never have a child of his, that I did not consider him suitable for me, and that it was pointless to love me. Even though he knew it was absurd to go ahead and have a baby at the age of twenty-two with a thirty-two-year-old woman, it was all very heartbreaking for him.

"By New Year's Day we were apart again, having just gotten back together in September. The abortion had been easy physically, but emotionally it was rough. When I got home that day I thought he was being totally unfeeling and unsympathetic to me. Any twenty-

53

two-year-old guy is so shallow. I was feeling very blue. I still felt there was some spirit trying to thrust its way through. Our love had gotten to the point where it either had to express itself that way or else nothing. It was too deep.

"I had always read in those magazines like *Redbook* and *McCall's* that our mothers used to have around that women used sex as a weapon. I found out then that men use sex as a weapon just as devastatingly. He became very good at that. Just marvelous. He would withhold it or be in a pout about something. He started to get very tricky sexually. He'd do things like make incredible love to me, and he knew me so well he'd know whether I'd had an orgasm or not, and then he'd finish just before I was about to come. Things like that. Just little ways of keeping you totally bananas, on the edge all the time. He became more and more violent. When we had an argument, he'd pick up something and throw it. We would just have finished building a beautiful wall, and then he'd take a wine bottle and throw it against it. I used to think, oh, my God, the next time it's going to be my jaw. I'm just an inch away from a punch. Not for one single minute did I ever relate it to the abortion. Now I would instantly. Now I know men much better. They are so much more fragile and sensitive than I ever suspected they were. I've come to see them as the really delicate creatures they are. So delicate. So much more than we are really. With all that violence, in retrospect now, it proceeds quite logically.

"I have a theory now. A man knows if you're aborting his child even if you don't tell him. Later, this third abortion I had, I never told this man I was pregnant. Not on the most subtle levels did I intimate it. But if one had a way of measuring things like that, I would swear that a man feels something when there's an abortion going on of his issue. I think they are much more connected than we understand they are. And I think somewhere on a deep, deep level a man feels a rejection of his seed. At the moment that machine goes in, wherever they are, they feel disturbed. They don't interpret it at all as anything, but they feel it.

"With Larry I didn't feel he gave a shit about the abortion. But I went to London two years later, and he was living with another woman there, and I went and visited them, and we were all being friends. She was a year younger than he was. There we were, the three of us sitting in her living room, and all of a sudden he started saying things like 'You know I always thought you and I were going to be together for the rest of our lives and I couldn't believe it when you went ahead and had the abortion.' I couldn't believe it. And he said he was completely devastated and upset. I was very embarrassed he was saying things like that in front of her. So I didn't pursue the conversation. That was the last time I ever saw him. He had a child by this woman and married her and now they're divorced.

"Now I've been through three years of a whole new awareness. If I had been in touch then the way I am now, I would have understood that my body was involved in a little bit of survival. That's what a child is. It's continuance. The body is striving to protect it, so the body is shocked by such an action. The body is offended and shocked and reeling and insulted. It's exactly like throwing a monkey wrench in the works. Probably a lot of the fights Larry and I had, had to do with the abortions, and neither one of us knew it.

"With the third abortion I never told the guy, but I maintain that he knows. I see him, and we're friends, and it's fine. There's no pain. But we don't make love any more. It was his choice. I think with a lot of men if they don't think you're 100 percent into them, or they sense a slight feeling of rejection, or that you're an independent person, they draw back. They become very hard to get sexually. That's how he got. After the abortion I went away for a month, and the first night I got back he came over, and he was impotent. That's what made me think, Aha, he knows. Somewhere in the beast side of him he knows that something was cut off. He feels cut off. And he had never been impotent before. He was always a very incredible lover. It was such a miserable night because he was really impotent, and I was so hurt. You know it's such a blow to a woman's pride. I find that one of the most devastating forms of rejection. You feel so ugly and unwanted and unfemale. We were both devastated by that and he'd never have anything to do with me sexually again. He might come over and see me, but it would be in the afternoon, and he'd only stay a few hours. He'd never touch me. Finally my pride got up about it. This had been going on for months. One night I got very aggressive with him and told him I was going home with him, which was a terrifying experience. I had never done that before in my life. It was as if he had been waiting for me to do that. I aggressed on him that night, and it was wonderful. But that was that. We never made love again.

"One thing that's come out of all this is that I'll never have another abortion. I've become much more involved with my body, my head and my roots, as part of the animal kingdom. And I know it's just nuts, it's bad karma, it's negative anti-life. It's a no. It's not allowing things to flow their natural way. I'm just never going to be pregnant again."

———————

Marigold Rojan, twenty-one, is making an appointment at Grady Hospital in Atlanta, Georgia, for an abortion the next week. She is very upset and cries frequently during the interview. Marigold wants to have the baby but feels it is unfair financially to her boyfriend, who took her in when she was eighteen and pregnant with her son. Marigold says that if her mother would help her, she'd keep the baby. But Marigold is too proud to ask.

"When I found out I was pregnant, first I wanted the baby, then I didn't. I've got a little boy already, and my boyfriend—well, by nature that little boy is not his. I was pregnant when I started going with him, and when I had the little boy, my boyfriend he signed the birth certificate. We both want a lot of things, and with one child we can get it, but with two, I don't know, because I'm not working.

"My boyfriend, he's said that he can't have children because he had the mumps or measles as a kid, so he was excited to find out he could. But we just can't take care of two.

"I'm scared about the abortion. I feel all kind of sad, and I'm scared I'm gonna break down and cry because I feel like crying now. We want to have one, but we don't want to bring a child into the world that can't be taken care of the way it's supposed to be taken care of. I'd rather have an abortion than to make it suffer.

"My boyfriend, he works for the Environmental Protection Agency, and we're going to get married. We all be engaged. But we don't have no mind for a date.

"It's not so good at home. I moved away from home when I was eighteen. My mother—when she found out I was pregnant, she like took a fit. She said what they all say: I'm not going to take care of it; you've got to get out of my house. Then I didn't even think about an abortion. It didn't even cross my mind. All my girlfriends was having babies, and I just wanted to have one of my own too. My boyfriend, he took me in.

"There were eight of us at home, four sisters and three brothers. But my mother was only married three times, to my oldest brother's daddy and my daddy and my youngest sister's daddy. I guess she thought about that when she saw I was pregnant. My older sister, she had a little boy when she was eighteen, and I guess my mama thought she wasn't going to take one more. All of us was at home. All of us.

"She doesn't know I'm here today. She'd kill me if she'd know. Everybody was hoping I'd have a little girl, because all her grandchildren—she got six now—they all be boys. My boyfriend, he told her I was pregnant, so she thinks I'm going to have a baby. I tried to talk to her when I was thinking of having an abortion, but she don't agree with it and she got kind of mad when I was trying to tell her, so I'm going to have to think about what I'm going to tell her after I've had the abortion.

"My boyfriend, he makes four dollars an hour, but we got bills to pay and stuff like that. For four years he won't want to admit that I made him suffer because I took away a lot of things that he had, because he's not but nineteen and I'm twenty-one, and he dropped out of school at sixteen to get a job to take care of me. I just think it's time for him to have what he wants because he done gave me all I wanted. I'm really doing this for him. I don't want to make him suffer any more than he has to.

"My mama ain't never really sat down and talked to me like mamas and daughters should, because I'm twenty-one and there's still a lot of things that I don't understand about life. Just to tell me. If he leave me, I'm in a really bad situation because right now I'm not capable of taking care of myself and a child too. I can take care of him and feed him and do all that, but just to be out on our alone, I don't think I'm capable of that. I just wish my mama had told me about everything—about life—or said to do this or that. In school I was running with some kids, and I ran away from home when I was fourteen and didn't come back till I was eighteen, and then I left again. I guess she thought I was the black sheep in the family because she gave me the hardest time of all of us. I feel she hated me. Sometimes she'd whip me. Sometimes she'd try and put me in a home. She did for one day, but then I ran away from there and they wouldn't take me back no more.

"I don't know why she hated me. I was good in school. But if I ask her for something—like I was on the basketball team and the track team and I needed some shoes—she wouldn't do it. But if my brother or older sister asked, she'd do it for them. I wanted to go on to college, but there's no way. Now she'll give me things, but it's not as if she's giving it out of her heart but just because you is her daughter. I don't want to be in any position to ask her for anything, because since I left home I never did ask her for anything. She's only kept my little boy three times. But she keep my little nephew just about every weekend.

"If I got along with my mother, then I could have this baby."

———

Karen Tuthill, twenty-three, is going to have an abortion, her third, in the morning. A receptionist at a Brooklyn law firm, she is on her lunch hour and breaks into tears several times. She suffered physically and emotionally after her first abortion, believing she had "killed" a child. Her second abortion was easy physically but worse emotionally.

"I was brought in up in Hartford, Connecticut, but I never made out with any of the guys in high school. I guess I was just storing it all up. My best friend, who looked like a cheerleader, had been fucking like a bunny since the age of fourteen, and she was dying to get me on the pill. But I refused. Then the day I graduated

58

she drove me to the gynecologist, and that was that. That fall I moved into the city where I went to acting school, and that's where it all began.

"I was hardly a virgin, though. When I was thirteen, I was raped by a guy in Rhode Island. My family and I had been staying at a farm, and because I was big for my age and had a big mouth, people thought I was older than I was. I talked my family into letting me stay on after they left because I had a crush on one of the fellows, but I didn't tell them that. We went to a big party in a meadow and I got completely plastered. I guess I came on like a rabbit. When I went into the woods to pee, this guy followed me, and when I came back on the trail he was waiting. I asked what he wanted, and he shoved me down on the path. I must have hit my head because it knocked me silly. When I came to I was awakened by an extreme pain in a region I didn't know could feel pain. 'So that's what that word means, that's what it's all about,' I can remember thinking. I tried to push him off, but I couldn't. So I went dramatic and lay there and moaned. That scared him off, and he ran away. I pulled myself together, went back to the party, and announced what had happened. Even though he was engaged to one of the girls at the party, they ran him out of town on a rail, and he ended up joining the marines.

"When I went back to my room that night I looked in the mirror and saw my eyes. I have very big eyes which had always had a certain gleam and an innocence. Now they looked evil. I've been ripped off, I remember thinking, and I'll never be the same. Nobody asked. They just took. I didn't tell my parents about it until I was eighteen. My mother was giving me some sort of virginity lecture, and I told her she was about five years too late.

"But I didn't make it with anyone again until I moved to New York. I felt sort of unattractive. I had an inferiority complex, I guess. But the first night I was in New York, the waiter at the restaurant we were at asked me if I'd like to go out. Hot damn, I thought. He chose me. It was scary, but I went and I did it. I think I went through every waiter in that restaurant in the next year. My roommate and I kept a scoreboard, and boy, we've been busy. It got so we couldn't remember the names and the faces. It finally tallied up to fifty different guys for me. It was fun.

59

"I settled down for a bit after that first year, but I sure wasn't a Polly Pureheart. And I got negligent about the pill because I didn't have any particular boyfriend. Then I suddenly went through a hot streak and discovered I had something growing inside me. I have no idea who the father was. And I didn't really face it until the doctor told me I was pregnant. As long as I hadn't heard it from him, I thought it wouldn't be true.

"Well, I freaked out and started crying. I went off to the Eastern Women's Center all by myself, where they gave me a local anesthetic and then a suction job. They told me the local would be less dangerous, and the general anesthetic would give me cramps and make me throw up, and that I'd have to stay there for hours recovering from it. The local, they said, was just a shot in the cervix, which has no nerve endings, and that I'd be out in forty-five minutes. And like an ass I believed them.

"There were around sixty of us, divided up into groups A, B, C, D, E, and F. They gave us questionnaires to fill out, and two cups to pee in. There was a sea of people all in there for the same thing. There were the criers, the gigglers, the palies, the I-don't-give-a-damns. The worst were the people all alone with no one to hold hands with. That was me. It was tough, but there you were. The groups became foxhole buddies, and we all went together to seminars on birth control. It was just like high school. Then we all sat around and rapped about how we'd gotten pregnant. They called me first.

"Suddenly I went all wobbly. They had to lead me out of the room and put me on the table. Instead of shaving my crotch, they spray-painted it with some orange disinfectant. It was like graffiti. Then I saw a long syringe and nearly died. But it didn't hurt, just like they said. The doctor said he'd have to dilate me three times with rods to open me up enough. So when he starts to work, the nurse starts asking me dumb questions like what religion I am and who the father was. God, the pain. I was screaming and the doctor was getting worried. 'Hang on,' he kept saying, 'It'll be over in a minute.' I kept screaming back, 'You said there'd be no severe pain and you lied!' Then they made me sit up and I didn't know if I was going to faint or throw up. The nurse gave me some smelling salts and led me over to a cot.

60

"On the way to the cot I saw all the horrified faces of the girls in the waiting room. I guess they heard me screaming.

"On the cot the cramping got so bad I had to stay there five hours. They gave me stale Lorna Doones and ginger ale and Tylenol for pain. I was wishing I'd had a joint. It was just inhuman scare tactics to make you feel so miserable you'd never come back again. I couldn't eat the Lorna Doones, but the nurse made me.

"Emotionally I felt terrible. I just didn't know how I'd gotten myself into this situation. I hated myself. I felt abandoned and lost. There was no one's shoulder to cry on, and I wanted to cry like hell. And I felt guilty about killing something. I couldn't get it out of my head that I'd just killed a baby. I couldn't get the upbringing out of my head that my mother and father had drilled into me, whether I liked it or not. Regardless of the current vogue and what you say to your friends about abortion, I couldn't take it. 'I wish I were married,' I remember saying to myself. 'Then I could have had it.'

"If my parents were dead, then I'd have had that baby. But they're here to remind me of guilt and lay on their disapproval. They're lovely people really, and practice what they preach. But they're very old world. And we're new world—or at least in between. My new world self to survive remains intellectual and not emotional. I can't catch up to myself.

"I had my second abortion after I'd been living with a guy for two years. I missed a couple of pills and got knocked up. I must have done it on purpose. I really believe that. I love children, you know. I've been a mother's helper since I was thirteen and spent a whole year as a governess. I was old-fashioned enough with this guy to want to have his baby, but not admitting it to myself. I was really half-assed.

"He was very sensitive. He sort of wanted to have the baby too, but then he said I better have the abortion. So I did. I had a general anesthetic that time, which was much easier. Afterwards he drove me home and I felt rotten, all sick and depressed. I felt hot and feverish. I lay down on the bed and asked him for tea and the sympathy that went along with it. He was out of the room for forty-five minutes and I thought I was going to die for needing someone. I went out into the next room, and there he was just

61

looking at the colors on the wall. Instead of getting me the tea, he had dropped acid.

" 'What happened?' I said. 'It's been a hard day for me,' he said. 'A hard day for you?' I said. 'I was the one who went through it. You just had to sit in the waiting room.' The little creep. I wanted arms around me and to be cuddled, and he thought he'd had a hard day. I went crazy.

"I started beating him up. I grabbed the lamp and shattered it on his back. Then I swung a baseball bat at him, but he got away. So I jumped on him and started beating him with my fists. I was bleeding all over the place and all over him. I beat the crap out of him. He ran out the door and I locked it behind him and shoved a chair under the knob to keep him out.

"I let him back in the next day. I guess we women are all fools, and I loved him no matter what. It wasn't till a month later that I started being repulsed by him. I started bitching at him and being contemptuous and resentful. Whenever we'd argue I'd never stay in the present but bring up everything I'd ever been mad at him for from the past. He'd let me down. We still made love but it began to peter out. It went from once a day to once a week to once every two weeks. And I started making love like a whore. I never got out of the missionary position and going down on him was impossible. I just lay there and gritted my teeth. But still I hoped it would all work out. Finally I felt like throwing up whenever he touched me, and I had to leave. That was a year ago.

"This guy, the one whose baby is being aborted tomorrow, I won't tell at all. He wouldn't have made love to me if he'd known I was unprotected. I'd run out of pills, but I didn't bother to get another prescription. I've fallen in love with him, but he says he doesn't love me. He says he can't love, but he treats me better than any other guy who says he did. Now I'm two months pregnant, and he doesn't know it. I try to be tough. I have two fantasies. One says to me: Grow up, be mature, you don't need him to drag into this mess. The other says: I want to tell him, but he might freak out and then I'd lose him, even though I really don't have anything to lose. But the looks he gives me, the tenderness—it must come from somewhere.

"So tomorrow I'm going back to the Eastern Women's Center. I don't want him to find out so I'll never know if he would have failed me. I just smile and act cheerful like the best sport in the world. Maybe it's bullshit and maybe it's psychological masochism.

"I'd like to get married and have a baby, but I doubt I ever will. I look too much for love and adoration, and I get them mixed up with sex. I guess I do it to get people to validate me. If someone frowns, I always think it's because they're mad at me.

"I never think about the babies at all. But I fantasize when I'm around little kids. I pretend they are mine. I live vicariously off of other people's children. I have regrets, and that's when they come in. I want. But I keep denying it. Every time I talk about it, though, I want to pound the walls and scream and beat the carpets.

"I remember a conversation I had with a friend who'd just had an abortion. It's just an embryo, I told her, preferring to use the clinical definition. It's not a being, just a bunch of splitting cells. My friend said, 'It's murder. How can you deny it's a life? It's murder, but it's justifiable homicide.' Now if I took that as my own philosophy I couldn't follow through with it. I'd have to have the baby. I agree with her, of course, but I just won't admit it. We've gotten very distant now.

"Maybe I should go to a psychiatrist, but I really don't have the money or the interest. Truth is hard to take, and I just don't know if I'm ready for it."

For some women, abortion can be a positive experience and a period of personal growth. Robin Terhune, thirty, an attractive travel agent in San Francisco, had a disastrous first abortion six years ago, after which she continued living with the man for four years without ever having intercourse with him again. Her second abortion, two weeks before this interview, started off just as badly, but Robin came to realize that her behavior was more destructive than constructive.

"I was having this real weird relationship with a guy in Vermont six years ago. Then he went off to Vietnam, and I felt obligated to sleep with him before he went. While he was gone, I went off the pill because I didn't think I'd need it, and besides, I hate anything that interferes with the natural rhythms of the body. I'm a health and sun freak, I guess.

"Anyway, he came back suddenly, and I felt real obligated to sleep with him again even though I hadn't taken any pills. I mean, my God, he'd gone off and gotten shot at, and I really felt I had to give him the American welcome home. So I did it, though I really didn't want to. I remember just shutting my eyes and breathing a lot and hoping he couldn't tell.

"When I discovered I was pregnant, I was really freaked out. I didn't love him, but we had this like weird dependence on each other. I told him I was going to get an abortion, and he went wild and got stoned, but he went with me to the place anyway. I just couldn't stop crying the whole time. They almost wouldn't do me. All I could think was that I was going to be a mother and that this child would love me and I was hurting it. I lay on the table and kept cradling my arms as if there was a baby in them. I could swear I heard it crying.

"Afterwards it got weirder. I stayed with this guy in Virginia for four years, and we never had sex once. Not once. I was repulsed by him. I couldn't stand to look at him naked. I'd look all over the room, study the curtains, anything so long as I didn't have to see his cock. Do you think I'm weird? We'd get into bed at night and he'd come over to my side and I could just feel my body get cold and dry up. I didn't even have any spit in my mouth. He was real understanding, which was even worse, but I just couldn't do it. My friends kept saying what a neat couple we were and why didn't we get married, and I thought I was going to go crazy.

"When the travel agency I worked for said there was an opening in San Francisco, I jumped at it and left him without even telling him I was going. And then this really weirder thing happened. I met this guy who was really no good and didn't work or anything, and we started a purely sexual relationship. We just fucked and fucked and fucked. I was taking the pill again, so I wasn't worried about getting pregnant. And it was the first time I'd ever had an orgasm. After a while I began to think I was turning into a whore, so I broke it off and didn't make it with anyone for about a year.

64

"Then I started to know this guy at work and pretty soon we ended up in bed. It was nothing like that other stud, but then this was a nicer guy. This time I was totally irresponsible about birth control. It was like I was just waiting to be punished. I set myself up for a real shitty thing. I didn't go out to do it, but I didn't do anything to not make it happen. I'm always dangling with fate. I was all hot to get pregnant. I don't know what it is. I just like it because that's the way it's supposed to be.

"When I got pregnant, it was worse than before because I'm thirty now, and I don't have much time left. But I just don't want to be a mother. I want to be pregnant. But I don't want the child. Isn't that weird? It was a lot more painful being pregnant this time, and I had a lot of strange sensations in my abdomen, and I was feeling tired all the time. And I started to get fat which really bothered me.

"The guy was really supportive. He wanted to come with me and hold my hand, but I just totally turned him out. I just wanted to roll around in my own shit. I really set myself up for a monster. I really wanted to punish myself, and I guess I was setting the guy up to be a victim, too. It was really a trip, but the worst kind because you have so much trouble getting out. So I wouldn't let him come with me, but when I get home I'm moping and crying, thinking why isn't he over here, why isn't he taking care of me. And I didn't give him any space to do that in the first place. He could do no right. Only wrong.

"I was terrified about my body too. The abortion was incredibly painful, and I was convinced they were damaging my body and I'd never get pregnant again. I felt like they were sucking my whole insides out. I just didn't want to be hurt. My legs were shaking so hard on the table I couldn't stop them. And I couldn't stop crying. It was partly the pain and partly that I was really disgusted at what I was doing. It was awful.

"I decided after the abortion that I was just tired of being uncomfortable, so I took all the nerve I could get together and put all my shit on the table. I was being impossibly snotty, which made him withdraw all the more and made it worse. Finally we had a twenty-five-pound bag of shit to deal with. But we did deal with it and I've been incredibly happy ever since.

"We just shared our sides of the story of anger, and his side was just like mine. I was just buried so deep in all my own stuff that I wasn't even including any possibility that he was hurt too. And that we had just been so irresponsible about our integrity to each other. I don't blame him at all. I think that we're both actually responsible for what happened. He just explained to me that he'd been feeling really ripped off because I'd been so bitchy in not letting him be there. He was really trying to put out for me, and I wasn't letting him. I was making him offer everything and not accepting.

"What we talked about was not pushing anything, and just seeing what happens, starting off with just being friends and being honest and being supportive of each other. Maybe from that we'll come together again, and we may end up sleeping together. We had a relationship, but it was never a very honest one. It was never on the level that I wanted it.

"So the way I feel right now, this abortion's really been a positive one. And maybe it's going to be okay, now."

—————

It has been six years since Florida Amos, twenty-three, had an abortion at the Special Care Center in Oakland, California. Today she is returning to be sterilized. Separated from her husband, Florida is the mother of two children, one and three, and doesn't want to have any more. On welfare at the time of her teenage abortion and still on welfare, Florida says black men just want to knock women up and not take any of the responsibility.

"The first time I got pregnant and had an abortion, I was seventeen and in high school. I thought about getting married, but the guy wasn't interested in marrying me. He wanted me to have the baby, but he wasn't about to support it or anything. He just wanted to brag about it, like a lot of black guys.

"I thought about abortion again when I got pregnant with my youngest daughter because they'd be so close in age. But my husband, he said, 'If you have the baby, I'll be right there by your side,' and then he tells his friends that I was expecting again and carried on about it to his friends, telling them I was going to have a boy this time. He was working on me right after I had my first baby to have another. He started bragging about the baby that hadn't even gotten started yet. Right after I had the baby, he said we have to do it again. But I was hesitant. He'd walked out on me when I was six months pregnant the first time, and I didn't know if he'd do it again.

"So I was just a little happy when I found out I was pregnant again. Mostly I thought about the future. How was another baby going to affect my life as far as, well, nothing's really for granted, not even marriage. The first thing that popped into my head, if this guy walks out and leaves me tomorrow . . . how? Which is exactly what he did, for the second time. I was five months pregnant when he left.

"I considered having an abortion then, but I couldn't. I kind of fell in love with the baby. His walking out made me closer to my two-year-old and the unborn child. It entered my mind, but I couldn't handle the head trips. The baby was moving then, always moving.

"I had my abortion here, when I was seventeen, and right now it's bothering me, being here. What would have happened if I had had that other baby? Now that I've had children, I've developed a respect for life. Now I look back and I'm glad that I didn't know then what it was to have a child. It's much harder to have an abortion if you've already had a child. I don't know if I regret the abortion. I have mixed emotions about it. I'm glad I did it because of my age then, and I would have had no source of income, really. But then when I look at me now—I'm on welfare, I'm alone—it wouldn't have been too much difference, you know? I would have been in the same shape a couple of years ago, only I would have known the happiness that a child can bring. I didn't get a chance to go out and party then, and I still don't party. All the reasons I had the abortion for, I still have the same problems now that I've got two children. They were just kind of delayed. If I had a seven-year-old now, it actually would be a lot easier for me. Then I wouldn't need to pay for child care. I'm sad really. I guess that's what is it. I'm sad.

"So now I'm getting my tubes tied. I have trouble remembering to take the pill every single day. I tried the IUD, but my whole body just rejected it. It was like having a baby. The doctor inserted it, and it was just like I was going through labor. He took it out thirty minutes later, and he told me my body just thought it was aborting. So I'm looking at it logically. I don't need any more children. Emotionally I love children, and I sort of enjoy carrying a child and caring for it. But now I've had my children, and they're growing up, and it's time for me. I have enough to do for them, and then after I do for them, I take care of myself. I never have any time doing my life. I can't take another one upstairs. I'd just crack.

"This time I'm through with my husband. He's only seen the new baby once, and when he tried to come back again, I said, 'Forget it.' I feel like right now I can make it just as well without him. He doesn't pay anything. Nothing. And I don't care to try and make him. He doesn't bother me, and I don't bother him.

"It may seem weird, but I'm having a kind of occasional relationship with another guy now, and we've talked about my being sterilized, and I told him he can go out and have as many babies as he wants just so long as he has them with somebody else. If a relationship develops between us, he can still go out and have as many as he wants. I'm not having any more babies. Period.

"Black men just want to knock women up. It comes from being a child when he sees his mother pregnant all his life. Up until the time he's an adult, his mother is nine times out of ten pregnant, and nine times out of ten, his father or her husband is not there. After a while, as he gets older, I guess he just assumes this is the thing to do. This is his role. And he thinks, basically, that men are here to reproduce and women are here to do the producing. It's going to be awful hard changing that notion. Seeing as the white people more or less control things, trying to put birth control in black men's minds just makes them reject it more. They think it's the whites trying to exploit the black man. Breed 'em out. The black men think they got to fight to protect their masculinity.

"The problem is women are weak to an extent. My mother always had a saying: 'A hard dick has no conscience.' Which really fits. But neither does a hot woman. Like when I went to bed with my husband, pregnancy never entered my mind. I was just hot. But at least soon I can be hot with a conscience."

68

Before 1973

Because abortion has been legal for such a short time, many young women undergoing legal abortions now have had illegal abortions in the past. Obviously, the differences are striking. Aside from the shock every woman feels when she discovers she is pregnant, the shock to a single woman when abortion was not immediately available quickly escalated into panic. For the lucky and affluent women with sympathetic doctors, abortions were quietly arranged in Puerto Rico, Mexico, Cuba, or as far away as England. In such settings, the procedures were safe, the staff was reassuring, and the women were secure in knowing that if there were any complications afterwards, their private doctors would take care of them.

For the less fortunate, however, illegal abortion was literally a matter of life and death. Much has been written about the abortion mills and quacks who practiced in back alleys. Even more has been written about the desperate women who would either operate on themselves or bleed to death after being butchered by an illegal abortionist, and for those reasons alone the fact that getting an abortion is now legal should be welcomed without reservation.

But many women sought out illegal abortions and survived. Aside from the shame and fear they felt prior to the procedure, and for many, the physical agony of the procedure itself, the aftereffects were remarkably similar to those experienced by women undergoing legal abortions. In situations in which the relationship between the couple involved was not strong to begin with, the abortion carried little aftermath of guilt. Where the relationship was meaningful, the abortion produced more ambivalence. The degree of severity of the illegal abortion, some of which were unspeakably horrible, seemed to have had little effect on the woman's emotions afterwards. There was the same need in some women to punish the male partner, the same need to retreat temporarily into celibacy or promiscuity, the same strengthening of some relationships and the dissolution of others.

Like pregnancy and childbirth, abortion, be it legal or illegal, is solely a woman's experience. The whole process of reproduction screams out the bottom-line difference between men and women—that though the pleasure of sex is shared, the physical result affects the woman only. And much as some men try to share in it, they cannot. Even wanted pregnancies create strains. Unwanted pregnancies multiply the strain a thousandfold. Finding an abortionist added untold stress on top of that. It is sometimes a wonder that women have survived at all.

Penelope Marsh was one of the lucky ones. Now thirty-six and single, Penelope had an illegal abortion in Puerto Rico ten years ago. Though she bought a fake wedding ring and lied to the doctor, the procedure was safe and easy, and Penelope felt no guilt about it. She never told her not-serious boyfriend about her pregnancy or the abortion. But two years later when she found herself in bed with him again, she suddenly got furious at him and sent him home. She's never seen him again. Penelope is a television reporter in New York.

"I had spent an agonizing two months in a hospital at the time undergoing tests for a brain tumor. The neurologist thought the increased pressure in my spine might be due to birth-control pills, so he took me off them. When I got out of the hospital, I felt I deserved some fun. I played Russian roulette with sex, and two months later there I was, preggers. I lied to my gynecologist, who is a very traditional man, and said I'd been on the sequential pill and it hadn't worked. Because he believed in the pill so much and was horrified it hadn't worked, he sent me to the Women's Hospital in Puerto Rico. But he couldn't look me in the face.

"I was very frightened. What if he hadn't sent me to Puerto Rico? How would I have gotten rid of it? As it was, I simply made a reservation and went away on a long weekend. I was terrified on the plane that I would die on the operating table and no one would know where I was except my doctor.

"I arrived at the clinic at eight-thirty the next morning, and the place was jammed with mothers and daughters all wringing their

70

hands. It was hysterical. The worst part was telling the taxi driver the address because he would know why I was going there. But I did it. After the doctor gave me a physical examination, he told me to go to a bank and bring back eight hundred dollars in cash, which I did. I also bought a little ring so I could tell the doctor my husband had been killed in Vietnam.

"When I woke up in the hospital room after the D and C, the doctor came in to see me and delivered a moral lecture. He also said he hoped he wouldn't see me there again. Can you imagine—after all the money he made that day? But my first feeling was one of relief. I had no sense of loss about what I'd done, and I'd do it again. The first person I told about it tried to make me feel guilty. She succeeded for a couple of minutes, but then I said, 'Fuck you.'

"I really love kids. My friends with children call me 'The Spoiler'! My only question is—did I allow it to happen? Sure I was irresponsible, but I wanted to be irresponsible. And I'm not sure I felt more secure knowing I could get pregnant. After all, I was raised to get married at sixteen anyway!

"My brother was furious I didn't tell him before the abortion, but it was just something I had to do alone. I didn't even tell the guy. Why bother? He was just a nice guy, and I didn't need the money. I saw him again a couple of times, and then two years later we ended up back at my apartment and we went to bed. Suddenly I got furious at him over nothing, and he asked me what the hell was bugging me. I told him I didn't like him and I never wanted to see him again, and he got dressed and went home. And I never did see him again. I'm very careful now. It's not something I'd like to go through again."

Life has been more harsh to Leslie English, thirty-two. She has one son, nine, has given up another son for adoption, and has had two abortions, one illegal and one legal. The combination of these experiences caused her to check herself into a mental institution in Ohio in 1969, and later to try to commit suicide. Now Leslie is a counselor at an abortion clinic.

71

*   *   *

"I was twenty-three the first time I got pregnant, and it scared the man half to death. I waited for five months until he felt more comfortable, and then we got married. He was in the service, but then he left and went back to college, and the adjustment proved too hard and we got divorced. My son was one and a half. I had been on the pill while we were married, but when we got divorced my family doctor said I wouldn't be needing the pills any more, and he wouldn't give me a prescription. I was dumb. I accepted what he said, and of course I got pregnant.

"The father of the second one was just a good friend. I never thought of having an abortion or giving the baby up for adoption, but presumed he'd marry me, which he refused to do. I brought a paternity suit against him. This was the second time I'd gotten pregnant with the guy shaky. I was tired of being left holding the bag.

"I went to a counselor to ask about my chances of proving a paternity suit and she said, 'No way, forget it,' so I dropped the suit. While I was pregnant, I went on welfare. But I knew emotionally I wasn't going to be able to handle the whole thing. It was too late to have an abortion, and very few black families adopt children. They already got too many. I was going to have the baby and put it in a boarding house until I could support it.

"Then a friend told me about her cousin who couldn't have children and who wanted mine. I never met her. The whole thing was arranged through a private attorney, who instead of giving me the money this woman had given me for my expenses, pocketed it instead. When my son was a week old, they took him.

"I bottle-fed the boy in the hospital. I had named him and everything. I was very upset by it but felt it was best. I had a lot of guilt. Would the child ever understand what I had done? My son now says he wants a little brother, and that tears me up.

"I saw my second son once, three years later. The adoption papers were about to become final, but the woman had finally gotten pregnant herself, was having marital difficulties, and wanted to give him back instead. They drove up to my house one morning in a station wagon filled with toys to deliver him. They were having a terrible argument in the front seat, and I looked at my boy in the back seat.

72

I felt hurt and guilty. I wanted to hug him, but I couldn't. I tried to avoid eye contact with him and ignore the fact that I was his natural mother.

"He was small and not as alert-looking as my other son. If I had taken him back, the two boys would never seem like natural brothers. And I wondered how people would react to me, knowing the boys had two separate fathers. I felt a lot of social pressure and refused to take him back. I saw him once more at a church function, and he still didn't look or act like my son. It made me feel better. Again I tried not to let him catch me looking at him. It was like a part of you was there, but not there. I know I'll have to tell my first son someday. I wonder how he'll feel about me.

"The guilt just wouldn't go away. I developed a bad vaginal infection, which the doctor said would mean that I could never have any more children. I was sure I was being punished. I felt so bad I checked myself in a state mental institution.

They wouldn't let me out for three months. It was a nightmare. They threatened to probate me if I signed myself out without medical consent. I didn't want that on my record. I just wanted to talk to a psychiatrist, and the only way I could afford it was to check myself in that way. Instead of letting me talk to a psychiatrist, though, they made me spend all my time doing arts and crafts. My whole personality changed. I started cursing and breaking rules. I had to find a tough part of me to survive. One night an orderly beat me. When I told him I was going to report him, he told me he'd say he'd caught me having an affair with another patient. It was a trip.

"When I got out, I was completely fucked up. I took up with a married man and didn't bother to use birth control because that doctor had told me I could never have any more children. I got pregnant and went back on welfare. I knew this time I had to have an abortion. A friend of a friend referred me. I went to a house in the black community. The woman who owned the house made her living selling hot clothes and renting a room to the abortionist. While I was waiting for the abortion, she tried to sell me a stolen suit.

"The abortionist finally came. She had a pan boiling on the stove with instruments in it that looked like hangers. I lay on my back with my knees up. I knew deep inside it was all wrong, but all I could think about was what else could I do. She stuck the coat hanger up me and scraped all around until I fainted.

"The next day I had to go to work, but I started having bad cramps. I took a bus home and hemorrhaged all over the street. My mother, luckily, was with me. I went crazy. I started to scream and cry. I ran into my apartment and bled all over the rug. I jammed a towel between my legs and there was a fetus hanging down between them, swinging from the umbilical cord. It was fourteen weeks and already formed. I knew from what I'd seen on TV that I should cut the cord, so I did. Then I wrapped it in newspaper and put it in the garbage can. Luckily my mother didn't see any of this, and to this day she still doesn't know. She only saw all the blood. I couldn't stop bleeding. I didn't dare go to the hospital, but she called the life-saving squad, and they took me anyway. I didn't dare tell them about the abortion. I thought they would send me to jail. I just said I'd had a miscarriage. The doctor could tell, though, and made me sign a statement that the hospital was not at fault.

"I was so shamed I called the guy I'd been seeing, and he was only terrified that his wife would find out. He never came to see me or even call me. Not one man had ever stood by me. I called the doctor who had said I could never get pregnant, and he said nonsense, that I was psychosomatic and just imagining the whole thing because I'd been in a mental hospital.

"I finally broke down and told the nurse what had happened, and the next day there were two detectives in the room to question me. But I couldn't tell on my friends who had helped me. They threatened to put me in jail, just the thing I'd been afraid of. I started harassing the married guy. I called and called and finally got the wife. She called the police, and the next time I called, they answered the phone. They they came over to the hospital and disconnected mine. I was so tired I couldn't do anything but sleep. When I woke up one afternoon, the wife was in my room. She had a strange bulge in her purse and said she had come to kill me. Then she said she really felt sorry for me and walked out of the room instead.

"When I got home, I took an overdose of tranquilizers. But then I thought of my son and called my mother. She rushed me to the hospital, and I had my stomach pumped. I was really emotionally

74

fucked up. I had hurt two innocent children and killed another. I was a good Baptist and felt really bad about myself. I slept with every and any man who came along after that.

"I finally got to a good psychiatrist and also got an IUD. I went a whole year without getting pregnant, which made me feel really good. I went back on welfare then, and finished college. I graduated in '74.

"Then they took me off the IUD because I bled so much from it and it made me anemic. I went back on the pill and missed a couple last year and got pregnant again. By then abortion was legal, so I came to this clinic and the nurse told me they were looking for a black counselor. I had a degree in social work by then, so I took the job. There was nothing punitive about the abortion I had here, and I can help other women now by making something positive out of all these experiences. Now I can give factual knowledge, which helps them make their decisions.

"I feel a lot better, but it's been very rough. My parents don't know about the abortions, just the child I gave up. I've never really told anyone about my life. I couldn't even tell my minister. The minister makes the atmosphere for the church in a black community, and he's very stuffy. The congregation would definitely ostracize me if they knew. They think sex is only to have kids, and they'd never understand this. The church is very important to me. And I don't want to let all the members of my congregation down."

When Ellen Herblock discovered she was pregnant at the age of nineteen, she panicked and asked every man she knew for help. Finally one came up with a nurse on the Upper West Side of New York who performed illegal abortions in her apartment. Ellen had to go to her twice before the abortion took, then hemorrhaged badly at home and expelled the fetus into the toilet. Twelve years later, Ellen has just had a legal abortion with no complications, either physical or emotional. Ellen lives in Newark, New Jersey, where she is a part-time computer programmer.

*   *   *

"I knew it was a bad day when I first got pregnant. I knew it was my fertile period, and I told the guy he had to stop and he did, but what I didn't know was that he had ejaculated already. Big surprise. I never thought I could be pregnant because I believed him. He had pulled out and said, 'Phew, that was close.' But when I called him two weeks later after I had missed my period, he confessed.

"It was the first reality I had to face, and I got hysterical. There I was, nineteen years old, having just moved out of my family's home and into an apartment with a roommate who was a virgin. And I became the loneliest, most depressed nineteen-year-old you can imagine without anyone to talk to.

"I walked around looking suicidal, thinking that if I looked bad enough someone would help me. I was sure if I had an abortion I was going to die. I'd just read about some really rich girl being butchered, so what was going to happen to me?

"Finally a guy said he'd help me. I asked men for help but not girls. I figured they'd be more judgmental than men. This guy told me about a Puerto Rican nurse up on the Upper West Side who was cheap, only ninety dollars, who induced miscarriage with some liquid or other so I wouldn't be tampered with with instruments. It seemed endless between the time I got pregnant and the time I found out about the nurse, but it was only six weeks.

"I called the guy who'd gotten me pregnant and he took me over. The nurse was nice. She said the cost of the abortion was the same as the cost of her supplies, and I believed her. She said she felt sorry for women in this position, which is why she did it.

"When I went it hurt a lot, like intense cramps, but I wanted it to hurt probably more than it did because the guy was there. I wanted it to be more traumatic to punish him. And of course the abortion didn't work. All the liquid fell out because I screamed and squirmed and carried on so, even though the nurse was trying to hold me down. I went back alone a couple of days later, and that time she asked me not to scream so I wouldn't upset the neighbors. I controlled myself that time because I didn't want to hurt her feelings.

"The abortion took, and I started bleeding right away. There was a great risk of infection, but I blocked it out. I didn't want to know about it. I tried not to feel very much of anything. I didn't relate to any of the facts that proved that I was a pregnant person. It was merely a problem and I was solving it.

"A few nights later I woke up in the middle of the night and knew something was wrong. I turned on the light, and the sheet was bloody from top to bottom. I ran into the bathroom and sat down on the toilet and something fell into the john. I was petrified. I didn't know if it was my liver or some internal organ. It looked like a ball to me, some important part of my insides. Then I rationalized to myself that I felt all right, that I was still breathing, so it was probably just the baby.

"I had to sleep in that bloody bed all night and then wait until my roommate went to work in the morning so she wouldn't see it. It's amazing what you can do. It was worse to me what she would think of me rather than what I thought of myself. It was a terrible experience in every way.

"It wasn't helped by the guy's family. His uncle was part of the Mafia, and he kept calling me before the abortion telling me I was a tramp and a whore and his nephew had no responsibility. And all the time I had to smile into the phone and take it so my roommate wouldn't know. He kept telling me I had to pay the piper, but his nephew was really nice about it and paid the abortionist instead. It was like being in the middle of the cyclone. So I just stopped feeling altogether.

"The next morning I washed the sheet in cold water by hand for hours to get all the blood out. And when I got to work they bawled me out for being late. Then I wrote the nurse a nice thank-you letter with some perverse manners my mother had pushed into my brain.

"I sort of forgot about the abortion afterwards, but I always felt guilty. The worst part of it was being secretive. It was like being the first on my block. I never went out with the guy again.

"In juxtaposition, the abortion I just had was over in five minutes. The doctor was nice, and I felt good and normal. Right afterwards I went to Bloomingdale's, then to a movie and had a bagel. Why shouldn't it always have been that way for women?"

Sally Thorton, thirty, had an illegal abortion at the age of nineteen, shortly before she married her husband Randy, a schoolteacher. They were living in Kansas City at the time, and Sally's sister and husband-to-be decided the time was not right for Sally to have a baby. Since that time, Sally has had one miscarriage and no other pregnancies. She is convinced that God is punishing her for having the abortion.

"I hadn't started on any birth control when I was a teenager. Randy was only the second man I'd ever slept with, and my sex life was just beginning to become active. But when we had slept together maybe four times over a two-month period, I thought I'd better go to the doctor to get some birth control. Our relationship was becoming serious and looked like it was going to continue.

"When I went to the doctor he gave me a complete physical and said that it looked like I was already pregnant and asked me whether it could be possible. I turned all red in the face and said yes. It was amazing. I hadn't even skipped a period but had just bled lightly. It was like a bolt out of the blue.

"I was very happy at the thought of being pregnant. I'd always loved kids. I didn't think of any of the consequences of being nineteen and single. Then I started thinking wake up, you're not a kid. Randy and I sort of knew we were going to get married, but not at that point. He was still in school. We were semi-engaged, but were not at that final ring-on-the-finger stage.

"My sister and Randy and I sat down to talk about it. One of them, I can't remember which, said I should have an abortion. I have a background of not making decisions for myself, but I still said I didn't want to have an abortion. Randy said he wanted to marry me, but he just wasn't ready for children at that time. He just couldn't take on that responsibility. I kind of went along and agreed.

"My sister produced the abortionist. It was a very bad experience. Randy dropped me off at this gungy little office, then left, because the doctor didn't want him there. I wished I'd had the guts to say I didn't want to be there, but I didn't.

"He took me into a back room which had a lounge sort of couch in front of a television set. He gave me some pills and told me to watch TV, and the next thing I knew I woke up on a table. The doctor was talking on the phone and was having a very personal conversation. I just didn't give a damn what he wanted for dinner. I must have made some sort of sound because he turned to me and said, 'Oh shut up, will you.' I felt terrible. I wanted to get out of there, but I didn't know whether he'd started or finished the abortion. He gave me a drink of water, which put me right back out again.

"When I woke up again he gave me a lecture about not taking a bath for two weeks or even washing my hair. I paid him three hundred dollars, and then Randy came to fetch me. At first I felt relief just to get out of that office. And then for three days or so I felt kind of down, but I wasn't sure why. Even then, I guess, I was trying to block it out. It took me six years and a year of therapy to even discuss it with Randy.

"We got married the next year, and for the first few years the abortion didn't bother me. I was on the pill then until 1970, when I went off it to get pregnant and succeeded. It was a hellish pregnancy. I bled a lot at the beginning and the doctor finally put me to bed. For five weeks I was flat on my back and the abortion just wouldn't go out of my mind. 'My God, did I do this?' I kept asking myself. 'Am I never going to have children?' I felt that God was punishing me on one hand, and that the abortionist must have messed up my insides on the other. Maybe it was a botched job.

"I began to get better finally. I went to my monthly checkups and was getting bigger all the time. The doctor always said, 'You're fine; come back next month.' Then when I was five months pregnant I was driving home from work and I felt the whole thing go. I'd had a backache for a couple of days, but that hadn't worried me because I'd had a backache more or less all the time since I'd gotten pregnant. I knew it was all over then and made myself keep on driving home so I could call my husband. 'He'll know what to do,' I reasoned.

"He came home and drove me to the hospital. The doctor there couldn't even find the fetus. What had happened was that I had probably lost the baby right at the beginning with all that bleeding, but the placenta had continued to grow as if it were still there. The doctor turned to me and said, 'I guess you know it's all over,' and all I could think was don't be like that. Be nicer to me. Help me. I felt really bad. I couldn't stop crying. The only thing that consoled me was the fact that with all those problems, there was probably something wrong with the child.

"Since then I haven't been able to conceive. For a year I took my temperature every morning and kept a chart so I'd know when I ovulated. My husband had a sperm count. I had a blood work-up and a thyroid test. I had minor surgery which entailed two incisions, one just under my navel and the other just above the pubic bone, so the doctors could X-ray my tubes. One turned out to be questionable but the other was perfectly clear. In another test, I had to come to the lab two hours after my husband and I had had intercourse to make sure the juices in my body weren't killing the sperm. They wanted to see if the sperm were still alive, if there were enough, and if they were getting up far enough. That test worked out fine too. The only thing they've found is that I don't ovulate every month. I skip every third month or so. There's nothing wrong with me physically. I haven't gotten pregnant out of guilt and fear. As much as I want to be pregnant, I'm frightened of having another miscarriage.

"We can't even adopt. Our names are on every list in the country, but there aren't any babies. I tried a Jewish home, but they weren't even taking any more names. When the Vietnamese babies were being flown over, I rushed to put my name on that list, but there were 1,500 couples ahead of us. I keep calling all the agencies just in case. But it's impossible. Now I'm trying for foster children, but that agency never calls me back.

"Every month when I get my period, I'm extremely disappointed. The doctor says to relax and forget about it and not to count the calendar, but I just can't. Every month I feel a great, great disappointment.

"At one point after the miscarriage, I blamed my husband for making me have the abortion. How could he have done this to me? Our marriage began to fall apart. We stopped communicating altogether. We were at the point that if we didn't start talking, we were going to kiss everything goodbye. The only thing left between us was hostility. Surprisingly, we never stopped sleeping together. I've never spent the night on the couch. Our sex life was never a problem.

"I didn't even know what was bothering me. I knew what all the miscellaneous things were, but I didn't know it was the abortion. I had totally blocked it out. My husband said, 'I know you're not going to talk to me, but you have to talk to somebody or else it's all over.' I went to a psychiatrist, and for the first few visits I would only answer his questions yes or no. It took me eleven months of therapy before I even told him about the abortion. He flew at me. 'Goddamn it, woman, why didn't you tell me nine months ago?' he said. But even when I told him about the abortion, I wouldn't say anything more than just that I'd had one.

"I've been in some sort of therapy ever since, and my husband and I can talk now about the abortion. It's saved our marriage. And I understand what the therapists are telling me, that I shouldn't feel so much guilt. But I just can't change my feeling. The guilt is punishing. I'm being punished by God because I did this thing ten years ago. I shouldn't have done it. I wish I wouldn't have.

"Now we use the pillow when we have intercourse. It worked for my sister-in-law, who couldn't have children until she tried that. She's having her third child in January. I've even tried smoking grass to relax, but it makes me leery. I've got to have control. I feel if I get too far out on grass, I wouldn't be able to get myself back.

"One thing for sure is that I've changed my mind about abortion. My husband still feels that every woman should have the right to control her own body. But I feel I can't have children, and that because of the abortion laws I can't even adopt one. I should probably join one of those anti-abortion groups. It would get me out of the house and give me something to do. I have all these maternal instincts and no one to give them to."

Second Trimester

Though no abortion is pleasant, second-trimester abortions, which take place after the sixteenth week of pregnancy, are far more painful both physically and emotionally. Because of the increasing number of first-trimester abortion clinics and the growing general sophistication among women of childbearing years, the incidence of late abortion has dropped to below 10 percent of the total number of abortions performed. But for the women who make up that 10 percent, the ordeal can be very traumatic.

Typically, the candidate for a second-trimester abortion is the least equipped to handle it. In a study of 200 women having first-trimester abortions and 200 women having second-trimester abortions in New York in 1972, the interviewers found the latter group to be younger, less educated, single, predominantly unemployed, and still in school. The majority of them were also experiencing their first pregnancies and were therefore less apt to pick up the symptoms that signaled pregnancy. They also had a higher degree of ambivalence about abortion versus giving birth, and often denied the fact of their pregnancies to themselves until it became too obvious to ignore. One thirteen-year-old girl kept dutifully wrapping up Kotex napkins and putting them in the wastebasket until her grandmother noticed she was getting fat. A twenty-four-year-old Puerto Rican woman was seven months' pregnant before she could face the medical conclusion. Even with the quickening of the fetus, skipped menstrual periods, and weight gain, she claimed she couldn't be pregnant because she hadn't had any morning sickness.

Emotionally, the second-trimester abortion patient is apt to be more dependent on others than on herself. According to a 1973 study entitled "Psychological Factors in Mid-Trimester Abortion," conducted by a doctor at the University of California in San Francisco, late abortees were found to have come from authoritarian families in which they hadn't been encouraged to make decisions on their own. These families also had a history of avoiding communication on emotional issues. The combination of these factors led these abortion patients to procrastinate about dealing with their pregnancies in

82

hopes of "an intervention by an authoritarian physician."

The aftereffects of the abortion were also more difficult than those following first-trimester abortions. Many studies point out that first-trimester abortees discuss their abortion experience in terms of "the pregnancy" or "the fetus." Late aborters, on the other hand, use such terms as "the baby" or "the child" and refer to the procedure as "labor," "delivery," and "childbirth." Instead of expressing their feelings afterwards as slight grief or loss, the late group often used the term "mourning." "There are any number of psychological problems and ramifications in second trimesters having waited so long, and they are going to have to go through the most traumatic medical type of abortion there is," says Frances Kissling, director of the National Abortion Council. "These are also the people who are least prepared to deal with the most trauma. They need more extensive counseling on a one-to-one basis. We concentrate on what took them so long to come to this decision to facilitate some solution to delayed decision-making in other aspects of their lives as well. In trying to make their abortions as much of a positive experience as possible, we try to relate it to how they will proceed from there on in in all their decision-making."

The numbers of women facing second-trimester abortion will probably continue to decrease. But where there are ethical or religious conflicts that cause women to delay, social barriers that limit access to medical care (for example, youth, ignorance, or the inability to pay), or inaccessibility to abortion facilities, some second-trimester procedures will be inevitable.

When Gwen Soltey was eighteen she became pregnant and gained forty pounds to try to hide her condition from her mother. Engaged at the time, she told her fiancé about her condition, and he walked out on her. Alone, Gwen flew to New York for a second-trimester saline abortion. Now twenty-three and pregnant again, Gwen is terrified she may have to face another saline abortion instead of the easier D and E procedure. At the end of our interview, the word came from the lab that Gwen could have a D and E, and the abortion was performed. Gwen now lives in southern California and is a factory assembly-line worker. Her boyfriend Andy manages a motel.

"When I found out I was pregnant this time I couldn't believe it was happening to me again. I've never missed a pill, which was the way it happened the first time. I was still in high school then, and I was terrified to tell my mother I was pregnant. She's the type of person who if I'd told her would say, 'Never come back in this house again.' So I ate and ate and gained forty pounds to try and hide my stomach. I finally broke down and told her, and I was right. She called me every name she could think of—bitch, whore, slut—which made me feel really terrific.

"I flew to New York for the abortion. It was hell. At first they said they wouldn't do it, said I was too far along. I was in the hospital for five days while everybody made up their minds. There was one nice nurse who invited me to come live with her if they couldn't take the baby and said that she would support us and I could pay her back by babysitting her kids. I really thought of doing it because I couldn't stand to come home. But they finally did it, and two days after they put in the saline, I had the baby. It cost me six hundred and fifty dollars, which was my life savings from babysitting.

"I really suffered from that. I was very much against abortion at the time. I thought I was killing a living thing. And it didn't help much to overhear them talking in the hospital when I had it, saying, 'Oh, it's a baby boy.' I was almost seven months pregnant, and I was born myself two months early. That got to me more than anything.

"For a long while afterwards I hated men. I had been engaged to the father of the first kid until I told him I was pregnant. He went out and got drunk and never came back. He just split and took off. I never saw him again. I felt just like a piece of dirt. That's how I felt I was being treated. It seems I can't remember when I wasn't crying.

"For two—no, three—years I just felt guilty all the time. I didn't go out with anyone, not even my girlfriends. I just went to school and came back home. School and back. Every day. My mother made it worse. She blamed me for everything. When my sister's boyfriend got thrown in jail, she told me it was all my fault because he'd been in a fight with a guy who was saying bad things about me. I finally moved out.

"This time I got pregnant on the pill again. My boyfriend and I decided on an abortion because Andy is going through a divorce and it would have put another trauma on him. This is harder for him than me. He just didn't want a baby. I really did want it, because I didn't think I could mentally handle the abortion, but he talked me into going to Planned Parenthood.

"They sent me to a really nice hospital. It was beautiful, all pine-paneled, with a color TV and music piped in. But they said there I was too far along and they couldn't do it. So the hospital referred me to another place, but when I got there, it looked like a garage. It was surrounded by factories and was right next to the railroad tracks. It looked more like a place you'd send your car to have a lube job over a pit, but Andy talked me into going inside. I stayed five seconds. I just ran out and left him there. Nobody could ever stay in a place like that.

"So we drove to Los Angeles and stood in a phone booth in Hollywood for four hours dialing every ad in the yellow pages to find someone who'd do a D and E. We found one private doctor who'd do it for six hundred dollars, but all the others were just saline. I decided in that phone booth to have the kid, which made me relieved, but Andy said he just wasn't ready for a kid. I am. The last phone call brought us here.

"I still don't know whether I'm too far along to have the abortion. If it has to be saline, I just won't go through with it. I'll just raise it alone if I have to. But what I really want is a D and E and to get out of here. Poor Andy has been through a lot and he just couldn't handle it. All I'm thinking about is him. He's really had a lot of troubles. I'm doing it for him."

Frances Alden, twenty-five, had a saline abortion in Los Angeles when she was nineteen. Though she had decided to abort when she was six weeks pregnant, the red tape involved in applying for financial assistance delayed the schedule until she was too far gone for a first-trimester procedure. Now an active feminist, Frances thinks of her abortion as a result of societal pressures, which do not include support for single working-class women who also want to bear children. Frances is presently unemployed and works as a volunteer in a Los Angeles hospital with second-trimester abortion patients.

"I was nineteen when I found out I was pregnant. I was using a diaphragm, but I didn't really use it because I didn't like it. I still don't like to use birth control. I feel like it sort of destroys the power of my fertility. I don't know how to explain that. But at one time I tried the pill, and it made me real sick, and I didn't want to have an IUD' cause I think they're very dangerous. So I was using a diaphragm, but I wasn't really using it. A diaphragm makes me feel like I have to keep my cervix or my reproductive organs away from everything.

"When I found out I was pregnant, I was real upset. At first I was numb, and then I thought, you're pregnant! How nice. I considered having the baby, but I also realized my class position as being a poor woman, and being real dependent on having to work and go to school to get ahead. My mother was a PBX operator all my life. But I was real happy about the idea that I could be pregnant. I had worried in high school about not being able to have children. A lot of times on TV, if you ever notice, nobody can have children easily. So if you have been brought up on popular media it's sort of a fear you might have.

"Then I realized I did want to have an abortion, and I came in to L.A. I didn't have enough money, 'cause it cost a lot of money then. I can't remember how much it was. I didn't have any money at all. I was just living on a shoestring. So I applied for Medi-Cal. I lied, said I lived in Los Angeles and used my girlfriend's friend's address. It took me almost two months to get that card. So whereas I had been about six weeks pregnant when I decided to have the abortion, and it could have been very simple, one, two, three, I ended up having a saline procedure because I was fourteen weeks pregnant by the time I had the abortion.

86

"I was going to be in a really wretched hospital for three days. I understood that they were going to inject this fluid into my uterus that would cause me to miscarry, but I did not know that much about birth. It was just a real weird scene, 'cause there were several women who were having these infusions that day. We were all sort of going in one after the other. The doctor was just real jovial about the whole thing. He was a really young person, and I had all this confidence in him, because I really had to. He said, 'Oh, it's not gonna be all that bad,' that kind of stuff. And then he went on to do the most brutal examination I've ever had. He didn't even say anything supportive, like 'Sometimes it takes more than one insertion of this needle to find the uterus.' I just got this horrible feeling that I was in this place where people really got off on being mean to each other.

"Then they put the saline solution in and put me in a room with several other women. We were all having these procedures. Before, when I had gotten bad menstrual cramps I had always gotten up and walked around, or run or done some exercises. But this time I was real scared. I thought that if I stood up, my insides were gonna fall out. I had this bloated feeling. I felt like I couldn't walk, like I had this fish bowl or something in my uterus. It was real uncomfortable. So I lay there, cramping and cramping. It hurt real bad, partly because I didn't know what was happening. We all worked to be supportive of each other, but most of us were really freaked out. People were crying because you felt so alone, 'cause you didn't know what was happening, and we barely knew each other. Nobody particularly introduced us. And it was just a whole difference in age, and class of people. People were sort of tentative about each other, frightened.

"I got the infusion in the morning and at the end of that night I started to miscarry. I realized what was happening, that the fetus was being expelled. I was laying there and it came out, and I could feel it laying there between my legs. I wanted to look at it, but I was kind of scared. I felt bad that I didn't look at it, because I wanted to at that point. I thought I should.

"My mother died a few months ago, and I was really glad I was with her when she died. I don't know how to say this, but I just felt like I should have looked at the fetus. And I was sort of curious. It lay there for about five minutes, and I called the nurse and said, 'Could you do something about this?' I was the second person to expel. I didn't scream or anything. I just sort of pushed down, and I really wanted it to just happen. I just wanted it to get over with. So the nurse said, 'We can't take it until the placenta comes out. After the placenta comes out, then we'll take it all away at once.' I was a good forty-five minutes laying there. I just cried, I was just laying there crying and crying and crying. And then I just pushed the nurse's button, I pushed and pushed, and they finally took it away. Then they had a doctor come in. He did this D and C that really hurt, and I thought I was gonna die. They just had an authoritarian structural assembly line way of health care there. So everybody had a D and C. I screamed. I didn't even have an anesthetic.

"I went back to school, and I've often thought about this. I didn't think about the abortion very much after that. It was over. It was an experience I'd think about occasionally. But I had to go back to school, I had to deal with things, and I was really busy. Mostly I felt real brutalized, like I had been treated like a piece of shit by the nurses and by the hospital and by the doctors.

"Now I want to have a baby. First of all, I'm more stable than I used to be. I have more of an understanding. The reason I had my abortion was because I was a poor working-class woman who was trying to go to school. There was just no way I could have that child. It was society. We live in an antipoverty society where my having that child would have totally ruined whatever aspirations I had.

"I had no choice. A lot of times we talk about a woman's rights, and I do think we have a right to choose whether or not to have children. But for many of us our class and our economic background pretty much makes the choice for us. We don't really have the free choice to have children when we want them. But right now I really would like to have a child in spite of it. I feel like caring for another human being and seeing this little human being born and raising it, and fighting for this person to survive. It gives you this incredible experience that you don't have if you're not a mother. It also makes you a stronger person.

"I was just looking at a little boy right now and realizing that if

88

I had had my baby he would be about his age. So I do think about it occasionally. But it just is. I don't cry about it or anything any more."

━━━━━━━━━━

When Sally Upton, now twenty-four, thought she was pregnant five years ago, she put off finding out until it was too late for her to have a first-trimester abortion and not far enough along to have a second-trimester abortion. Deciding instead to have the baby, she asked both of the men she'd been sleeping with if one of them would marry her, but both refused. Her saline abortion in upstate New York was very traumatic, and she developed a severe infection afterwards. Now married, Sally wants very much to have a child, but can't get pregnant. Sally is a social worker in Cleveland, Ohio.

"When I thought I was pregnant I was so terrified I couldn't face it. I kept putting off finding out whether I was, so when it was finally confirmed it was too late for me to have a suction abortion and not far enough along for a saline abortion. I had to wait four weeks, and I thought I was going to go crazy.

"The roughest thing was facing my mother. I was nineteen then and needed parental consent for the abortion. She gave it, and I flew to Boston to visit my brother, hoping to convince a doctor there to do it right then, but he said no, I'd have to wait another two weeks.

"I flew home and thought maybe I'd get married instead, but both of the guys I'd been sleeping with said they didn't feel like it and didn't want the responsibility. They both convinced me I should have the abortion. I wasn't very assertive then. I felt terrible. On the flight from Boston I'd gotten so uptight that I started to have a terrible nosebleed, and the plane was going to make an emergency landing. There was a nurse on board who finally calmed me down so we didn't have to land.

"When the time came for my abortion appointment in Ithaca, New York, I took the bus to New York with my mother. It was a nightmare. I was very nauseous, and we had to spend hours waiting in layovers. I couldn't sleep at all on the bus and my nose began to bleed again. My mother kept saying 'Oh, my poor little baby—are you okay?' It drove me nuts.

"When I got to the hospital, I was exhausted. They didn't explain anything to me and I wasn't counseled at all. They admitted me and prepped me, then put me in with another young woman who was also having a saline, and another who was having a miscarriage. We were on the same floor as labor and delivery. They gave us a local anesthetic so we were awake, and I'm not aware of how long it took. It seemed like a very long time.

"They told us if we walked around it would come sooner, and there was no place to walk except up and down the hall. Every time we walked, we would pass the nursery filled with little babies. Other women would say to us, 'Did you have a girl or a boy?' but neither one of us would admit we were having abortions. We just walked away. It was tearing me up, knowing what was happening to the baby inside me. The other woman was even more upset. She had even bought baby clothes for her baby, but her mother made her have the abortion instead. I was trying hard to support her, but every time someone asked which baby was mine in the nursery, I just broke down and cried.

"I got through the abortion with a strength I never knew I had. The pain was really bad. I talked to people who weren't even there. It didn't go normally. After being in hard labor for maybe twelve hours, the doctor had to go in and remove it with forceps. I was numb, and didn't get out of the hospital for four days.

"I flew home in a puddle-jumper feeling physically weak and sore. I had to be met with a wheelchair in Cincinnati, and I told everyone that I'd had surgery in New York. It happened over spring break, and I made it back to school, but I was existing on Darvon. I started having severe cramping, and the police took me to a Catholic hospital where they didn't even examine me, but just gave me a pain shot. They referred me to another doctor who removed a piece of the uterine lining and showed it to me. But I still felt bad. I went to the health service at the university, and a woman doctor there said I had a terrible infection in one of my ovaries and gave me an antibiotic.

"When I started feeling better, my mother got very upset. She thought I was getting off too easy. She started walking around the house all night wringing her hands and would cry for an hour before I went out on a date. Then when I came home, she'd still be sitting in the same spot, crying.

"I just wanted to forget it, but after a year I started having anxiety attacks. I didn't think the abortion was causing them though. I thought that was all past. On the anniversary of the abortion it got really bad. I started to shake and cry. I huddled on the floor and felt like I was screaming, and my breathing became heavy and uncontrolled. I started having two or three attacks a week, and it was scary. I went to a counselor at the university and finally talked about the abortion. I said I wasn't sure I had done the right thing and that I felt guilty. He said the way to make decisions in life was to look ahead two years and see where you want to be. And I realized then I didn't want a two-year-old child. I wanted to finish school.

"The experience was a turning point in my life. I was then forced to make decisions. I married someone very supportive. He knows all about the abortion. I never saw those other two guys again. They were neither supportive nor understanding. One called and said he felt we should talk about it, but it never came off. Now I'd like to have a child. But I can't get pregnant. I keep trying and trying. I just can't."

3

Married Women

Not surprisingly, married women have a far lower abortion rate than unmarried women and account for only 27 percent of the total abortion picture, according to the Center for Disease Control's Abortion Surveillance Branch. Married women in stable relationships are far more apt to practice contraception successfully, and if they become pregnant accidentally, far more likely to carry their pregnancies to term. While there are societal pressures on a single woman to abort an unwanted or even a wanted pregnancy, married women are under pressure to carry a pregnancy to term. Estimates from the 1970 National Fertility Survey indicate that 15 percent of all births in that time period to married couples were "never wanted," the greatest proportion being among families who already had three children or who were in lower economic brackets. In a society which is still pronatalist, a "grin and bear it" attitude toward pregnancy and birth among married women still prevails.

For a married woman, then, the decision to have an abortion is more difficult than it is for a single woman. The same factors are involved—the financial burden, the emotional commitment to both pregnancy and the raising of the child, and the relationship between the partners—but for middle-class women, abortion is primarily a life-style choice, which can cause an aftermath, however temporary, of guilt. "The older you are, especially for women who already have children and aren't desperately strapped for money, the harder the decision is," says Francine Stein, who works for Planned Parenthood in New York. "For women who have completed their ideal family size, the decision to abort can be excruciating. It's a life-style choice, and we are not taught to think in such a self-centered way."

Although most marriages are not made or dissolved by an abortion, the fact of abortion alters the relationship. A 1973 Canadian study comparing the responses of husbands and wives to unwanted pregnancy and abortion revealed wide disparities between the two. Administering the Minnesota Multiphasic Personality Inventory test to seventy married couples both before an abortion and six months afterwards, the authors found that before the fact great stress was exhibited by the women and very little by the men. One explanation for this, suggested by Stewart Meikle of the Department of Psychology at the University of Calgary, and Richard Gerritse of the Department of Psychiatry at Foothills Hospital in Calgary, is that the physical state of an unwanted pregnancy is an "immediate and continuous reminder to the woman of the true state of affairs." By going off to work, the men could distract themselves from the immediate stress for at least eight hours a day.

The stress on the woman also put a strain on her relationship with her husband, and in many cases the wife underwent a temporary personality change. Instead of drawing the couple together as they faced a crisis situation, the pregnancy forced them apart. "The effect of an unwanted pregnancy on the women was sufficiently great to swamp whatever personality similarities they had previously shared with their husbands," the study continued. "The implication here is that far from an unwanted pregnancy drawing husband and wife together, it seems more likely to put distance between them." Postabortion, however, the stress slowly disappeared until when the test was readministered six months later, the similarities between husband and wife had actually increased. In that study anyway, abortion seemed a positive act in marital relationships.

Among the married women I talked to, the variables in the decision-making process and in the aftermath were far fewer than those among the single women. Of the eleven women whose interviews follow, five had little difficulty reaching their decision and no appreciable trouble afterwards. All but one of the five had already reached their ideal family size, and with the support of their husbands, had

93

little difficulty dealing with their abortions. Only one woman had no children at the time of her abortion and does not plan to, a joint decision she and her husband made before they married.

The other six married women were more troubled. One, a teenager pregnant with her first child, was being forced to abort by her mother-in-law. Another was tormented by the thought that she aborted a daughter, while still another suffered the same anguish thinking she had aborted a son. One, who hadn't been able to have a child since an abortion eleven years before, blamed her childlessness on the guilt that followed, while another, having been through the death of one child, five miscarriages, and an abortion, was having her tubes tied.

In only one instance did a marriage break up before the abortion, but almost all the relationships went through a period of stress. A few have never recovered, but the marriage is still limping along. In these strained relationships, the women use the abortion as a weapon.

Shelby Winters, eighteen, cannot stop crying. Her face, under a tangle of blond curls, is red and swollen, and she is surrounded by a pile of damp Kleenexes. In her blue jeans and football T-shirt, she hardly looks old enough to be able to conceive at all, but she is scheduled for an abortion the next morning. Married for a year to a farmer and living with his family in Indiana, she is being forced by financial and in-law troubles to abort her first child.

"We got married last year and went to live on his family's farm. His mother—doesn't care for me at all. As soon as she found out I was pregnant, she wanted me out of the house. My husband had to quit technical school to get a job so he can pay for us to live somewhere. The job he got only pays $2.25 an hour, which isn't enough to get a house on and is certainly not enough for a baby.

"My mother-in-law says a baby would hold us together, and she is waiting for the day when we'll break up. She wants to keep her kids at home around her. She just let her twenty-six-year-old son get married. She's afraid I'll take her other son away from her, I guess.

"My brother-in-law says if I don't get the abortion I'll be so stupid he won't even want to look at me. He told his wife if she gets pregnant, she should get out of the house.

"My husband doesn't demand that I get the abortion, and says that if I really can't go through with it, he'll find some way.

"I can't go to my father for help. My father thought I was pregnant when we got married. He said he'd pay for an abortion until I told him I wasn't pregnant. He wanted me to wait until I had a career or married somebody rich. He can't believe I'm married to a farmer. My husband won't talk to my dad at all because my dad's so sarcastic to him. If I ever went to my father for help now, he'd make me spend my whole life paying him back. My mom lives in Albany, New York, somewhere, but I don't know how to get hold of her.

"I think abortion is best for both my husband and me. I'd like to get a little bit of something someday. I had to quit high school in the eleventh grade, and I don't know how to do anything.

"The problem is deep down I want to keep the baby. I realize it's not the smart thing to do. The abortion will give us more of a chance to get something. But I think about the baby all the time, about my little girl. That's what I had always hoped it would be if I would have had it. If it had been born, what would she have looked like? I just guess I feel bad that when my next one comes along that I would have had another one that I loved . . .

"I come in tomorrow. I'm going to go through with it. I hope I feel better than I do today. I love the baby. I love my husband. I just think it would be better for him if I have the abortion. I'll get over it. I'm sure there'll be a lot of times when I'll think about it, but we got so many problems now. So many. I know I can have another baby someday. But it's this one I love now. I just love her so much . . . But my mother-in-law says we got to be off the farm in two weeks —if I keep on having my baby."

Mary Murphy is lying under a plaid blanket in the recovery room of an abortion clinic in Ohio. Thirty-three, Mary is the mother of four children, and on welfare. Obviously nervous, her fingers play incessantly with the top of the blanket while her toes never stop wiggling. But she is clear about her abortion.

"I had no trouble at all making the decision to have it. I just didn't want to have another baby. I have four kids already. I couldn't afford another. I'm already on welfare. There was no question about it.

"It was a clear-cut choice and I feel better already. The kids don't know about this and I'm not going to tell them. It's my business and not theirs.

"I don't feel any guilt. I don't feel no nothing except tired. It was simple and the only thing to do."

———

Carol Polaski, twenty-four, is very pale. Married to a carpenter, Carol has a four-year-old son and has just had her first abortion. She is staring at the ceiling in the recovery room of an Ohio abortion clinic and seems very composed. But as she begins to talk, the tears begin leaking from her eyes into the pillow. She feels she has abandoned a daughter.

"I had the abortion for financial reasons. We just don't have enough money for another child. Oh, it hurts so much. I hurt really bad. It hurt so much in that room I almost jumped off the table.

"I was very upset when I found out I was pregnant. I knew what I should do, but I wasn't happy about it. I'd really like to have a baby. But there is no way. It was my idea to have the abortion.

"At first my husband was totally against it. He said you can't do it—I won't allow it. But something changed his mind. In a way I was hurt even though the abortion was my idea and it was the only thing to do. I guess I wanted him to talk me out of it, to reassure me we could make it. Instead he was cold. I wish he could have been more feeling. He didn't even bring me here today. And he says he can't get off work to pick me up.

"I've felt closer to him lately anyway. I wanted to be around him more. He assured me we could have another baby someday. I want

96

a daughter. All I've thought about is that this is a daughter. I want one so bad. I feel so sad. I feel like my daughter just went down the tubes. I feel like I abandoned her. Oh, I feel so bad. I'd never do this again."

Flora Winsted, forty-four, had little difficulty reaching her decision to have an abortion, her second in two years. The mother of eight children and the grandmother of a one-year-old, Flora feels it would be unfair to her family, herself, and her husband to have another child. She and her husband, an appliance repairman in Kentucky, had no difficulties after her first abortion, and Flora doesn't anticipate any after this one. A jovial woman, Flora had her first abortion at the same time that her daughter, then fourteen, did. It seemed an ironic way to bridge the generation gap.

"Our eight children weren't planned. They just happened along. My husband and I are very passionate. I always say to him, 'You're going to have one foot in the grave and come back up and say, "One more time!" ' We don't miss many nights. I'd say we had relations five times a week. We're very compatible, and I love it. If he doesn't get it at home, he'll get it elsewhere, you know. I tell him when he wants sex with someone else, he has to take all eight kids out the door with him.

"When I found out I was pregnant last year, I was disgusted with myself. I guess we were just careless. My husband didn't want me to take pills. My mother has cancer, and no one can prove the pills don't cause it. The IUD? I'm not sold on them. Anything like that can cause something. I can't help but think they're not good for the body. And the diaphragm. My second one is a diaphragm baby. So I leave it up to my husband, and we both watch the calendar. He hates the rubber. He says it's like taking a shower with his boots on.

"When my daughter came to me and said she was pregnant just at the same time I found out I was pregnant, my husband and I were very upset. But it took my mind off my problems, and it created a funny feeling in between me and her. I had my abortion first so I could see it was okay, then I took her in. She hasn't had any bad effect from it, or at least she doesn't talk about it. We just forgot about the whole thing. I never told her about my abortion. I only told our oldest daughter, and she told me to go right ahead and have the abortion, that we were too old anyway. She said we had no business starting all over again.

"I wasn't happy about it though, then or now. My husband asked me what I wanted to do this time and I said, 'You know.' He said, 'You make the arrangements.' He would have been willing for me to have the baby though. He has mixed emotions about abortion. He's a very conscientious man and works very hard for a manufacturing firm. Financially, it's very difficult for us. And he's going to be forty-seven soon. It would be a hardship for us and a hardship for the other children if we had more. It just wouldn't be fair.

"My husband's like me. We were both raised in religious homes, real Protestants. When you're raised that way, you're never really sure you've done the right thing. But the abortions were the best thing for our lives and families. You have to take your own way of life into consideration. You can't worry about what other people think. It's not their lives.

"I was pregnant another time, too, just two years after the eighth kid. I wanted an abortion then, but no one on our side of the river would touch it. At two and a half months I miscarried. I made up my mind then I would never have another child. They thought if I had carried it, there might have been something wrong with it. I was never upset with my husband for getting me pregnant. It takes two to tango. He felt he was at fault with the last two and I thought I was. We shared the blame together. He's been threatening for three years to have a vasectomy, and now I think he'll finally do it."

———————————

It has been two weeks since Maria Concepcion, twenty-three, had her abortion at a Brooklyn abortion clinic, and instead of feeling better, she feels worse. A native of Honduras, Maria and her husband, a medical clerk in Brooklyn, have a daughter eight months old and decided on an abortion this time because of financial reasons and the young age of their daughter. Maria's resulting grief has put a great strain on the marriage.

"I had stopped using the pill because it caused me to have headaches and nausea. My husband used condoms sometimes, but still I couldn't figure out when I got pregnant. I thought my time was safe.

"At first I decided to keep the baby. I had had a prior abortion which I hadn't told my husband about, which depressed me very much for months later. I had so much guilt. I love children so much. I have a seven-year-old sister whom I practically raised and love so much, and I wanted so much to have that first child, but we weren't financially ready. The first time I never thought whether the baby was a boy or a girl.

"This time I hoped the baby was a boy and that I could keep it. My husband and I discussed it and discussed it. We had to convince ourselves to have the abortion. It makes it much harder when you already have a child. You realize it's a wonderful thing to go through a pregnancy and then have a baby dependent on you.

"This time I couldn't help thinking it was a human being, a living being. At first my husband wanted to keep it, but as the weeks went by and the morning sickness got so bad I couldn't take care of our little girl, he changed his mind. She is just beginning to crawl.

"The new baby would interfere with everything. We want to move to the West Coast, for example. We were convinced that the abortion was the best thing rather than the right thing. If you asked me how I felt about abortion I would say I was against it. I feel very hypocritical.

"The abortion hurt worse than when my daughter was born. I fainted on the table. I just kept shivering from the cold. I kept wondering whether the child felt any pain. When I got home my daughter kept crying and crying, and I wondered whether she sensed what had happened that day.

"I thought afterward it would hurt more. But my husband and I decided not to talk about it, and it worked. I regret the abortion even though I know it was right. It's hard. I admitted it to my husband last night. I still have doubts. He told me not to think about it. He doesn't want to talk about it. He's sure it was a boy.

"Sometimes I blame him for having let me go through with it. I think he should have said we could have made it with another baby. We made a selfish decision. We didn't tell anyone about it. They would have thought badly about us.

"The guilt came up when we first made love and I cried and pushed him away from me. And we talked about it a little then. At least he admitted the abortion had happened. But I had expected him to say, 'Have the baby.' I wanted him to say, 'You're going to have this baby.' And he never did. As time passes I'll stop blaming him, I guess.

"I dream all the time I have a boy two years old along with my daughter. I am walking in the park with them. When I wake up, I feel sad. One day last week I was alone in the house, and I felt so lonely. Then I cried. I hadn't cried before that. It would be better if my husband and I talked about it.

"Every time my daughter cries, I feel she's crying for the baby. She has never cried so piteously, night after night. It breaks my heart. I find myself hugging her, kissing her, holding her. She's at the stage where she wants to roam instead of being hugged, but all I want to do is hold her.

"I resent the fact that I've got an IUD in me now. I resent that I can't get pregnant. Maybe I just want the decision taken out of my hands, like a woman being raped.

"I felt every part of me functioning when I was pregnant. I felt complete, and I miss it. The first three days after the abortion, I felt empty. I still find myself patting my stomach. That's what I used to do when I was pregnant. I think back about the places my husband and I went when I was pregnant, and I want to go back to all the same restaurants.

"Sometimes I've been pretending I'm still pregnant. I'm still eating coleslaw and pickles. I can't stop. But I'm dealing with the abortion. I really am. Really."

100

Melanie Foster, twenty-seven, had her first abortion two weeks ago and feels no regret at all. She and her husband, who is twenty-one years older than she, decided before their marriage seven years ago not to have children, so the decision was made well before her accidental pregnancy. She and her husband like their life the way it is and are not willing to make the sacrifices necessary to raise a child. They live in a suburb of Atlanta and don't plan to tell anyone about the abortion.

"I wasn't using any contraception when I got pregnant. I believed the doctor who said I couldn't get pregnant because I had a tipped uterus. But he must have been halfway right, because that was five years ago and it has taken all this time to prove him wrong.

"I woke up one morning and started throwing up, but I didn't really have any concept that I was pregnant. My husband realized it before I did. He was more aware of the changes in me than I was myself. He didn't say anything. He just felt it.

"When I went to the doctor and he confirmed it, I felt disbelief and a confusion. Did I want to have it or did I want to get rid of it? I think it upset my husband more than it did me because I didn't know what I wanted to do. I never really felt pregnant. I never really had any sensation of something growing inside of me. I just had a great deal of pain in my stomach. That's all it was to me. I was just hurting. What I really wanted to do was just get rid of the pain and the discomfort. It was like I had hurt myself or something, and that's all it was to me. It wasn't that it was a baby.

"My husband and I discussed it, but we had made the decision before we were married that we didn't want to have any children. My husband's a great deal older than I am. He's now forty-eight, so that by the time the child was grown he'd be almost seventy years old.

"I guess I'm suffering a little bit from women's liberation. I like my career and I know that for our life style I have to work. We would not have the luxury that we have now. We would just exist. I know it's a very selfish attitude, but we like the things that we do. We enjoy

101

them. We have friends that have small children, and it's all they can do to support them and then they have nothing else. They can't even plan for their education because they don't have enough money to put aside for it. A child is not just a baby. You've got it twenty years at least. It's your responsibility, and we just knew that neither one of us was really willing to do that. With the hours I put in—I leave home at six-thirty in the morning and it's usually six before I get home—it wouldn't even know that I was its mother. Who would be the mother figure? The person who would raise the child and give it its background and everything, because I wouldn't be there to do it.

"On the other side, I thought a lot about the difference in age between my husband and myself and that someday I am going to be alone. And that is the only thing, another selfish reason for having a baby. I don't want to be alone in the future. But that was the only thing that has ever crossed my mind to make me want a child. It's just that I don't want to be alone when I get old. It's companionship. But then you've got no guarantees about that. Some people never see their children when they get old, or the child hates them, or they go off ten thousand miles away and all you can do is send them cookies.

"The thing that frightened me the most was the procedure. My husband came with me. I would not come by myself. And I think that was just the fear of the unknown, of not knowing what exactly was going to happen. I think that maybe if I'd had other children and simply didn't want another one I wouldn't have had that fear. But everything was happening so fast. I found out on Saturday that I was pregnant, and I had the abortion on Tuesday.

"I had more problems adjusting to the physical problems of the abortion than the emotional ones. I had an allergic reaction to the anesthetic and stopped breathing. They had me on that respirator for forty-five minutes until I could breathe again, and I felt so bad those next few days that as far as having any regrets, I didn't. I think I felt more of a trauma from the respiratory arrest than anything else. As far as the baby was concerned, it was like before. I had gotten rid of something that hurt. It was not that I'd gotten rid of a living creature. I didn't feel it before, and I guess that's why I didn't feel it afterwards.

102

"My husband and I are closer now because we went through something together. It was the both of us. We sat down and talked about it, we made a decision, and we decided to go the same route. There was no conflict. And during the pregnancy, I think he was more concerned about me than he had been in the past. And so far he still is, so it's been a positive experience.

"I don't anticipate waking up in six months and wishing I'd had the baby unless there's some severe trauma like my husband dropping dead tomorrow. Mostly I look forward to making love to him again because I've missed that intimacy. It's hard when you lie down beside a man every night and you're used to having a relationship and then you stop. Our sex was spontaneous. It's not that we had sex every Thursday night. We've never had any schedule. I think I'd revolt against anything like that. It's when you have the mutual feeling that it's good.

"Now I'm going on the pill because I really don't want to go through this experience again.

"I don't ever plan to talk about this. There's only my husband who knows about it. The people I work with think I've had a miscarriage, and the people who work with him don't even know I was pregnant. It's not something I would discuss openly with my friends. I don't want to subject myself to their baggage if they want to tell me that they don't like it, or they think it's wrong, or even if they think it's right. I don't go with their baggage, and I don't expect anyone to go with mine.

"To have an abortion in the South is looked upon as happening to a girl who has no choice. A married woman, especially a white woman—it's frowned upon. It would be expected of a black married woman in the South. There would be nothing thought of that. But there's a whole bunch of racial prejudice still in the South. There's no point denying that. I think that a lot of white people think blacks don't have the same emotional feelings about a child, that they don't think blacks have the same emotional feelings about much of anything. And they just accept that what would be acceptable for a black person to do would just not be acceptable for a white person. A white married woman in the South is just not expected to have an abortion, or to rule that part of her life. She is expected to accept whatever

103

comes along and take it from there. It didn't make it much harder for me to make my decision, because I don't go along with a lot of things anyway."

⸻

Juggling a career and family has caused great stress on the relationship between Florence Ottinger, thirty-five, and her husband, a criminal lawyer. The parents of two children, twelve and eight, they live in New Rochelle, New York. An economist, Florence commutes to the city and has a live-in housekeeper to look after the children. Three years ago Florence's husband got drunk at a party and raped her when they got home. Her resulting pregnancy ended in abortion and a lasting anger at her husband which led her into having an affair. Now Florence is considering having another child to try to cement their failing relationship.

"Our first child was born seven months after our wedding, but it wasn't a shotgun marriage. We were engaged, we had the church all lined up, and the minister all picked out. I wasn't displeased when I found out I was pregnant. We discussed then having an abortion, but we dismissed it. Abortion was illegal then, and we were getting married anyway. The baby was conceived out of love and passion. We were never closer than we were then. I was on such a high. If abortion had been legal we probably would have had one. But then there was all that scare talk and everything was so hush-hush.

"It was ironic, however, that my father gave us a picture of himself with a shotgun across his lap for a wedding present in front of everybody. Everyone laughed and I didn't dare look at George.

"Four years later George got out of law school, and we finally went on a honeymoon. I got pregnant again immediately, but it wasn't the same high as having our first girl. There was no comparison. I was sick all the time, but I loved it anyway. There is something about being pregnant. You just sit there and you're doing something. After they're born I love to nurse them, to hold them, and let them sleep on my stomach.

104

"I went back to graduate school. We had very little money so I also taught and audited various courses at Columbia. Things began to go badly between George and me. His work and play always came first. He could get home at five-thirty to play tennis, but not to be at our daughter's birthday party. I joined a feminist rap group and started falling in love with another guy.

"George and I went to a party one night, and when we got home he was so impatient to screw me that he wouldn't stop long enough for me to put in the diaphragm. He held me down and in fact raped me. When I found out I was pregnant, I was furious. I remember thinking it was impossible to have another child, especially one of George's. We were both working too hard. It was such a struggle. Only the housekeeper was delighted I was pregnant.

"I don't even remember discussing the pregnancy with George. I just told him I was going to get an abortion, which was legal then. I was going to do it all alone, drive myself there, check in, and come home all alone. It was part of my shtik not to need him then.

"I called my obstetrician, but he's Catholic and was shocked. So I went to Planned Parenthood. I went on my own and had a suction abortion. It sounded exactly like my vacuum cleaner. It was ghastly and graphic, like the hose had something caught in it. I should have put cotton in my ears. But I had no feelings about the baby. I didn't think of it as a baby. I had no emotional attachment to it. Hell, you can make one of those things every month. Once it's born I wouldn't give it up. But a fetus is unique only in the statistical sense.

"I drove home alone that afternoon. I wasn't upset or trembling and had no regrets. It was no different from getting a filling at the dentist. Now I could go on and do other things.

"I was pissed off that I had needed to have an abortion. George had suppressed all memory of how I got pregnant. I could have fought harder, I guess. Maybe I was saying, 'All right, you bastard, I'll get pregnant and you'll have to pay for it.' I didn't feel spited at George though. The babies are mine, not his. But I couldn't deal with another one. I had too many oranges in the air. I care so much about the children that they are an enormous burden. I just couldn't go through another one and do graduate school besides.

"I drifted into an affair with a professor at college. He had a brilliant mind, and our relationship was very heady. He kept telling me I was going to make it, that I really have it. He made a lot of things bearable, but in no way was our affair intellectually defensible. You still end up incurring more pain than pleasure, which is probably the only reason why marriage as an institution survives. George keeps wandering too. He's clearly looking for more exciting sex. And how can I be challenging after fourteen years?

"Now we're talking about having another child. It would be nice for George to have a son, and we'd make a reasonable effort to jimmy the odds. I gave George an ultimatum to finish the affair he's having now or it's all over. The child we're talking about now would be a love commitment. After all, I keep meaning to have my tubes tied, but I haven't, which means I'm leaving the option open. But this baby would not have anything to do with the baby I aborted. There is no correlation."

Ariel Balkind, thirty-six, sits tensely, chain-smoking. Married to a lawyer in New Haven, Connecticut, Ariel lives in Boston five days a week, where she is a medical student. On weekends, she flies home to her husband and two teenaged children. Ariel has had two abortions, one six years ago in England, another two years ago in Connecticut. These two experiences have caused her to have a deep resentment toward her husband and a sharp sense of conflict within herself between the traditional American wife and mother and the emerging professional woman.

"I think I was using a diaphragm at the time. I don't do tremendously well with contraceptives and have had some trouble with all of them. I have no problem with fertility, though. I have no problem getting pregnant at all. And suddenly six years ago I found myself pregnant with two kids in school.

"I could have been persuaded to have that baby and then to have another one which would have meant two sets of kids, two separate families, and which also would have meant no medical school now. .

"The night after my pregnancy was confirmed, my husband and

106

I went out to dinner, and my only emotion was anger. I was angry that I was going to have to have an abortion. He could have persuaded me not to have it, but he didn't. Though I wanted him to talk me out of it, I also didn't want him to. In the back of my mind I wanted to be able to escape from him, to get divorced, to leave him, just to go home alone. I did want not to feel trapped.

"We had been talking about taking a vacation, and I found out that England was having totally legal abortions performed in hospitals and clinics. It was still illegal here, and the thought of it being safely done abroad appealed to me. We flew to England, I had the abortion, and then we went to Scotland for two weeks.

"I didn't like having the abortion one bit. I felt very martyrish. There I was having an abortion, and there was my husband not having one. I resented him enormously for that. The emotions of it were terribly difficult for me too. There is that whole maternal thing, that by having an abortion you're not fulfilling your feminine role or your destiny. The social pressure on single women who get pregnant makes it easier to have an abortion and not think about it again.

"My feeling at that time was not one of shame, but of sadness. I tried not to think of the fetus as a baby, but I did. I wanted it over as quickly as possible emotionally. Mostly I wanted the option of divorcing my husband. That was the prime reason for the abortion. He never realized it at the time and still doesn't. We've been married sixteen years, and we've had a very difficult time.

"I didn't feel all that super-duper after the abortion, and we had a fairly miserable time in Scotland. He was solicitous toward me after that, which was pretty rare for him. Usually he's very dependent on me. He couldn't bear being alone in London while I was in the hospital, so I had to leave a day early just to keep him company.

"The resentment didn't go away. I kept thinking that this was something not everyone has to go through, so why should I. My husband should have said, 'I'm definitely going to have a vasectomy.' In the same way I should have said, 'I'm going to have my tubes tied.' But I haven't. And he hasn't. We all play such destructive games.

"Four years later I woke up pregnant again. By then I was in graduate school studying neurophysiology. I was angry. God had to do this again? I had to have another abortion?

"This time I made my husband make all the phone calls and the arrangements. I was furious, furious, furious. He likes to call all the shots, but never to carry them out. I was absolutely furious at him and made him do all the dirty work. I disclaimed any responsibility for the pregnancy. I felt I was absolved of all this. He should have had that vasectomy. I was totally irrational.

"I didn't feel like missing three days of classes or not feeling well for a day. Because I was older and had made that choice before, it was easier this time, but only slightly. I kept thinking it's my body, it's my baby, it's me. God, the resentment. It was a tremendously emotional thing.

"I don't regret the abortions, but sometimes I put myself back into the American dream and think of myself with two little children now instead of being in medical school and making myself exhausted and neurotic. Why can't I be like other women, who I guess are happy and contented making lunchboxes and curtains and are not possessed by the devil to do the ridiculous things I do.

"I don't think for many women abortion is as blithe an experience as women are led to believe. I know I'm not totally unique, but how many women going into it know what to expect? I have no moral handle on abortion—none at all. I've never been able to work it out. Is there a right and a wrong? I don't know what to tell my own children.

"But one thing is certain. Abortion has an effect on your life. I've never stopped blaming my husband. I always throw it back at him whenever we have a fight now. I accuse him of making me have the abortions, or I tell him it was far more painful than it actually was. The subject only comes up once or twice a year, but whenever it does, I have all the ammunition ready."

Sally Ordway, thirty-eight, is married and lives in Lexington, Kentucky. She has had a series of maternal tragedies. She has had five miscarriages; she has one living child and another who died at three. When she became pregnant at thirty-seven, Sally couldn't bear the pain of another miscarriage and aborted the fetus instead. Her husband, the owner of a paint company, supported her. Now she is at a clinic in Ohio having her tubes tied.

"I've been pregnant seven times in my life and only have one living child. My daughter Jennifer died five years ago, and I had three miscarriages before that and two since. I swore with the last one I would never put my feelings on the line again. We had moved to Lexington from Chicago and had rented a house with an extra bedroom so we could try again. But I miscarried again. I can remember lying in the hospital listening as the nurses brought all the babies out to their mothers, and I made the decision if I ever got pregnant again I would have an abortion.

"Ten months later, I discovered I was pregnant. I was using foam and my husband was using a rubber, but we had a birth-control failure. The decision to have the abortion was no decision, really. I had made it in the hospital the year before. And at thirty-seven I didn't feel capable of starting the bottle-and-diaper routine all over again. But mostly I decided not to take that risk again. With so many miscarriages, I decided to be in control of the situation this time. I had no religious or moral hang-ups, and my husband supported my decision.

"I was very angry when I discovered I was pregnant. When I was younger I was unable to get pregnant, then I kept losing them, and finally, now that I am older, I am unwilling to go through with it. My husband probably felt anger and bitterness too, but didn't express it. My luck was backwards.

"I was terrified of the pain I anticipated at the abortion. I never thought about the baby. Having had all those miscarriages and flushed so many fetuses down the toilet, it's not a baby to me. It's just a medical procedure. But then I was only eight weeks pregnant. I could never abort a fetus that moved. Physically I felt great after the abortion. There was hardly any pain, just a little cramping. I kept thanking God I was out of that situation and that my uterus didn't have a hole in it. I was proud of myself that I had gone through with it. I had made a big decision and followed through with it. I was definitely proud.

"I felt no sadness, no sense of loss as I did with the miscarriages.

109

I was relieved that I would never have to face that agony again in my whole life. Now I'm getting my tubes tied. Then I won't ever have to go through another abortion. As it is now, I sweat it out every month.

"Nobody knows I've had an abortion. I worked for a while in an abortion workshop after I had had my own abortion, and the local newspaper ran a story on the program with a picture of me. I sent the clip to my mother, and she wrote back and said she liked the article and the picture was cute, but that she wasn't going to show anything about abortion to any of her friends and hoped very much I wouldn't send the clip to any of them. I guess she doesn't want to know. So I won't tell her."

When Missy Brown got pregnant six years ago at the age of twenty-two, the relationship between her and her husband deteriorated rapidly. Finally realizing that she didn't want to raise a child alone, Missy decided to have an abortion. Four months pregnant, Missy flew to New York and had a difficult saline infusion. It took her over four years to reestablish a satisfying relationship with a man. Now Missy, a clerk in a Dayton, Ohio, department store, is planning to have a baby during the next two years whether she is married or not.

"I've wanted a baby since I got my first doll as a little girl. But when I got pregnant, suddenly my husband and I weren't getting along so well. I was real touchy and oversensitive and I didn't feel so good either. My husband wasn't giving me anything I needed, so we decided to get divorced. It was terrible. Just terrible.

"I didn't break down or anything. In fact I handled it very well. My husband and I were fighting about everything and I didn't want to have this baby and bring it up alone. I also thought I might resent the baby because I resented its father so much. I felt bad because all my life I'd wanted to have a baby and suddenly I couldn't have this one. I hated him.

"My obstetrician said women who want to have babies and have

110

abortions instead become frigid, so instead of helping me find an abortionist he sent me to a psychiatrist. I went to my sister-in-law's obstetrician, and he arranged for me to have an abortion in New York. It was my first trip there and my sister-in-law came with me. I paid for her flight and the abortion and it took all my savings, close to eight hundred dollars.

"The doctor came in with this needle. It looked like it was capable of having a quart of liquid in it. He stabbed me in the stomach with it. I have a chunky stomach and he couldn't find the right area so he kept stabbing me again and again. I've never felt such pain. It hurt way beyond crying. It hurt too much to cry.

"The pain was finally unbearable, but they didn't give me a pain-killer until that evening because it slows down labor. In fact, I spent two days in labor, with severe contractions the whole time. But the pain blended in with the shots so I couldn't tell what was hurting. They wouldn't give me any more painkillers.

"The whole floor was having saline abortions, and only one other woman had a fetus before I did. We were all lying there moaning and groaning. The pain was so bad I felt I had paid my price. I have no guilt. But I didn't think pain should be the price you have to pay to get rid of guilt. But I guess it was all right to have the pain.

"Finally it happened. I said I couldn't stand it a minute longer, and they put a bucket in the bed under my ass. It felt like a bowel movement, and then they took it away. They said the placenta was left and they tried to squeeze it out of me but nothing happened. So they finally took me to surgery and gave me a D and C. They knocked me out. It was wonderful to be unconscious.

"After I went home the thought of having a man sexually turned me off a lot. But it wasn't all due to the abortion. I had married my high school sweetheart, and I was a virgin bride. Now suddenly here I was divorced and in the midst of a sexual revolution. I felt very uncomfortable.

"It took me three years to sleep with a man again, and then it was an experiment, a one-night stand. It was okay, but not good enough to do it again for another year. It was real weird for me. Then I found a guy I liked, and we had sex and it wasn't the ultimate greatest, but it was all right. Now I'm fine, but it sure took a long time.

111

"A saline abortion is certainly to be avoided. It was the worst thing that ever happened to me. My relatives still don't know. They think to this day I had a miscarriage. My husband didn't help either. He said abortion is murder, but then he's Catholic. I finally turned him around by saying, 'Just think, Mac, you won't have to pay child support for eighteen years,' and he said, 'Well, that's one good way to look at it.' The next day I left for New York. That did it. He couldn't give me anything. I never told him about the abortion. He found out later, but we never talked about it. He was a hard-hat construction worker, and he just couldn't deal with it.

"Now I want to have a child. I don't feel it's necessary to be a complete woman like I did when I was a kid, but I do feel a little left out. In the next two years I'm going to have one whether I'm married or not. The neat thing about being a woman is that I can have a kid any time I want, and a man can't. I feel real privileged about that."

4

Men

You see them in the waiting rooms of all the clinics. Nervous and apprehensive, they leaf through tattered copies of old magazines, leaving the stories unread. For the most part, they avoid eye contact with one another, and when the fight to concentrate on the magazines is lost, their eyes remain fixed on the floor. An abortion takes a long time, between the counseling, pregnancy and blood testing, the procedure itself, and the waiting in the recovery room, and the men are sometimes left hanging for three or even more hours. When the suspense becomes unbearable, one or another will approach the reception desk and ask about the condition of the woman he accompanied that day. His fears allayed for the moment, he returns to his chair.

Abortion is very hard on the men who wait in the clinics. By the very fact of their being there while their wife or girlfriend is having her pregnancy terminated, they are showing support and commitment. But they have nothing to do but wait. Sometimes the wait becomes unendurable. In Ohio, one young man who was opposed to his girlfriend's abortion found out when her first appointment was and canceled it. He woke up three days later to find her gone; he discovered her car in the parking lot of the abortion clinic and stormed in, demanding to see her. After the couple had been counseled, he sat in the waiting room and cried for two and a half hours. Suddenly he went berserk, pulled the fire extinguisher off the wall, and started smashing in the glass partitions between the office cubicles. The clinic had to have him removed by the police.

Other men take less violent routes. In a recent case in New Jersey, an unemployed carpenter took his objection to his nineteen-year-old girlfriend's desire to have an abortion to court and had a Supreme Court judge issue a restraining order on her plans.

"I know she has a lot to lose—her family, her education," said John Rothenberger, Jr., twenty-three, who offered to marry his girlfriend. "All she has to gain is me and our child—a human being." The restraining order came too late, however, as the woman, a student, was actually having the abortion when the order was served on her sister. It would appear that Rothenberger's plea was more emotional than legal, however, because the U.S. Supreme Court decision in 1973 gives women the absolute right to abortion during the first trimester of pregnancy. The right to abdicate future motherhood is guaranteed. The right to insist on future fatherhood is not. And to some men, that is very disturbing and unfair.

Increasingly, more and more clinics are also becoming disturbed that they offer so little except innumerable cups of coffee to the men who sit and wait. Overworked already, their counselors have no extra time to counsel the men, except when counseling couples. And often true feelings don't come out during counseling because it is so close to the point of abortion. Men see their roles under these circumstances as being totally supportive of the woman and her needs, and tend to discount or suppress their own. Fear about the physical condition of the woman both before and after the abortion was found to be the overriding concern of 400 men interviewed over a four-month period at Parkmed in New York in 1975. This anxiety would tend to override any ambivalent or guilt feelings the man himself might be having at the time. As a result, he is apt neither to disclose his feelings nor to receive any attention as a result. It is the woman's body that is going to undergo a certain amount of trauma, not his. And in many cases, this adds to his unexpressed guilt and anger and can fester in him for months afterwards.

Trying to head off these problems before they occur, two counselors at the Special Care Center in Oakland, California, initiated an experimental program in male counseling last year. Engaging over 100 men between the ages of fourteen and forty-seven in group

114

dialogues while their female partners were having abortions on Saturday mornings, the counselors first gave the men a tour of the clinic, then followed it up with a detailed description of the abortion procedure itself, using slides. The counselors urged each man to discuss his relationship with his partner and how he and she had arrived at the abortion decision. The men were encouraged to air any disagreements with their partner that had occurred along the way. The program went on to focus on birth control, in the hope of involving men more in the methods used, and in so doing to reduce the risk of being in need of another abortion. With the IUD, for example, it was suggested that the man check the woman after her period each month to make sure the IUD was still in place. With the pill, the role of the man was not to monitor its daily intake but to take a vitamin pill at the same time that his partner took her birth-control pill every day, so that it became a ritual. With the diaphragm, the men were instructed how to insert it themselves, while couples using foam and condoms were urged to have the woman put the man's rubber on him while he applied the foam to her. "The point is to incorporate birth control into sexuality and sexual play instead of treating it as a separate entity," said Abro Sutker, one of the codirectors of the program.

The emotional aftermath of the abortion was the final point of the male counseling. Helping the men to learn how to be supportive, the counselors suggested that for the first few days each man not ask his partner any questions about the procedure, but just be there for her. After that time, however, the men were told to encourage their partner to start talking about it. The men were also counseled not to be alarmed by any sexual hostility after the abortion but rather to expect it, since the whole abortion experience had started in bed and getting back into it was a reminder. To ease the transition back into a sexual life, the counselors suggested that the man initiate a conversation about contraception with his partner before they had intercourse. That way, the counselors pointed out, the man was letting the woman know that he didn't want her or himself to have to go through another abortion. "That sort of dialogue would free a couple up and take away the pressure," says Sutker.

Though the evaluation of the program was not complete when I spoke with the counselors, the initial response was favorable. Giving the recipients a scale of 1 to 5 to rate their reactions, the overall response to the program added up to 4.6. Eighty-six percent of the respondents said that they thought the guidelines for shared birth-control responsibility would make a difference in their contraceptive habits, while 60 percent thought the guidelines for emotional support after the abortion would make a difference in terms of their relationship. Though there must be other counseling programs for men, this was the only one I found in all my research, and it was eventually discontinued because of lack of funds.

Not every man, of course, wants to become more involved in birth control or in abortion. Withdrawing into masculine isolation, they consider contraception and indeed all aspects of reproduction to be the responsibility of the woman. Absolved of any responsibility, these men do not do time in the clinic waiting room but think their involvement can be written off by paying for all or half of the abortion costs. Other men don't even do that, washing their hands of any responsibility whatsoever.

But for the ones who care, the effect can be devastating. In my research, several of the men became impotent—a few with the woman involved in the abortion, one or two with all women. Some anguished that they were powerless to stop the woman from aborting, even though they had wanted to marry and raise a family. "Helpless" was a word heard often in describing the situation. "Anger" was another. But the most common word was "relief," as it was in all the interviews. Terminating an unwanted pregnancy—be it the man, the woman, or both who wish to terminate it—is easier than carrying an unwanted fetus to term. And post-abortion, after the arguments and doubts, life, however altered, goes on.

———————

Derek Thompson, twenty, is aimlessly reading magazines in the waiting room of an abortion clinic in Cincinnati while his seventeen-year-old girlfriend is having a pregnancy test. An employee of an electrical company in Kentucky, Derek is anguished over whether she is pregnant and what they should do about it if she is. Like many men, he feels helpless, caught in this situation.

"She had a pregnancy test two weeks ago here, and it came out positive, but they wanted to make sure by trying again. I am hoping so much she isn't pregnant so we won't have to make the decision. That's all I have in my head, all the time. Should we get married or should we have the abortion.

"For me the best thing is to get married. But she's so young it wouldn't work out. She's just seventeen last week. I think I'd like it if we did get married, though. That way I'd be with her more. I really love her, and I would have married her anyway when she got a little bit older. I feel like it would be wrong to tie her down now, but I also feel I could handle it. But I'm not going to talk her into it.

"The baby bothers me, too. When she told me she thought she was pregnant, I was happy in a way. I'd like to have a son to do things with. When I make love to her now, I try to keep it out of my mind as much as I can. But she feels if she does go ahead and have the baby, she's going to miss out on a lot. She wants to go to college, and she can't face telling her mom and dad. That's the worst thing.

"If she were having the abortion right now, I'd be scared out of my mind. It's something you've got to live with all the time. I'm still trying to decide what's best, and I guess the abortion is right in the long run. She'd always be worrying she'd be missing something, and that would bother me. I'm sure I could talk her into marrying me, but it just wouldn't be right for her. I wish a whole lot this had never happened. We'll never tell our parents. It's between her and me. I feel closer to her now. I have to be for her sake. And that's a positive thing.

"My brother had to get married, and he's not real happy. I just don't know. It's so confusing.

"She wants to take it all on herself, do all the worrying and arranging. And it's not fair to shut me out like that. I want to share it with her. After all, the man's half of it, isn't he?"

Sean McKenzie, twenty-five, looks like an ad for California. His eyes are bright blue against his tan, and his mustache flows into his curly hair. He is extremely agitated in the waiting room of a Los Angeles hospital where his girlfriend may or may not be undergoing an abortion. She is hoping that the doctor will determine the gestational age of the fetus, and thereby also determine who the father is. If it is Sean, she plans to have the baby. If it is not, she plans to have an abortion. After this interview was concluded, she found out it was Sean's baby but went ahead with the abortion anyway. When I last saw Sean, his face was frozen in anger.

"We don't know if I am the father of the child. There was another man involved. That's bothering her very much. She told me if she knew for sure I was the father, she wouldn't want to have the abortion; she would rather go ahead and have the child. That's why I was intrigued with knowing how pregnant she was. About two months ago there was another man, but if I knew for sure it was my child, I would rather her have the child. We don't believe in abortion, really, but she didn't want to have the baby of someone she didn't love and was only with for a night.

"I blame her, and she blames me. She says if I hadn't yelled at her and given her a hard time that night, then she wouldn't have gone out with him in the first place. And I said, 'Well, what a great Christmas present you gave me.' It was a heavy thing. The story was that she woke up Christmas night and was crying and wanted to talk to me. I was in a bad mood, and I was sleepy, and I started yawning and telling her she was a spoiled brat. I was really insensitive to her feelings at the time. Then she got really upset, and it got like a snowball and we couldn't stop it. Then I started getting mad because I knew at a certain point in my rantings and ravings, 'There goes Christmas; man, the whole thing's blown.' Finally, it was an impasse, and I had to leave. The next day she went out with this other guy. It was like instant karma. So I'm mad at her and she's mad at me,

118

because 'If you hadn't done this, it wouldn't have happened in the first place.' So it may surface again.

"I have a lot of strong feelings about being a father. Part of me has a philosophy that says if a child is going to be born, when it's time, he'll be back. It's the reincarnation kind of thing. If he came into this fetus now, then he'll just hang around and wait for the next one. Part of me believes that, but the other part is thinking well, what the fuck, what if this is the right child, who is this gonna be, who is this little boy or this little girl, who are they, and why are we telling them they can't come into the world? I have an image of the child I'm gonna have someday, and I feel like I know him, and it's kind of frightening that at this very moment that child maybe is not going to be here. Stopped before he began.

"But there is her career. We didn't want to have a baby because of her career as a model. She's doing commercials, and she wants to make a lot of money, and if she had a baby it would sort of put a stop to those plans. The responsibility would bear more on me as far as affording and taking care of everything. I told her that's what I wanted, that's what I'd like to do, and part of her wants to do that too, to have the child, if it is mine.

"We have lived together for two years, off and on. She's made the decision to go ahead and have the abortion if she doesn't know who the father is because she's here and all ready for it. The way she sees it is, it's a lot of pain to go through to have a baby. It's nine months of being weak and fragile and having to eat the right foods and morning sickness. She's already feeling a lot of that, feeling pretty lousy every day. And so for that part I think she just wants to get it over with and be free again, and when she has a child, to do it consciously.

"I will have a boy someday. I know his name, I have a feeling for that child. I don't want to tell you his name, I just have a feeling. That's why it is very strange, because if it's this one, maybe it's the biggest mistake I've ever made. That's the thing. This may be my chance, and if the child is there, maybe he's going now, and maybe I'll never have that chance again. I don't know. That's the thing that's frustrating, is you don't know that. That's the rub. I don't

119

know how the forces that be work, really. I don't understand them.

"I would rather it not happen, but I don't want to run in and stop it, because it's her body and it's her free will. Let what's gonna happen, happen. That's a hard decision to have, but it might be the worst decision she's ever had or the worst decision I've ever had. But it might be the best thing she's ever done; maybe if she had the baby right now, it would be horrible. Maybe the kid would be miserable, we'd be miserable, we don't know. Maybe it would be the most beautiful thing that has ever happened to us. You can't tell. So I just gotta accept what's happening. If she decided at the last moment not to do it, I would be feeling fantastic. I would say, 'What a relief!'

"I don't think I could possibly resent her after the abortion. I'm not that macho. In the movie *Godfather,* Al Pacino really socked it to his wife when she had an abortion. I just worry about the kid. How would I feel? I mean, it's a life there. And some people can view it very detached, right? In a way I can. In a way I say to the kid, 'Well, you can go back to limbo now and wait around for another year, and be pissed at me when you finally come.' You know, that kind of thing. He's gonna be mad . . . say, 'I wanted to come out of here in 1976 and you didn't let me come!'

"When we go home today we plan to cook some rice and visit and relax, sit around. But I'll go through a lot just trying to figure it out. Trying to wonder if it was the right thing to do. Just more or less regretting, wondering if, if. Because sometimes I wonder, what the fuck, I'm twenty-five, she's twenty-seven, if you're not gonna have a child now, when are you going to have it? What's the excuse? It's really a fantastic thing to bring a life into the world, to teach him and show him, and let him experience life.

"At the time of the other abortions I guess I felt strongly. During the very first one, I really didn't think about having a child. Because I'd been with the girl three or four months and she was playing games, and we weren't really close.

"In high school I had a girl that had an abortion, and then a girl up North that had two. She had both kinds. She had the saline abortion, which is a pretty heavy experience, because she had it in a hospital in San Francisco, and it was very heavy. It went that long just because of negligence, irresponsibility, on both of our parts. I

120

don't really remember if we even considered having it or not, but it was just that we let it go too long.

"So I think part of my thinking is that as far as a family goes, I'd be a big daddy now with a family of four if it wasn't for all these abortions. And here another one is coming, and going, and it makes you think, sure.

"I'm totally against abortion. It's like a paradox. It's like I'm against hurting people, but if someone comes to attack me, I'm going to hurt him if he tries to hurt me. It's the same thing. You have morals, and things like that, but in some cases, you can't live by them. But you have to accept some things, right? It's not my body. If it was my body, I could make the decision.

"If I were a father of four right now, I'd love it. I love children. If I was rich enough I could have a harem and have them all there. Take care of all the kids. In the old days they used to have a hundred kids at a time, right? One guy and a hundred wives—sure, why not go back to all that? I believe if someone has the money, there shouldn't be a law against how many wives or husbands a person has. That's completely a personal choice. If he can have forty children, I think that's his prerogative. I can afford kids now. It would be a beautiful thing. To me it would be the most adventurous and romantic thing I could do right now, to have a child with her and for us to live together.

"It's very complicated. Just the fact that I said I don't believe in abortions and I've gone through with this is another paradox. I would rather not see any harm come to a living being. I definitely believe that they're a seed, and they've been planted, and they will grow up; and at the time they're in the womb, they're pretty much programmed as to what they're gonna look like and be like as they get older, although the environment has an effect. I think the child's performance and life is already pretty much like an arrow; the bow is strung and he's ready to come out. It's a life.

"I hope our relationship survives this. Part of me doesn't believe in the theory that says the system is all gonna collapse in a year anyway and we're just gonna take off for the hills, with our knapsacks. What are you having an abortion for? What's a career? What are you worried about? This world isn't gonna last that long, you know? Let's just go, let's have this child, it's God's plan."

═══════════

Seated in the waiting room of an Ohio abortion clinic, Ralph Wisnowski, twenty, has an unread magazine in his lap. He is very pale and anxious and seems close to tears. He flinches every time someone new comes into the room, for fear of being recognized. His jeans are clean and pressed, his shoes are polished, but in his haste to get his girlfriend to the clinic, he has forgotten to put on his socks. A practicing Catholic, Ralph is torn between his girlfriend's decision to have the abortion and his religious beliefs. Inarticulate and awkward, Ralph wants only to get back to his father's farm in Kentucky.

"I really love kids, and I was hoping she'd decide to have it. I really wanted to get married, but she's still in high school, so I guess it wasn't much fair to her. And I feel really responsible for all this. I knew she wasn't using birth control, but we'd only made love twice. Those are the breaks, I guess.

"I knew she was real afraid when she found out she was pregnant, but I didn't know what of, so I tried to be real nice to her. She's kind of stubborn, anyway. She really wanted this abortion. We both cried, I guess. It was real important to me for her not to have the abortion, but I didn't let on. I didn't want her to feel she was hurting me.

"I'm fairly religious, a Catholic. I'm totally against abortion. But it was what she wanted to do. And she's got to have the say, doesn't she?

"I'm not going to talk to the priest about it. I just prayed and prayed a lot. I asked forgiveness. I wasn't sure what to do. I was really confused. Even though I pray, it doesn't make it right. No, I'd never go through this again. I just want to go home."

122

Willard Novak, thirty, is a construction worker in Los Angeles. He is obviously ill at ease in the waiting room of an abortion
clinic, where he is biding his time while his girlfriend has an abortion.
For a while he played Pong with other men in the waiting room; then
he paced restlessly up and down. He has a daughter by another
woman and wants desperately to have a son. But, he reasons, he can't
afford to have a baby now or even to get married. Medi-Cal is paying
for the abortion.

"It was about a coupla years back when me and this other
girl—you know, she got pregnant so she thought maybe I'd settle
down with her. I was going to, but she had too many boyfriends for
me, so I had to move on. But you see, I had the kid, so I just take
care of the kid. I ought to pay the mother money every month, but
I prefer just taking care of my baby. I go over and get her on
weekends, mess around the streets, park, beaches, stuff like that. It's
a lot of fun.

"Me and this girl here today, we got together in '75, and messing
around together, one thing led to another.

"The thing about it is that birth-control pills have an effect on her.
At one time she was telling me that they had to pump her stomach
or something because the birth-control pills messed her up. So she
don't take them. She's scared of them, really. So I got to be more
careful myself, but sometimes it's hard, you know. I wore something,
but it just slipped out. So she got pregnant.

"I wanted a baby real bad, but I be realistic about everything. I
think about it, and figure, well, we can get us a kid in time. I'm not
planning on getting a wife for a while, to tell the truth about it. I can't
afford it. Couldn't afford the kids. But I wanted her to have this kid,
because it works itself out sometimes. This'd be my second kid. But
we had to make some kind of decision there quick, 'cause it was
getting late. It's about a month, so we made the decision to come on
down.

"If she had the baby, I could keep the baby with me, which I was planning on. And her. We gotta stand together and say start all over again because she had some bad luck on her own. Her personal affairs—well, the guy she used to be going with, I just wanted to be different, you know? For me too. I wanted to build a life with her. Just start whole new from scratch. It would be harder with a baby, though. In another year or so maybe we'll be ready enough to have one.

"I think she wanted to have the baby. But I had to look at it that she wanted to go to school, and she's working too, and having the baby would mess the whole plan up. 'Cause she'd have to come out of school, and since she's so far in it, it wouldn't make no sense in her coming out, for in a year or so she'd be out of school, she'd have a steady job, we'd have our finances together. Get us a good budget, and we'll see about having a baby then.

"A boy, that's what I kinda want. Just one boy, that's all I want. It's going through my head now. I believe if she hadn't come down here today, I wouldn't have let her come down, because I wanted a boy. Still do.

"I had about a week, two weeks, to think about it. But I didn't make no agreement on it to myself. I just went along with the program, really. But I still have doubts. I don't really care for it, abortion and stuff. But in some cases it do help, because of the individual situations people have, because some people can't really afford it. Some girls get pregnant too young, too quick, and then abortion is good, 'cause having a baby so young can mess up your life. If she too young to take care of herself, or too young to go get a job, or have responsibility and she don't know nothing yet about debt, it's too soon to have a baby.

"Maybe my mind is knocked out right now, but in myself I don't think the abortion is gonna affect me. But like I say, I never been through this before. This is the first time. Again and again, I think about the little baby. I don't know. I'm just different from some fellows I know. About kids. A lot of them have kids, and they don't really care. They just got a baby. Something to talk about. But I'm a little different. I brag about my own. I wish I had a whole houseful of kids, you know? I just need a houseful of money.

"I think it's gonna work out pretty good. I'm gonna establish on

124

my job. I'm trying to buy this house, and get a home and stuff, like we get everything squared away and have a lot of babies. I believe that boy's gonna get born, sooner or later."

━━━━━━━━

It has been three months since Fred Pasanski's girlfriend had an abortion, and he is still troubled. Though he had no problems about the abortion itself, as his relationship with the woman was not very serious, still the thought of it keeps cropping up in his mind. His sex life and his relationship with his girlfriend have slowly faltered, and now he is having periods of impotence with other women. Sex, which had been a frivolous pleasure before, now bears with it commitment, and Fred is not ready for that. A college dropout, Fred, thirty-one, lives in Lancaster, Pennsylvania, where he is a garage mechanic.

"Sarah and I weren't actually living together. It was an I'd stay at her place or she'd stay at mine kind of a thing. She was my main friend or current girlfriend at the time. I don't think I was ever in love with her. It was just after many years of knowing her, we became intimate, which was kind of strange.

"I dumbly never considered the question of birth control because I assumed she was using it because I obviously wasn't. We kind of ignored the situation. It's funny. I just ignored it.

"She must have had her suspicions before she checked it out at the doctor's. Then she came right back and told me. It was like a bolt out of the blue. I was surprised, for sure, but in my mind there was never any question of what she'd do. Obviously, it was the realistic thing. My response was automatic. There was a curiosity, of course, as to whether I could produce a kid, but I always sort of assumed I could, so her conceiving was no ego boost.

"She wanted to have the kid, but it seemed totally unreasonable to me. There was no way I could handle any part of a kid right now. I have enough trouble keeping my own life in a straight direction without taking care of a kid. I just couldn't handle it. I didn't think it was good for her either. If I'd been in love with her, maybe I could

125

have settled down, but it would have been the kid controlling our lives.

"I could tell she was agreeing about the abortion realistically, but she was obviously having different feelings from me. I guess there are obviously different feelings between mothering and fathering. It wasn't going on in my body. I could only help financially. It must have been closer to her than to me. I just blotted the possibility of her having the kid out of my mind.

"I took her to the hospital. Christ, it was awkward just sitting there in the corridor. The nurses always seemed to be giving me a knowing wink. I wanted like hell to get out of there. So I split and came back to pick her up when the whole thing was over. I didn't want to stay around. Visiting people in hospitals makes me nervous.

"I went home and drank a couple of beers. I assumed everything was fine, so I didn't worry. I never thought about the baby at all. A baby's not a baby until it's born. And little babies don't do anything for me anyway. I never felt we were doing something inhumane. It only made me feel guilty knowing she cared and I didn't. I felt guilty for not feeling more about it.

"When I picked her up, I felt nothing but relief. I was happy to get it over with, and I hoped we could get back to normal. I got champagne to celebrate. She was trying hard to be cheerful. The atmosphere was 'Let's cheer up and let the whole thing slide by.'

"But it didn't. Since then our sex life has slowed down. We haven't slept together much lately. The first couple of times I can remember thinking, We've got to be careful. I can't remember whether we were just fooling around or doing it to climax, but I can remember thinking, This is dumb. But we were half-joking. We'd get all turned on and start to do it, and then quit.

"She doesn't turn me on physically as much any more. Right now I haven't been sleeping with her lately. Or really with anyone. With one lady friend I find myself turned off right in the middle of it because my mind begins to wander. I don't think, What if she gets pregnant, but, Here we go again.

"I've been impotent a couple of times, too. I just couldn't get it on. I wasn't drunk, but I don't know if the abortion had anything to do with it. It would be worrisome if I thought it was becoming a common thing. It's something to think about, for sure. Little thoughts pop up in my mind in moments of passion, which is disturbing to say the least.

"With some people abortion might cement things. It would be their own special little secret. But my guilt is that she's put more into the relationship than me. The abortion was just one more trial. Maybe it has changed my sex life, but I don't know. I hope not.

"I've pretty much put the abortion in the back of my mind, but it's still there. As a matter of course I try to think good thoughts instead of bad thoughts, and I get away with it most of the time. But the bad ones can creep up on you. The abortion itself was probably the least of all the problems. But it's the situation around it that makes you really think how you feel about the lady. This is life-and-death stuff."

Though three years have passed since Robert French's wife had an abortion, he has never forgiven her or himself for letting it happen. The father of two girls and the stepfather of a ten-year-old boy, French, forty-three, deeply wants a son of his own, and the thought that the fetus might have been a son haunts him. Though he supported his wife throughout the abortion and appeared to agree with her, he never aired his deep sense of loss. The hostility and lack of communication between the couple has now led them to the brink of divorce. French, a stockbroker in San Francisco, is a man caught between the old concept of woman as wife and mother and the more difficult concept of woman as wife, mother, and professional. He is hopeful they will get back together. Thoughtful and articulate, he is obviously still very upset and broke down twice during the interview.

"I don't think my wife was using any birth control at the time, mainly because we slept together so infrequently. She felt that a) the pill had complications because of its chemical content, and b) she had gone back to the diaphragm, which she resented using. I think she resented it because when she thought that we might make love she put it in, and when we didn't make love she felt foolish. It

127

soured her and disappointed her. Also, she felt that it was a one-sided deal, that it was the woman who had to use birth control. I refuse to wear rubbers. Rubbers are very insensitive, and putting them on is the fastest two-handed game in town. That night I didn't know whether she had a diaphragm on or not. I didn't think about the circumstances at all.

"We made love rarely because there were tensions in our marriage, which were unresolved. There were a lot of things unsaid that inhibited sex. A lot of the things she was doing disturbed and interrupted my life. Her job filled her life substantially. There was no room left for me. I wanted attention and wasn't getting it. I think I was punishing her by not sleeping with her. I don't know whether she wanted to sleep with me or not. I never asked her. We never talked about that kind of thing, and we should have.

"The night she got pregnant was the first time we'd made love in maybe two months. We'd gone to one of her assignments, which was to promote a string of discotheques. I was slightly surly and resentful I had to go. It wasn't something I had conjured and wanted to do, but off we went.

"While we were there, she did her job and I sat and had my head pounded by insensate noise. Finally, we went to the last one, and it was a zoo of a place, a cellar someplace. There were people crawling all over each other and a couple humping in a corner by the men's room. You could get stoned in the men's room just by smelling the air. I felt a disgust at the degeneracy of the place, but that wasn't important. It was two A.M. I had a job that required my being on the top of my game, and I wanted to go home. We were in a seedy part of town and the crowd was fairly rough, lurching around half stoned, half undressed. I felt wrong leaving her alone there. She could have gotten in a lot of trouble or at least have been scared. I didn't want to leave a woman alone under those circumstances. It would have been very irresponsible.

"But she kept working, and I was alone. Finally I was really furious. I was half drunk and madder than hell. It was close to three when we got home. I went slamming up to bed and turned my face and body as far away as I possibly could from her. She got in and came creeping over and was being affectionate and sexy. I spun right around, and we made love fairly rapidly but quite passionately. It was as passionate as our lovemaking had been in some time. I had emotions working. It was a combination of anger and sex that stimulated me. I don't know how she felt.

"I wasn't paying particular attention to her feelings at the time. I don't recall if she had an orgasm. And I almost always knew when she did, and I tried very hard to make sure she was pleased.

"Six weeks later I came home one night, and she said immediately, 'Let's have a drink.' We sat in the living room and she said something to the effect that 'You'll be glad to know your pencil still has lead in it.' I didn't understand her. Then she said, 'I'm pregnant,' and that was when my emotions became deeply ambivalent.

"In one sense I was deeply proud she was pregnant. I was proud I'd made her pregnant, and the idea of having children was terribly important to me. We had two girls, and I'd always very, very deeply wanted to have a son. When we first approached our marriage six years before, we'd talked gaily about raising a baseball team of boys, and we had two girls, both of whom I loved passionately. I recalled that her gynecologist had told me that the chances of a third child being of the same sex were 66 percent to 33 percent. My immediate reaction, without any attempt to use conception methods to determine having one sex rather than the other, was that this child had been created arbitrarily and that the gynecologist's odds would prevail, and we'd have another girl.

"She said, 'What should I do about it?' And I said, 'The one thing we don't need in our life is another Mergatrude.' My feeling was that if there were any reasonable chance it would have been a boy, I desperately wanted it. But the oddsmakers had told me it wouldn't.

"I was cold and rational at the time. As our life was then, things were stretched pretty thin. We had three children in the house, and she was working hard. I was trying to balance in my head the pluses and minuses of another child. If it could have been a boy, I would have said I very much wanted the child. If she had insisted on an abortion anyway, I would have been very upset and fought to have the child. If she had needed my consent for the abortion, for example, I wouldn't have given it.

"She wanted an abortion. I don't know what was going on in her

129

head, but I don't think she wanted another child at the time, be it boy or girl. I guess I was presuming she was listening to the same oddsmakers. She knew my feeling about having a boy, and I think she shared it absolutely. Had it occurred to her it might have been a boy, she might have had a different view.

"She said, 'Shall I have an abortion?' and I said, 'I guess so.' She made all the arrangements for a week later. The whole week I was extremely jumpy and preoccupied. People at work kept asking me why I was so preoccupied. I kept twirling the decision over and over in my head. A lot had to do with the women's movement, of which my wife was a part and which presumed a woman's ability to go out and make a good living without being dragged down by familial obligations. I felt this child would hurt that. She was just beginning to ascend in a good and important job. Pregnancy and all the things that go with it would have knocked the shit out of her career, it just having taken off after the birth of our second child.

"The contradiction was that under any circumstance, I wanted the child. Period. Regardless of sex. And I was swinging on a bridge that it might be a boy. I would do anything for that regardless of her career. I was forced rationally to believe the goddamned oddsmaker because that's the way I think. Emotionally I felt shitty. I felt just terrible. I've always wanted lots of children. I just wanted more. I feel a very deep commitment to each child.

"On Saturday morning we went off to the abortion clinic. There were all kinds of people there, all seemingly sad, which might have been my own emotional transference. The men seemed very nervous. I was very nervous. It was the build-up of all the ambivalence I felt all week. And was the whole procedure safe? There were serious things about to happen to her insides. What was going to be the effect on her body? All these clinics are bullshit. They all have nice reception rooms, but behind them is the risk of permanent harm and death. It's a scary procedure.

"I was also nervous because it was not clear to me that this was what I wanted to do. My wife and I were being very stiff upper lip about going in because we'd made up our minds and it was an 'I'll see you through anything' sort of thing.

"We sat there and waited. There were all sorts of boobs and

incompetents hanging around saying, 'Miss So-and-so, it's your turn.' You can't trust those people.

"And then she left me. The minute she went through those doors I had the feeling, 'Oh, God, I don't want this to happen.' Besides the rational reasons, all the emotional reasons happened at the moment she went through those doors. All the reasons that I'd conjured up that this was a good idea were stripped away. I had committed myself and her to this course of action for all good reasons, but without thought to the emotions it was causing. My whole emotional makeup went *phutz*. I felt bare and had a gut anguish. I stared at those doors she had vanished through in the hands of an incompetent, and I felt that I desperately wanted to impel myself through them and grab her away, but I did none of that.

"Instead I drove home and scurried around our house doing things to make it pleasant for her return. I set out a table in front of the fireplace in the bedroom and got the fire all ready to light. I made myself very busy for the two hours she was in the clinic. I got some soup or something for her lunch.

"I picked her up at the hospital and brought her back and tried to make her happy. She was very weepy and weak. When I came into the clinic, I brought her a piece of jade she had always wanted from Gump's. I wanted to give her something to hold onto as a token of my affection and love for the terrible thing she'd been through. I tried to tend to her. I didn't need tending to. I hadn't had an abortion. She didn't need me at that point doing a boo-hoo-hoo act. She needed help for herself.

"In retrospect I think a lot of damage was done to our marriage. My fault was in not articulating sooner that it was a child of mine I wanted born. Mostly I was responsive to her life. She wanted to go on working, and there was the women's movement. I was not assertive enough about what I wanted, which was the child. It's pretty hard to have children without a woman, which is something the women's movement tends to ignore.

"In a sense I blamed her for the abortion. Without her requirements for a career, the pregnancy would never have been an issue. I would have said, 'Fuck it.' I love kids. But there was an intensity about the moment regarding women and careers. I paid too much attention to that and not to what I wanted. I don't know how she would have reacted if I'd said this was a child of mine and I wanted it. Instead, I lost control of my own will and didn't say how much it would affect me.

"I left it to the oddsmakers so it wouldn't hurt so much that it might have been a boy. I've been tortured by that thought. I had a desperate need to know what that fetus was, could I have ever known it. Had it been a boy, it would have killed me. At the same time I couldn't have borne knowing. At the same time I wanted to look into the discharge pan, I far more desperately *didn't* want to look into that discharge pan.

"Two weeks later we went to Hawaii on vacation. We were walking down a path at night, and she looked at the palm trees and the flowers and said something about how beautiful it was and how sad not being able to show it to another child and having denied that bit of beauty to a soul. I felt desperate. That was the first chance we'd had to get out of our preoccupied selves and to think about the consequences of what we'd done. It just about killed me, and her too, I think. She wrote a poem and left it in the room. I read it, and I cracked completely. I openly wept for half an hour while she wasn't there.

"I didn't start making love to her again for a long time, and since then we've made love even less than before the abortion. I felt that this child had been sacrificed to her work, and I resented her work from then on. Her work and our emotional life were always at odds. I blamed her work for the sacrifice I felt I'd made.

"From then on our sex life was a real strain. We rarely made love, and when we did, it was very hard. In the summer of 1974, we didn't make love once. From then to the next summer, I was impotent with occasional lapses. The next summer I pulled the twin beds together in our summer house, but we didn't make love but once. I don't know why.

"Other strains had developed. There was even greater attention to her work, greater focus on her life and less on mine. There was no time for us. I had started having affairs outside our marriage where I was not impotent. Between the spring of 1974 and the fall of 1976,

132

I made love to my wife maybe four or five times, and then just because I felt I had to.

"I don't think she killed the baby. The life we were living at that time did. We mutually killed the baby. Because of our own selfish circumstances, we caused the child to die. A child, regardless of sex, who would have been a hell of a child. He or she would have been a fantastic kid, and if it had been a boy . . . The abortion killed a part of our life together. A terribly important part was our children and the ones we were going to have. And this killed the next fantastic one . . .

"She's switched jobs now, and her career doesn't suck the life out of everyone else's time. Our relationship is pretty good. Were she to say, 'I'm content with my life and my soul, and would you like to have a child?' I would say, 'Immediately,' and hope like hell it was a boy. But she hasn't said that, and we haven't discussed it. Nor have we made love in six months.

"I go to a psychiatrist now, and she and I have gone to a psychologist together and I've removed a lot of the wounds. But you never know when they're going to open up again. The eight-year-old son of a close friend was killed in a car accident recently. I went to pieces. Couldn't handle it at all. It took a while to realize that my despair was the grief of the loss of my child, whom I had never had a chance to grieve for and bury. Three years later, I wept openly for hours about the kid who had been killed, a kid I didn't know very well— but then I didn't know mine either. I'm still not sure I have buried that fetus.

"Two years after the abortion a lot of these tensions came to a head. Since that time, despite acknowledged affairs by both of us, we've been trying to weave back a fabric for our continued life together, and I think there's hope for the future. But if she had another abortion, I couldn't hack it. I would go crazy.

"This new breed of women has got it all wrong when they decide not to have children. What these intelligent women owe the world is not just what they do or are—they owe the world a legacy to pass on. To take all the genetic superiors out of the world is to leave a world of moribund morons behind. But they never even consider

133

that, and it would be political suicide to say it.

"I'm not against abortion per se. Abortion depends on the parents. Some people want children and some don't. I want kids. Sure I've got two of them. This was another one."

———————

Three years ago Ralph Sanders, now twenty-six, had a bad year during which he was responsible for three unwanted pregnancies with three different women. None of the women was important to him, and neither were any of the abortions. Rather than drawing him closer to any of the women, the abortions in fact made him dislike them as they became emotional and dependent on him. Ralph likes "superwomen" and dislikes children, and at this point in his life has no intention of marrying and settling down. He thinks he is lucky to have been involved in only three abortions, given his free-wheeling life style in New York, where he is in public relations.

"They were all terrible chance things. I had just started dating the first girl, and she got pregnant the first and only time we made love. I thought that in this day and age women would have the wits to protect themselves, so the subject never came up. It was pretty dumb of me, I guess. But obviously I thought the woman would know the consequences. She told me too late. All of a sudden, right in the middle of making love, I thought maybe she wasn't protected. I said to her, 'Can you take this?' which was probably too cryptic at the time. She misunderstood what I meant and said yes, so we plowed ahead to logical consequences. Then she told me and I said, 'Well, let's cross that bridge when we come to it.'

"When she found out she was pregnant, there was no question in our minds that she'd have an abortion and that I would pay for half of it. I checked around and found that the Women's Services were the most reputable place in New York. I went over there with her, but the first test was negative and we had to go back again. That time it was positive.

"I wasn't in love with her, or she with me. She was just a friend from down the block whom I'd been out with four or five times. I was more concerned with her nerves than with the abortion. She was much calmer about it than I ever thought she'd be. I felt closer to her because of the common bond anyone develops in a disaster circumstance. But I never considered marrying her.

"The abortion kept getting put off. First there were the tests, then the next time we went they wanted cash and I only had a check. The next time I was out of town, so she went alone. I remember one woman saying to me that all women want to be pregnant. Not necessarily to have the baby, but to be pregnant. And the night before the abortion this girl said to me she really liked being pregnant. It reminded me of a college chum of mine who got slapped with a paternity suit.

"I saw her the night after the abortion. She was feverish, which is a predictable illness about the whole thing. I wanted to take her out to dinner, but she didn't feel well. We discussed the abortion at length, but I can't remember what we said. I probably blocked it out. But our relationship changed. She got very dependent on me, and I guess in retrospect I could have been more responsive and supportive, but I wasn't. It wasn't out of malice or fear, just immaturity and lack of thought. I still had a lot of college thinking and didn't give women full credit for being the people they turned out to be when I was older.

"I treated her coldly and was unmoved. She was a weaker person than I thought she was. I had an idea of career women. They were not emotional and could handle anything. I thought they were super-women. You often hear women intellectualize about abortion and pregnancy, but when the shit hits the fan, it's awful. I expected everyone around me to be strong and react calmly, and I was disappointed when she didn't. After the abortion she wanted to continue the closeness that was manufactured by her being pregnant, but it was artificial. She came on very strong, and I wanted to run. The crisis had passed, but she was still demanding the closeness that had been accelerated by the abortion. I backed off like crazy. And I never made love to her again. When she turned out to be not a tower of strength and not a dynamic woman and just a plain girl, my interest waned. I felt turned off.

"Four months later I met up with an old friend from college, and she turned out to be another dynamite woman in sheep's clothing. She was married to a guy who pandered to her, but I didn't. I thought I gave her a chance to grow. She left her husband to come to New York. I wanted her more as a friend than a lover, but she wanted the opposite. She had gone off the pill after she had left her husband, and we took a chance. We lost, but she never told me she was pregnant. She had the abortion on her own and then told me she thought she was being a tower of strength, the woman I wanted. I admired her in one sense, but was pissed off in another. Had I known, I would have been allowed the chance to be supportive, which I hadn't been the last time. She finally told me about the abortion so she could say, 'Hey, look what I did for you.' I've slept with her since, but not often. I'm terrified she's still carrying a torch for me. But she's happier now. She's hardened and gotten some seasoning. It's had no long-term effect on our relationship.

"The third abortion happened almost simultaneously. I'd been putting the make on a stewardess who was sleeping with four other guys at the same time. She told me she was pregnant because I guess she felt she could trust me. I never had a relationship with her other than we slept together a couple of times. So she went off and had an abortion. She just blinked, and that was that. I didn't go with her or pay for it. It was very casual. I didn't feel it was my responsibility.

"After all, if you're young, single, in New York, and fucking around, these things are inevitable. Given my track record, I was lucky it happened so few times.

"I've changed now, though I'm still attracted to dynamic women. The fact that they were carrying my babies didn't bother me at all. I don't like children and don't want to be around them. My sister has a baby, and I can't stand being with him.

"If I get all burned out on Manhattan at the age of thirty-five and leave and change my life style, then I'll probably get married and have a family. But I can't imagine it. I'm having too much fun. My only residual guilt is that I wasn't more responsive. But then, it's not my style. If somebody walked in here right now and told me my parents had just been killed, I'd say, 'Thanks very much for the message.' The only twinge I felt was when the second girl sent me a Father's Day card this year. It was a joke, I guess. But not really."

136

When Samuel Martin's live-in girlfriend got pregnant, there was no doubt that she would have an abortion. Both of them were very career-oriented and neither wanted a child or a marriage. Though they both agreed, the abortion still caused resentment and feelings of guilt, surfacing in the tasteless jokes they cracked about the fetus. Three years later, they split up, though Samuel says it had nothing to do with the abortion.

"In my case, everyone knew the rules before we started the game. There was no question about having the baby for either of us. I also was not a likely candidate for a husband. But what bothered me was being part of the problem but not part of the cure.

"It was a difficult time. I knew what had to be done, and I also knew how she would react to it intellectually and to some extent emotionally. But still it was a new situation. The uniqueness threw Joey off so neither of us finally knew how to react. First she wanted the pregnancy to be her problem. Then our problem. Our responses weren't consistent. When the time finally came, she went alone. We split the medical bills—and the refund.

"She moved back in when it was over, and we had no problems at all in bed. I think she resented me, but then she would have resented having the child even more. She got whiny about it. But once the physical pain passed, the abortion became merely an episode. Later we broke up, but there was no connection.

"There was some kind of tug at the thought of the baby. It was not a fatherly one, but one of unease. We both cracked tasteless jokes about it months later, like how they disposed of it or whether it would have survived in salt water. Neither one of us wanted to confront that we had wiped out something alive. So we played games. It's just like war when you end up calling the enemy gooks.

"It really wasn't that difficult. I'd been through it before, but in a different way. When I was thirteen I knocked up a fifteen-year-old, who ran off with her seventeen-year-old boyfriend and got married. I didn't see her again for seven years when I ran into her and her kid in a department store. He was cute. But I didn't look at him too closely. I didn't want it to register. It's easier to forget a kid you never saw.

"You can arrange just about everything in your life—your schooling, your friends, the amount of money you earn. But in relation to pregnancy and cancer, you just can't. They are unfixable."

===

Abortion had just been legalized in New York when Charles August discovered his girlfriend was pregnant. Both students at the time, they were superficially for abortion, but Charles was deeply troubled at night by thoughts of the child. He never articulated them but instead supported the girl, who was very depressed. After the abortion he admitted his feelings to her, and they agreed that abortion was much more of a moral dilemma than they had previously thought. A year later Charles became impotent with her, and they broke up, though Charles insists it was because she was a better student than he was and not because of the abortion. Five years later, Charles is still disturbed about the abortion and has never resolved his feelings about it. He is single, and a journalist in New Hampshire.

"Suzy and I were at a summer program in Vermont to learn French. It was a very difficult summer. We could only speak in French and I was over my head academically. We also had very few friends there. We had been living together at Columbia University, but here in Vermont it was considered risqué.

"She was using the diaphragm, and maybe it wasn't in right or something. I knew she was pregnant before she did. I went by the clinic where she'd had the test the day before, and the result was in early. They said positive, and I was shocked. I had no idea how to deal with it. Up to then I thought it had been a false alarm.

"The abortion law had just been passed in New York, which made me kind of relieved. But I was worried about Suzy. She had exams right after lunch, and the best acting job I ever did in my life was not letting her know the result. Then I found it difficult to tell her. Finally I made a joke out of it. I bought a little bean-bag frog and put a sign on it saying: 'It's not my fault, I'm only a frog.'

"She laughed at first. It was like spanking yourself before taking a hypodermic needle. It was a distraction. She was forced to laugh, but it was very traumatic. She spent the rest of the night looking at herself in the mirror. It was very cerebral.

"Then she began to feel sleepy all the time. She started to sleep more and more. At the end she slept maybe fourteen hours a day. People began to notice and figured it out. There was a lot of holier-than-thou attitude coming down on us.

"I called the Feminist Repertory Theater and asked them where to go, but nobody lifted a finger to help us. Suzy was withdrawing more and more into sleep and depression. When she wasn't sleeping, she was crying. Finally Planned Parenthood gave us some referrals, and we ended up in the Bronx.

"We were staying with my parents then, and they could tell something was wrong. My parents—it was not their finest hour. 'What's wrong with Suzy?' they kept asking, and I kept telling them she had the flu. Finally I confessed, but the confines of their own morality forbade them to help me out. And the feminists hadn't helped either. I was all alone.

"Ideologically we were both for abortion. But in our own case, there was a great deal of ambiguity. There was the reality of this little person who was mine and hers who probably would have been a good kid. Late at night I thought about killing my own little son or daughter, but I also knew that it was a problem that had to be corrected.

"At the abortion center everyone was crying, so immediately Suzy perked up and became courageous. She had thought about the possibility of our getting married, but she was still realistic about it. At the time of the abortion I felt immensely sad. I felt I'd been shouldering an enormous part of the emotional and physical burden. I'd made all the arrangements and worked everything out. Suzy just wanted to wake up and find it over, which was exactly what she did.

"I can remember one weekend before the abortion. We had spent it with friends in the country, and I was driving back in the pouring rain. Suzy was in the back seat alternating between sleeping and crying. 'I cannot lose control of this car,' I kept saying to myself, 'and

I cannot lose control of this situation. Just keep looking through that windshield and get this car back to New York.' That's the way I felt about the whole situation.

"After the abortion Suzy was immediately better. We lived together for another year after that. And our sex life together didn't really change. We hadn't made love for three months prior to the abortion, and couldn't for six weeks after it, but at least we could talk together about it. We both had the same psychological reaction. We had been for abortion. But we were conscious that we had killed something, or rather had not let something live. We decided it was much more of a moral dilemma than we had realized.

"I'm still for abortion until they invent a substitute, and I'd do it again. It's only permissible considering the alternative, which is basically fucking up three lives. Suzy used an IUD after that, and we took better care. She felt relief and gratitude, and I felt all right about it, too. Men like to shoulder responsibilities, and I had. Our relationship picked up. We had no recriminations about that period.

"We broke up a year later. She had six years of French, and I was always trying to catch up. We had lots of problems we pretended were not there. We spent the summer in France, and suddenly I felt emasculated. It was important for me to take the leadership role, and I couldn't with her. Suddenly I lost all desire for her, and I became impotent. At first I'd just avoid her, and we'd joke that we were just like some old married couple. Then one night we started to make love. I wasn't impotent, but it was obviously a chore. There were tears, and that was it. She left to take a bus to the airport, but there wasn't one, so we got back together again. Six months later we broke up for good.

"The abortion tore at the fabric of our relationship, which was already strained, though it helped our relationship in other ways. I clearly wish it hadn't happened, but regardless, we still wouldn't have been together. Last week I saw a cartoon that was a picture of a couple with a huge monster lying on the floor between them, and under the picture the legend read: 'We deal with it by talking about it.' And that's just not true.

"In a different world, abortion would be wrong. In this world, it's a necessity of evil. There are too many people, too many fucked-up people. But that's just a rationalization. It could happen again. But it's nothing I could ever feel good about. And that surprised me. With men, I think, there's a confusion between potency and virility. At least I feel more manly for having made a baby. But I still have the residual feeling of having killed something, a life that was already impinging on mine. I've never resolved it."

———

Shefta Mercouri, now twenty-six, wasn't sure he wanted his girlfriend to go through with an abortion six years ago, but she insisted and he went along with her. He was surprised when shortly afterward a song on the radio made him break into tears, a song that still makes him feel bad. Though Shefta says he and his then girl-friend were closer after the abortion, they drifted apart and eventually split up. Now married and the father of a baby boy, Shefta is scared even to talk about the abortion because he feels he might be punished by having his son taken away from him. Shefta is a taxi driver in Brooklyn, New York.

"Oh boy, I remember that night; it was pouring rain and I had to drive her way upstate to get the abortion. I wasn't sure I wanted it, but she was still in high school and I was in college and we just weren't ready for it. She was the one who really insisted on the abortion.

"I waited outside the place with a friend of mine who'd driven up with us. He had lent me the three hundred dollars to pay for it. Afterwards she had bleeding and pain, and we had to go to our family doctor, which was very scary. We told him it was something else, but he didn't believe us.

"A little while later I was driving the cab and this song 'Where Are You Going, Billy,' came on the air and I started to cry, and I don't cry easily. I still can't hear that song without feeling bad. What would he have looked like now? They told her it was a boy. She was two and a half months along, which is pretty late. We broke up six months later, but the abortion had nothing to do with it. We were closer afterward than before, but then we just started drifting apart.

We never talked about the abortion. We just tried to forget it.

"I'm definitely for abortion and would do it again if necessary. It's better than having a son who's almost an orphan or putting him in an adoption home. It wouldn't be right for someone else to bring him up.

"Now I have a stepdaughter and a boy who is four months and six days old. I try not to think of him in relation to the other baby. You get rid of one—you get another. But I feel guilt whenever I look at him and especially when I hold him. I took the other one away. Maybe someone will take this one from me."

At fifty-one, Fritz Manson, a successful insurance agent in Pawling, New York, estimates that he has been responsible for at least nine abortions. Each of his two wives had three abortions at their insistence, and various odd couplings led to the other abortions. He was not upset by any of them, nor did he feel much emotional responsibility, as he believes birth control is in the woman's province. A miscarriage suffered by his second wife, Manson claims, was more traumatic than any of the abortions. The father of three children, Manson keeps planning to have a vasectomy even though his declining interest in sex may make it unnecessary.

"I was nineteen when I married Samantha, and she was eighteen. We were forced to marry when her stepfather found us in bed one Sunday morning and turned purple with rage. 'I'll give you one week to correct this situation,' he said, and one week later to the day we married in Elkton, Maryland. It turned out she was pregnant when we married, but we didn't know it at the time.

"We were both very frightened when we found out she was pregnant. She was still a student at Barnard and I was earning practically nothing working for an oil company. It was 1946. Abortions were hardly legal, and our gynecologist wouldn't do it. He sent us to someone who would, however, and because Samantha had a bad

142

heart, we were able to get the three signatures from all the honchos who had to sign.

"She went off to the Harkness Pavilion at Columbia Presbyterian Hospital in New York, and I brought her flowers and chocolates. I never gave a thought to the child, either that time or the others.

"She was always getting pregnant. If I put my shoes under the bed, she'd get pregnant. She used the diaphragm, but it kept slipping out of her fingers when she tried to put it in. We both used to try, but our fingers would get sticky from the cream and the damn thing would spring across the room. I couldn't stand the diaphragm then and can't to this day. My present girlfriend uses one, and honestly, I can't even sleep with her. The smell and the taste prohibits you from descending below the navel. And I can't stand wearing rubbers. It's like washing your feet with your socks on. Samantha got pregnant again two more times, and back we went to Harkness with the same signatures because of her bad heart.

"The fourth time she got pregnant, we both agreed it was time to have a baby, though she wanted it far more than I. I was very anti and very disagreeable about it, but we'd been married three and a half years and had created a happy home, which I was loath to give up. I wanted to create a home life, but that didn't include children. I wanted to be the center of attention. I went through the pregnancy reluctantly.

"Stephanie was beautiful but a nuisance. Our apartment was hot and noisy. I never liked small children. Samantha had a very hard time and bled a lot, but luckily it didn't affect our sex life, like what happened to a friend of mine whose wife hemorrhaged after childbirth—he was impotent with her for the next twenty years and still is.

"When Samantha got pregnant again, I knew I didn't want any more children, but again she did. I quite wanted to have a boy though, so I let her go through with it. I've always thought it was a woman's prerogative to have a baby or not, but I've also felt that if a man really puts his foot down, she'll give in. Clark was born in the midst of a hurricane, and after that it was just more noise, more hot nights.

143

"Then Samantha ran off with another man. He was much richer than I was at the time. I was good about the children, though, and saw them every other weekend. It always made me feel guilty. I thought they deserved a better lot.

"The next abortion was the girl in the office next to me, whom I used to screw on the sofa in her office from time to time. She was a sexy little wench, and it was great fun to poke her. She got pregnant, the little idiot, because she wore no birth control at all.

"That was my first illegal abortion, and it cost me one thousand dollars. I drove her home to New Jersey afterwards, and she was so calm about it you would have thought we'd been to the films. I felt nothing but relief. She even paid for half of it, which was very advanced for 1951. I can't remember if I screwed her again, but I doubt it. She was never cross with me. After all, I'd looked after her.

"Then there was a woman who lived around the corner from me and whom I'd run into at night when we walked our dogs. She invited me and my dog up one night, then said I'd knocked her up. I gave her some money and told her to get it done, and she made a frightful scene and said she'd sue me in a paternity suit. I never saw her again.

"Then I went on an orgy in Greenwich Village. There were six girls and six men. The girl I was with said that I had been the only man in her life, so it must have been me who got her pregnant, so I gave her two hundred and fifty dollars, and that was that. Now I began to ask everyone if they were using birth control, but women always say yes, whether they are or not. They probably all wanted to marry me. After all, I am heterosexual, nonalcoholic, and hardworking.

"My second wife was completely opposite from my first. She already had two children by her first marriage and was determined not to have any by me so that I'd be a better father to her children. She always said she used birth control, but she didn't. Instead, she'd take a douche afterwards, but often fell asleep instead. As a result she got pregnant three or four times and had abortions each time.

144

Finally I put my foot down. This time I wanted a child because I thought it might cement our marriage. I really loved her at that time. But it was nine months of misery. Sarah was impossible. Everything was wrong from morning to night. She was totally crabby. She really didn't want that baby.

"She was good to our daughter after she was born. And for a while she was better to me. Then she got pregnant again, and again I insisted on having the child just in case she might feel better about the whole thing. She tried to get another abortion, but the doctor simply refused, saying there was absolutely nothing the matter with her. So instead she miscarried, an act that took five months to end. She bled all that time and at the end went to the loo and saw a leg hanging down into the toilet. The doctors took the child, and I felt nothing but relief that the ordeal was over.

"We went to a marriage counselor then to try to work it out, and both my reluctance and my conflicting desire to have children was at least partially explained. My father was a frightfully irresponsible ne'er-do-well who saw me around five times in his life. He deserted my mother when I was three, and the only memory I have of him is being terrified of his booming voice. I rarely saw my mother either and can only remember her kissing me good night. I lived with my nanny while my mother was being supported by her various boyfriends. I was sent away to boarding school at the age of six and always had a terrible feeling of rejection. My mother subsequently remarried and became a drunk. What terrified me about having children was that it entailed for me a commitment not to reject them. And I still craved attention for myself.

"The counseling didn't help my marriage much, though, and my wife slowly tipped over into alcoholism herself. We were divorced ten years ago.

"Now everyone is on the pill and knows what to do with themselves. Thank God. And it's only laziness on my part that I haven't gotten a vasectomy. I've lost a lot of interest in sex in the past four years. Perhaps it's age or the fact that I believe sex is a commitment. And there's no one I want to make a commitment to. If I did knock up another girl, I'd certainly go through with another abortion. It really doesn't bother me at all. It's much easier to have an abortion than to have a child."

⸻

It has been eight years since Max Randolph's girlfriend had her first abortion, and eighteen months since she had her second. As they were both in high school during her first pregnancy and abortion, they decided they were too young to marry even though Max was willing to. Frightened by the idea of abortion, Max did not accompany her or give her any support, which made him feel guilty for years afterward. They broke up, got back together four years later, and she got pregnant again. This time she wanted the baby and so did he, even though this time he had no intention of marrying her. She began to miscarry and had to have a therapeutic abortion. They stayed together for another year and broke up again. Max never told her how hurt he felt about the loss of the child. A taxi driver in Los Angeles, Max, twenty-seven, says the abortions had nothing to do with their break-ups and he now wants to marry her. She, on the other hand, won't even speak to him.

"The first time we were both in high school, and we were just too young to be having babies. I wanted to marry her, but we weren't ready for it. I guess I wasn't ready for much. When she went for the abortion, I wasn't around. It was frightening to me. I made excuses that I had to be at football practice or something, but in reality it was fear that kept me away. I felt guilty for a long time.

"She was scared of the abortion, too. She was a weak person then, and it bothered her that I wasn't there. She didn't take it out on me, but I could tell she was disappointed that I wasn't there. It made me irritable just thinking about it. I'd fly off the handle at her over any little thing. It took me four years to understand all that I had learned during that abortion and afterwards.

"When we got back together and she got pregnant again, we never discussed the first abortion at all. In fact, we never have.

"This time she decided to have the baby even though I wasn't committed to marry her. I'm sure she thought we would get married anyway. She really let me know at that time that she was in love with me, but I don't know, I just felt stubborn. I was real proud of that pregnancy though. Real proud.

"But then it all started to go wrong, and she had to go into the hospital and have an abortion. It was all because of the first abortion. Psychologically and physically the first abortion had been such a shock to her system she couldn't carry another child. Her body had become conditioned to aborting at a certain period, and that's all there was to it. I made sure I was there for her the second time. I wasn't going to take that guilt again.

"We stayed together for another year, but then we began to get on each other's nerves. We didn't ever talk about the abortion except for the big letdown it was to her. To me it was like a huge hurt, but I never told her that. It would have been better if I had told her. It makes a difference to tell the truth because I began to resent her for taking all the disappointment on her and not letting me have any of it. For a while, though, the miscarriage and abortion brought us closer together, but now we're apart.

"I love her and really want to marry her now. But she won't speak to me, and if she sees me on the street, she runs into a store to get away."

147

5

Couples

Abortion means different things to different people. To some, it is merely the solving of an immediate problem. To others, it is the taking of a life. To the lucky ones, it is the best solution after all the pros and cons have been carefully weighed. But one fact remains constant: It takes a man and a woman to become pregnant, and in the face of a viable relationship, it takes a man and a woman to decide to abort, to go through the abortion and to live with it and with each other afterwards. Some succeed. Others don't.

Many clinics offer counseling to couples seeking abortion and talk with the man and the woman either separately or together. But there is concern that the counseling comes too late. By the time a couple arrives at the clinic for an abortion appointment, their minds are for the most part made up, and rather than welcoming discussion of their motives, they clam up and refuse to reopen a painful subject. Though the clinics are satisfied that they have fulfilled their obligation in helping the women and sometimes the men feel comfortable with their decision, often the counseling is looked upon as merely a courtesy, part of the abortion procedure that the patients are expected to go through. How the people really feel rarely comes up, either in front of the counselor or with each other, before the abortion. And often, as the previous interviews show, even after the abortion, couples, married or not, continue to keep their doubts or anxieties to themselves, each telling the other what he or she thinks the partner wants to hear.

Abortion can have extreme effects on the people involved. In one case Judith Wallerstein of the School of Social Welfare at the University of California at Berkeley followed one unmarried couple for eighteen months after the young woman, a student, had had a therapeutic abortion in 1972. The young man, a Catholic, had spent the night of the abortion sleeping in the car outside the hospital. Unable to shake his subsequent depression and guilt, he began to have nightmares, thought of himself as a sinner, and went to a priest for relief, but found none. As a form of self-punishment he invited a homosexual attack and began to think of himself as a homosexual. His distress lasted until a year after the abortion and then cleared up.

The young woman, on the other hand, appeared to have no distress. She felt only relief, according to Wallerstein, as her boyfriend was doing the suffering for her. When he recovered, her attitude changed immediately "because her own need for punishment was not contained by [her boyfriend's] illness." She began telling everyone about her abortion and was plagued by guilt that her mother would find out and think the less of her. Finally, eighteen months later, she sought counseling.

Counseling is not always effective, however. There are various neurotic and hidden reasons why women get pregnant in the first place, reasons which would not surface in the limited time the clinics have with their abortion clients. In a study of twenty-four couples with unwanted pregnancies in 1959, Hans Lehfeldt, clinical professor of obstetrics and gynecology at New York University, found a plethora of reasons for the women's pregnancies, even though the women were intelligent and knowledgeable about birth control. In his study of "Willful Exposure to Unwanted Pregnancy," he states that twenty of the couples were under stress because of marital infidelity, severe illness or death of people close to them, fear of sterility, premenopausal panic, a protracted engagement period, religious conflicts about contraception, the fear of remaining single, impotence or immaturity in one or in both of the partners. In many of the couples, either the man or the woman was undergoing psychotherapy at the time of the pregnancy. Though contraceptive failure was the pinpointed reason for the pregnancies in these couples, Lehfeldt discounted it as the cause. "These patients have such ambivalent feeling about pregnancy that neither contraception nor pregnancy offers a solution," Lehfeldt wrote. "They want both, so they alternate between contraception and exposure."

Ambivalence toward pregnancy does not always mean ambivalence toward abortion; there is a great difference between being pregnant and the ongoing fact of birth and child-rearing. Numbers of women seek out pregnancy to prove to themselves that they can conceive, and just as many men need to know that they, too, are capable of reproducing. There are also numbers of women who enjoy the state of being pregnant and the actual act of childbirth, but who have little or no desire for parenting. Reaction to grief or anticipated grief has been acknowledged as a familiar cause for unplanned pregnancies when the condition rather than the result is wanted. In a 1976 study in New Haven entitled "Grieving and Unplanned Pregnancy," three investigators from Yale University found that 1.7 percent of 402 women seeking abortions at Yale–New Haven Hospital in a given period had become pregnant within two months of the diagnosis of mortal illness or death in one of their parents. "Women become pregnant when grieving in an attempt to cope with specific emotional pain—that of loss or threatened loss of a close person and the individually relevant sequelae of such loss," wrote the authors, "—not because they wish to have a child as such at that time." Among the grief group, the women who had lost fathers were seeking closeness and release in intercourse, the authors suggested, while the women who had lost mothers were actually seeking pregnancy. In all the cases, however, the pregnancies were terminated by abortion.

Whether the women in the couples I interviewed had become pregnant for neurotic reasons or from contraceptive failure, as most of them claimed, the result was the same. Though the joint decision to abort was not particularly difficult to reach, the responses of the couples to the actual abortion were not so simple. In one couple, the unwanted pregnancy and subsequent abortion pointed up the failings in the relationship, yet the couple remained together for three more years though they never made love again. In a teenage couple, the abortion merely irritated the woman, as it precluded her from having sex for two weeks afterwards, while her male partner, matured by the experience, committed himself to never being involved in an abortion again. In an interracial couple, the man decided never to tell the woman that he was mourning the child, was against abortion, and resented her for having one, while the woman continued to think he was glad she had gone through with it. Only one couple appears to have been relatively unscathed. Thinking the whole thing through together, they sought out a clinic where he could be present during the procedure itself so that he could share as much as possible of what she was enduring. Together they appear to have eliminated as much residual guilt and anger as possible. Perhaps all clinics should be persuaded to invite or even insist on couples going through the abortion or at least the counseling together.

Betty Spalding, twenty-five, has just had her first pregnancy confirmed in an Ohio clinic. Now she and her husband, Gordon, twenty-nine, are setting up an abortion appointment for the next week. Looking and acting like the ultimately modern couple, the Spaldings are dressed in the latest fashion and talk rhetorically about their decision and the upcoming abortion. Betty's smile becomes a bit fixed, however, when Gordon goes too far. Betty, a student, and Gordon, who has just opened his own business in Kentucky, appear to be heading for trouble.

Betty: "I'd been on the pill for the last two and a half years, but went off because I started having headaches. I tried to be very careful, but obviously unsuccessfully.

"Around six weeks ago I was sitting in class when suddenly I felt nauseated. I thought, Oh, no. Then I thought some more and decided maybe I'd have the baby. When Gordon and I talked about it, though, we decided we weren't ready. We weren't emotionally ready."

Gordon: "I tried to think as far ahead as I could after Betty told me the news, and a baby just didn't fit in. The decision to have the abortion was really very easy."

Betty: "We discussed the alternatives, and decided having the baby would have been far more traumatic than having the abortion.

151

I don't feel any guilt at all, but I wish I'd never gotten pregnant. I really don't want to go through the whole experience. I wish it had never happened. But if I get pregnant again, I'll probably have another abortion. But Gordon would probably kill me if I did get pregnant again."

Gordon: "I feel real easy with this decision. It just doesn't upset me at all. The biggest hassle is the inconvenience, having to drive over here for the pregnancy test and everything."

Betty: "I think it's a bit more emotional than that, don't you?"

Gordon: "Maybe on your part, but not on mine."

John and Carol Anderson were very composed in the waiting room at Planned Parenthood in San Francisco where they were waiting for Carol's name to be called in the morning abortion line-up. Both in their early thirties, they had called over ten clinics before they found one where they could go through the abortion procedure together. Each of them felt it was important that John share in the abortion experience. They had discovered Carol's pregnancy just before they left Providence, Rhode Island, where she is a nurse and he is a psychologist. Rather than wait to have the abortion when they got back, the Andersons chose to get it over with in California so they could enjoy their vacation as much as possible. It was performed on their first wedding anniversary.

John: "It's the wrong time for us to have a child. We've talked a lot about having a family, and it will be another year or so. We were switching birth control methods, and Carol became pregnant. It would be good for neither us nor the child to have it at this time."

Carol: "It's not financial, it's just the desire. There would be great interference at this point in our lives. We're both in training positions. I'm a nurse, and John is a psychologist. We're in a very highly pressured environment in our work situations right now, and we feel even though we would like to have a child at some point, we would like to be ready to devote the time to it."

152

John: "The decision to have an abortion itself wasn't hard. It's hard reconciling the feelings after the decision. The conclusion was that we want some more time for ourselves before we have a family. A bigger family.

"I don't know that my feelings are different as a man. I think my feelings are mixed. One is that I want to have a family. It's good to know that Carol's fertile, and that we can conceive, because we've had friends who've tried and can't. Being around that, and knowing how much they would like to have a family, in a way this abortion seems selfish. But I've known that I was virile before. This isn't my first abortion either, although in that one I wasn't really part of the couple. It was more frivolous at that time. And I didn't go through the whole procedure with her. Those were a little bit the darker ages, the 1960's."

Carol: "I think I have similar reactions to John. We've discussed the fact that I feel a little isolated in experiencing the physical symptoms. It's been an unpleasant time for me, having all this constant nausea, and I have tended to be very introspective and aware of my own feelings and my own body. I think it's somewhat alienated us because I've had that isolation feeling. Knowing that we wanted to terminate the pregnancy wasn't something that we were sharing in quite the same way.

"I had the same initial feeling of elation because we could have children together, and we really very much look forward to that. It was mixed with sadness because it was the wrong time. It's our first conception of a child, and it's sad that we can't experience that child. But we both feel very strongly that it's not the right time, and we both feel very strongly that once we raise a child, we know what we want the circumstances to be. It's just not right now.

"My first abortion was a couple of years ago. It happened to be during the end of a previous marriage. It was very poor timing, and there again I made a definite decision that this was a bad time to have a child. My husband didn't accompany me. I found the support of the nurses to be much more than I had anticipated. The fact that I felt so strongly about not having the child really helped me to get the strength to do it. I didn't want him there. But I want John here. We tried a number of different places. Actually we had to drive four

153

hours to get here today. There were several places that were much closer, but there it was unheard of to have a joint experience. It was very important to us to have something that we shared."

John: "I was involved in the conception, I was involved in the decision to terminate, I've been involved in the feelings, and I want to be involved in the resolution. That's the way our life is.

"I'm not anxious about the procedure per se, I think being there conveys the message that I'm supportive."

Carol: "At one point we considered for convenience my going in without him. I became increasingly anxious to set up an appointment. I realized from my past experience how important timing was. But because of the isolation that I was feeling, I felt that it was especially important to have the resolution come about together. It could help us to regain the closeness we felt before we started this experience. It's been a couple of weeks now since we found out. I really feel like it's something that would be unfinished for him and for me if he weren't a part of it. It's not something that you can just talk about and understand. You need to share."

John: "I think this will bring us closer together. The last week has been a very hard time for us. The work situation that we're in from day to day really puts the pressure on us. The pregnancy has added a lot to it. I think one thing that we've known all along is that there are times in our own way when we need to be alone and be quiet. That was one of the things that we wanted to do on our vacation, to get away from the pressure cooker and lie back and get bored. If we had postponed the abortion until the end of the vacation, when we were back in Providence, it would have weighted our discussion the whole time. I'm looking forward to the end of today, when we can put this behind us, and work at getting relaxed."

Carol: "We found out I was pregnant two days before we were to leave on our vacation. It was early enough that we could have waited until we got back, but we decided that we didn't want the pregnancy to go on. We really needed a relaxing vacation with nothing on our minds."

154

Sonia Rothbard, seventeen, and Steve Hendricks, nineteen, have been going out together for a year. A senior in high school in Kentucky, Sonia was lying on a bed in the recovery room of an Ohio abortion clinic, having just had an abortion, while Steve, a produce salesman, tried to take a nap in the waiting room. Unlike the other women in the recovery room, who looked drawn and tired, Sonia was wiggling with impatience to leave. Dressed in painter's pants and a T-shirt that read *"Voulez-vous coucher avec moi ce soir,"* Sonia was giggling with another young woman on the next bed. Steve, on the other hand, was depressed and angry. This couple, like the couples that follow, were interviewed separately at their request.

Sonia's story: "When I found out I was pregnant, I felt very defensive about the baby and all confused about what I should do. The father is my steady boyfriend, and like I love him a lot, and I thought it would be fun to have the kid. I wanted to protect it in my stomach, sort of. I really felt like having it.

"It gave me a sort of handle on my boyfriend too. I teased him about it. Whenever he got out of hand a little I'd say, 'I got your baby inside of me,' and he'd say, 'Oh shut up,' because he just didn't want to hear about it.

"He's more upset about the abortion than I am, I guess. Today is his nineteenth birthday, which doesn't help. And he was so nervous that he got to my house at six A.M. so we'd be on time for our ten A.M. appointment. We stopped at Burger King across the street. I knew I wasn't supposed to eat, but I was starved, so I gorged on two hamburgers and a shake. He couldn't eat anything.

"I felt a little sad on the drive over here, but the people here at the clinic have made me happy. Now I can't believe it's over with. It's not something that's going to bother me. I'm not going to think of it like that. I'm not going to confess it, either, even though I'm Catholic. As long as I confess it to myself, who cares about the priest. He'd just make me say ten prayers, and that would be that anyway.

155

"When I get out of here, we'll probably go celebrate or something. The only thing I'm disgusted about is that we don't get to do nothin' for two weeks."

Steve's story: "Sonia stopped using the pill, and she didn't tell me about it. Boy, I was mad at her when I found out. She just had the idea it wouldn't happen to her, that she was special. Those damn pills are sitting in the glove compartment of my truck. I found them when I was looking for the map of how to get here.

"I was shocked and mad at myself and her when I found out. I never considered marrying her, though. She's just a kid, not out of school yet. And I just started work at the produce store.

"She sure was something when she found out she was pregnant. She's no mother, that's for sure. She teased me about it. She kept making little jokes about little Stevie. I didn't want to hear it. Then she decided not to get the abortion. Then I really went crazy. I got mad. One way or other, she wasn't going to have that kid. I thought she kept changing her mind just to spite me. Even on the drive over, she was trying to put it to me that I was making her have the abortion, but I'm sure she wanted it just as much as I did. She's just a kid. A kid.

"There was worry the whole time she was pregnant. I slept with her every night for the last two or three weeks. She said she had bad dreams and didn't want to be alone. She babysits my sister, so she'd just stay over. I never made love to her, though. I felt different about her with the kid and all. I cared more about her in a different way. And I still feel the same.

"I'm glad it's over with now. All that worrying. If we'd had the kid, we wouldn't have been ready. He shouldn't have to suffer for it. It wasn't his fault.

"She's going on the pill now, and damn it, she's going to stay on it. She didn't want to take it before because it made her fat. Next time I want to be ready for a kid. And I might marry her. I just might.

"Today's my birthday. I'm nineteen today. It doesn't bother me, but it's probably going to make me remember it."

156

═══════════════

Linda Zimmerman, a twenty-four-year-old fashion designer, and Graham Grant, twenty-five, an aspiring actor, have been living together for three years in New York. As Linda had great difficulty tolerating different forms of birth control, she got pregnant twice and has had two abortions. Her first abortion at a New York hospital was incomplete, causing her great physical pain and creating anger and guilt in Graham. The couple agree entirely on abortion, even though the unwanted pregnancy made Graham relieved to know he was virile. Their only problem has been Graham's feeling of anger at the hospital's mishandling of the first abortion and his feeling that the women's movement has led women to believe that abortion is "hassle-free."

Linda's story: "I've always had great trouble with birth control. The pills made me bleed, I've got a tilted cervix so I can't use a diaphragm, and I've tried three different IUD's, all of which were very uncomfortable. Both times I've gotten pregnant have been in between trying out different kinds of birth control.

"I've been living in an illegal marriage for three years, at least that's what the rest of the world thinks of it as. He's an actor, and we're in no position financially or emotionally to have a baby. We barely make enough money to support ourselves, let alone anyone else. And we're still too early into our relationship to be tied together.

"When I found out I was pregnant the first time, I wasn't that worried about it. But I should have been. I went to a city hospital where I waited all alone in a green room for two hours. I hadn't eaten anything because I was going to have an anesthetic. When I woke up in the recovery room, I was throwing up, and when I looked down, I realized they had taken the nail polish off my fingernails to see if my nails had turned blue. It was my first time in a hospital since I was born, and it was a frightening experience.

"They sent me home and told me I'd feel better in a day or two, but I didn't. That was a Monday, and Thursday was Thanksgiving. I went off to my family for Thanksgiving dinner and was in such pain

157

I counted to a thousand and back three times to keep from fainting from the pain. I must have turned bright green, but I just told them I had the flu and they believed me. When I got back to our apartment I went into the bathroom and crumpled up on the floor in agony. Graham took me to the hospital emergency room, where they didn't even bother to examine me but just gave me painkillers.

"I was up all night with the pain and went back to the hospital in the morning. This time the doctor did an in-office scraping to make sure everything was all out and sent me home again. By Saturday night the pain was so bad I felt I was going to kill myself. It was like the worst cramps you've ever had multiplied by five hundred. I dragged myself back to the hospital, and this time they admitted me. The next morning they gave me a D and C, and I felt much better —until the bill came. It was four hundred dollars, which is the price of two abortions. Having botched the first one, did they really think they could get away with charging me for cleaning up their mess? I wrote and told them I'd sue for malpractice and never paid them anything at all.

"I never felt anything about the fetus. Before the abortion I'd had one or two thoughts about it, but in my agony I only thought about myself. It's much easier not to think about the fetus, after all. The world would be a lot better place if there were fewer babies in it. That's the important thing.

"I went back to the hospital two weeks later to have the IUD inserted because they'd forgotten to do it after the D and C, but it hurt so much I had to have it taken out. It's hard for us to have sex now. It's all a drag. I'm going to try the rhythm system with a temperature chart, I guess. I've tried foam, suppositories, everything. God, a woman's body is a drag.

"The rhythm system isn't foolproof, though, because six weeks ago I got pregnant again. I guess I got mixed up. I knew I was pregnant even though the test came back negative. I had morning sickness and my breasts swelled and I absolutely freaked out. I was really petrified. I still couldn't fit a baby into my life either financially or emotionally. But the thought of all that pain again blew my mind.

"I had to get it done right away. I couldn't even bear to wait three or four days. I went to Parkmed, and the difference was incredible.

The people there had feelings. They're not robots and zombies. They ran another test on me and examined me, explained about the anesthetic and offered us either a local, a general, or none. And all for one hundred eighty-five dollars. I chose the general, they stuck the IV in my arm, I blacked out, and it was over. There were no side effects, no dreams, no nothing. In the recovery room there were people to help me. Then they gave me cookies and sent me home. I spent the weekend relaxing and had no cramps and just mild bleeding.

"I didn't think about the fetus that time either, but again was more worried about myself. I didn't think of it as killing a baby but like an operation on my arm or something.

"Graham and I have something between us, and we don't need to create anything else to make us feel more fulfilled. If we're financially secure five years from now, maybe things will be different. But right now, things are fine the way they are."

Graham's story: "I had thought up to the time that Linda got pregnant that I might be sterile. As far as I knew I had never successfully propagated, and it upset me. It was a status thing in college among the guys. They'd boast, 'I've got a kid here and a kid there,' like they were carving notches in a gun. I didn't think of myself as less virile, but I was preoccupied with the cocksmen in college. So my first reaction to Linda's pregnancy was relief, but immediately my concern shifted.

"I felt very bad except for the fact that my fears about sterility had vanished. I shared completely in her feelings. I almost got sympathetic morning sickness. My body felt as if it were going through some sort of change itself.

"I felt closer to her. It was an intimate experience. We never even discussed having the baby. The abortion was taken for granted.

"We had a lot of trouble with birth control. I find the IUD uncomfortable. I can feel the string and it causes irritation and pain to my penis. She has tried everything, even vaginal suppositories, but they took ten minutes to melt. All forms of intercourse that can't result from foreplay become clinical and doctorish. It's something outside each other's personal world, and sex becomes almost a fetish

159

and you might as well have black boots and a whip. The pill spoiled everybody. And then the problems with the pill began.

"The first abortion was a disaster. The hospital completely fucked up, and so did I. Three days after the abortion we went to a party and I got drunk. Then Linda hemorrhaged at four A.M., but I was so groggy I didn't go with her to the hospital. I barely remember her leaving. I felt great guilt for not being more supportive. I shouldn't have been in the position where I just grunted and rolled over.

"I felt really frightened for her and furious at the hospital. I had no desire to share her pain, but I felt her equal partner in this, and it was completely out of my hands. I felt my hands were tied. I was paralyzed and angry. If every abortion were like that, we'd have a large and boisterous family by now.

"I really decry the anti-abortionists, and I suspect if you did a survey you'd find that the people who are against abortion are for capital punishment. They're all for the beginning of life, but not for the continuation of it.

"And where does life begin? Is a 'fetus' a living thing? And what about onanism? Is spilling your seed a mortal sin? Is the egg or the sperm individually not life? Do they have to be joined? I can't correlate all this in my mind.

"Abortion must stay. The world population is going to double by the year 2000. By then murder will probably be punished like a traffic violation. But abortion is hard on the woman. Somebody should have found a treatment by now which would have made everyone sterile so then you could take a drug to make you have children. The whole thing of birth control is backwards. And why does a man have to propagate to know if he's virile? Why aren't there free sterility tests like there are free pregnancy tests? It's all backasswards."

———

There are many problems in the relationship between Reginald Brown, an unemployed construction worker, and Sally Bush, a student, in Memphis, Tennessee. Reginald is black, separated from his wife, and the father of three daughters. Sally, who is white, comes from an old Memphis family and is divorced from her husband. Her family does not know she has been living with Reginald for over a year and was very upset by her divorce. Because their relationship is so fragile, Reginald did not tell Sally when she became pregnant that he thought abortion was murder, nor that their shared tension both before and after the abortion caused him to hate her for a period. He has decided never to tell her how he really feels. So far he has succeeded. Sally feels he is happy about the abortion, though she admits there was tension over it. She feels it was just like any medical procedure. They have come to the clinic because Sally has been bleeding ever since her abortion two months ago.

Sally's story: "I don't think my relationship with Reginald changed at all over the abortion. It was before I even found out I was pregnant that I woke up feeling so bitchy and stuff. I couldn't eat and I had morning sickness and I was just taking it out on him. I wasn't trying to. I just did. I'd just wake up griping, and he could tell that I didn't feel good because I was always depressed. But when I found out I was pregnant and we decided on the abortion, I felt better.

"I didn't blame him for making me pregnant because we knew it was going to happen. I was married for three years and I never took birth control because I was kind of not wanting to get pregnant but if I did it was okay. We were kind of using the rhythm method for three years, and I never got pregnant.

"Reginald didn't want me taking birth-control pills. He thinks they're bad, so I quit taking them for a few months. It was taking a big chance, but we tried other things like withdrawal or sort of using the rhythm method because my period's always been real regular. So we'd skip that week right in the middle except when we really wanted to. So when it happened, it wasn't any big shock.

"He was telling me he was for the abortion and he was, but in a way he wasn't, but he thought that was what I wanted, so he was going to be all for it. I couldn't tell if he really wanted it or not until afterwards it seemed he was glad it happened. I stopped being bitchy right after the abortion. And my feelings for him didn't change, at least not consciously. And I didn't feel any different when I slept with him.

"Some times it would be better than other times. I was studying

161

real hard in the first quarter, and all I wanted to do was study and read. I'm just finishing up my master's. The abortion didn't really affect us at all except for the fact that I've been bleeding ever since. He keeps talking about a vasectomy, but I know he's not really serious.

"I don't know if I'll marry Reginald. There are a lot of problems. He's black. And my parents don't know we're going together. His mother knows. There's all that we have to think about too. Because when we tell them, I don't want to be pregnant. My parents are old. They're in their sixties while my friends' parents are in their fifties, and when I got divorced my mother, who's a librarian, stayed out of work for a couple of weeks because she was so upset. She gets real upset over a lot of things, and I wouldn't want to tell her a lot of things that would put her right over the edge.

"I don't know. It's so confusing. Why, I can remember in the eighth or ninth grades I never even saw any black people. We never even ate in the same lunchrooms or restaurants. I remember going into a rest room once and my mother jerking me back, saying that it was for nigras. It's sort of real unbelievable to me that I had an abortion and it was a black or sort of black baby. Everything's gone so fast. Real fast.

"Reginald and I haven't talked about the abortion at all. We've talked around it, like I'm still bleeding and all, but we never say why. I was thinking about that today, like coming in here. Even being in here today, I still feel real detached from anything here. It's just like coming to the doctor for any old checkup and just not thinking about it."

Reginald's story: "The abortion was her idea. I don't believe in it. Period. I would rather that she had had the baby, but she's the one who's got to contain it, she's the one who's got to go through all the trouble, so she said she wanted the abortion and I went along with it.

"I have to agree that at the time she got pregnant, I didn't really want a baby. I had just been laid off. It was a bad time, and we really couldn't afford it. At the time we were also both married to someone else, and it would have been a bad situation actually. My first reaction was, 'What am I going to do now?' It was kind of hectic.

"We didn't argue about it. Mostly I just listened and thought to myself that whatever she decided to do I'd go along with it. I didn't discuss my feeling with her then or now because it might upset her. I just walk around and keep it to myself. We had discussed abortion about a year ago, and she knows I don't believe in it, but as far as she knows, she thinks I was in full accord with this abortion.

"I feel awful, actually. I saw a movie on TV the other night, and I started wondering whether it was a little girl or a little boy or what it would look like. Things like that. But usually I just try to put it out of my mind and hope that she doesn't find out that I was against it.

"I was against her for a while, too. Sally is basically a very, very sweet person. She does the things she thinks you like to do, because she wants to make you happy. But during the period that she found out she was pregnant, and then she had the abortion, and then for three or four weeks afterwards, she was an entirely different person. She was hard to get along with, she never wanted to do anything. She didn't want to talk about anything, and she acted as if she didn't want me to be around. We would be sitting in the apartment, and it was like who was going to get up and get out first. There wasn't any physical hostility, but the mental hostility was there. It was as if we both hated each other, because when she found she was pregnant, you would gather that I had done something wrong to her. Everything I said and did made her hostile. If a piece of lint fell on the floor, she said I was making a mess. If she went for a drink of water from the icebox and the bottle was empty, it would be my fault. I'm surprised I was able to stick it out.

"Our sex life didn't change at all afterwards. No, wait. I guess the abortion did create some problems. Right after she had it, I was sort of impotent with her. I guess I'll have to back up a little bit. Because after she first had it, I guess I hated her for about three or four weeks. I didn't want to be around her. I didn't want to talk to her. I didn't want her to be near me because it was still really on my mind. It was real heavy then, but it's all over now. It's all gone. It's almost as if it never happened. But it was rough. I don't like to sleep with women I don't feel anything about, and I just didn't want to be bothered with her.

163

"She was going through a period then where she really needed to be loved, and I just didn't want to be bothered. After a couple of weeks I didn't think about it too much, and it all got back to normal. I just kept it all to myself. She's an emotional person, and I wouldn't want to make her unhappy. She thinks that we both made the decision, but if I tell her that she made up the decision on her own and I just went along with it, she'd be all upset, so I just won't tell her at all. Not ever.

"To my mind, the only man that can totally agree to an abortion is a guy who's just dating a girl he doesn't feel anything about. If he has any feelings at all about her, I would hope that he wouldn't agree to it. If a man loves a woman, I don't think he would agree to it under any circumstances.

"In a way, black men think about pregnancy as a status symbol, but I like to think that I'm different from everybody else. I don't think it should be as one-sided as it is. But I don't think there's that much difference between white men and black men. They all expect a slave. She's supposed to work and come home, clean, see about the kids. She's not supposed to go anywhere or have any life of her own, have any fun or anything. I'm not like that. I don't think a woman should be dominated. But the abortion left a deep hurt on me, because I'll always wonder whether it was a boy or girl and what it looked like or what it would be like when it was grown. I've got three girls, and I want a son bad. And I often wonder whether that was him. If I get angry enough I'll probably think she murdered my son, but just to myself."

Nancy Kingsley and Sean Thomas lived together for seven years in a part-time marriage relationship. Nancy, now thirty-six, is a public-relations executive in Washington, D.C., but on weekends she commuted to Sean's house on the Maryland shore, where he was in real estate. It was a comfortable and convenient relationship for both of them until she became pregnant four years ago. After her abortion, though they lived together for three more years, they never made love again. It was only after they split up that they were each able to talk about the abortion. Nancy, recently married to a television producer, has decided never to have a child and has since had a menstrual extraction. Nancy found it easy to talk about her experience. Sean did not.

Nancy's story: "The night I got pregnant was really a scene. It was my birthday, and Sean had invited my mother and another friend over for dinner. Everyone got plastered. My mother was particularly hateful to me that night, and I remember driving her home and then coming back and announcing, 'God damn it, I'm so upset I'm going to get drunk,' which I systematically proceeded to do.

"I was using an old diaphragm at the time. I had been on the pill for nine years, and it had begun to disturb my body. I was spotting in between periods and feeling a general discomfort, so I quit. I had tried an IUD, but two weeks after the doctor put it in he had to take it out because I'd gotten pelvic inflammatory disease, which can have horrendous complications. He said I wouldn't be able to have another one inserted for six months, so there I was back with my old diaphragm.

"This night occurred during that interim six months. Though I had the diaphragm, I didn't have any spermicide ointment, and when we made love, which was more violent than loving, the diaphragm ripped. When I discovered the rip the next morning, I was more amused than anxious. I had never gotten pregnant before, even when I was trying once when I was married. I thought that maybe I'd never get pregnant, that maybe I was sterile. So we both laughed when I showed Sean the rip. 'What will we name the baby?' I joked with him. We both laughed. We weren't tense at all.

"I skipped my period and went to my doctor for a pregnancy test, but it came back negative. I felt different, though. My breasts were bigger and tender and I was mildly nauseous. I was sure when I went on a business trip and my body felt entirely different. I was depressed, anxious, and confused in not knowing what to decide. I had the clear-cut choice of a legal abortion with a doctor whom I truly liked and trusted, which made the decision even more difficult. I wasn't being forced into having the abortion. I had the money and the time to have the baby, and I had flirted before with the idea of having a

165

child, but now I was growing farther away from that concept and more into continuing my career. What did I really want? What did Sean really want? He was not the type of person who will straight-out answer you and tell you what he wants. I thought about the problem every morning when I woke up and every night when I went to sleep. The emotional decision was far greater than the physical one.

"If I decided to have it and raise it myself, would Sean help me out financially, and if he did agree to and then lost interest, could I count legally on him? Could I force him? Also, if I had to give up my job, then I wouldn't be able to afford anything for myself. And if I kept on working and paid for a housekeeper every day, I'd have to stay home every night because I had no one to share the load with.

"My instinct from the beginning was that Sean didn't want to get involved in it. He didn't want to get married to me or anybody else. And he wasn't interested in babies. I kept him posted the whole way. The message he kept giving me, overtly and subtly, was not to make a decision until the pregnancy became a fact. I felt very strongly that the decision should be mutual. It was not my right to abolish this baby alone. He said it was my ultimate decision, as I would have to bear the baby, which in one way was a copout and in another way, very nice.

"When it became definite I was pregnant, we sat down and I laid out the options. I would move to the country with him, get married, have the baby, and find something to do. Or I could live with him, have the baby, and not get married. Or I could have the baby anyway and continue living our dual lives and bring the baby on the weekends. Or I could get an abortion and wash my hands of the whole thing.

"I never considered what effect the abortion would have on our lives. Things weren't going that well between us then, anyway. He wanted me to come down and be his hostess, go places with him and be his girl, but he had never made any emotional commitment. I got the feeling he didn't want a baby around, but he never came out and said it. After a while, during that night, I began to feel humiliated, as if I were pleading with him. He was drinking while we were talking and probably got drunk. I felt very rejected. What I probably wanted him to say was 'Quit and come out here and live with me and

166

have the baby,' and if he had, there was a 90 percent chance I would have done it. I would have fallen right into his arms. But never once had he told me he loved me, and he didn't that night either. He always said he was incapable of love, even though I showed him all the ways he was loving me.

"At the end of the discussion, I felt shitty, but I didn't cry or anything. It was a very businesslike conclusion. At that point I decided to act fast. I was uncomfortable at the thought of being pregnant. And our relationship really wasn't good. We hadn't been doing well sexually for a year before that. If I hadn't made advances toward him, we wouldn't have made love at all. I was very disappointed at his reaction to the pregnancy, but I wasn't surprised. It was just proof that, shit, he doesn't love me.

"I took the day off from work and had the abortion. Sean refused to come with me or have anything to do with it. He was very firm that he couldn't cope with the mechanics of it. I guess he was afraid he'd have an anxiety attack in the doctor's office and drop dead or something. When he couldn't make that effort, it was the last straw.

"I had a close homosexual male friend then who gave me all the support I needed. He wanted to come with me, to pick me up, to do anything he could. I chose to go alone, but he called me four times that afternoon and then took me to dinner and the ballet. I told him every gory detail and how the abortion felt like I was being raped, that there were strangers taking over the functions of my body. It was humiliating, degrading, and much more painful than I had anticipated. My friend died four years later of cancer, and he told me while he was dying that he felt just the same way I had, that he was being raped by strangers.

"I felt terrible after the abortion. Sean had asked me to call him, and I did. He was reserved but relieved I was all right. I had a tough time at the ballet. The last dance was a circus scene in which there were a lot of children dancing around. One was a little girl around seven or eight who had strawberry blond hair, pigtails, and freckles. I shed a few tears in the dark and thought, I've just killed my own child. I've always wanted a girl, and she looked just like me. It made me feel really bad. I felt really bad lying on the table right after the abortion too. I felt horribly sad at what I'd done and started to cry.

My doctor held my hand and said I'd feel better about it soon. He assured me I could have another child when it was the right time for me. But I was still all psyched up because I had thought I was going to feel relief that it was all over, and instead I felt very depressed. A couple of weeks later a friend of mine brought her newborn baby over to show it off, and I felt very sorry for myself and sad, but I couldn't tell her. I was very embarrassed by the whole thing. I had been brought up in a Catholic culture where abortion simply didn't exist.

"I went down to Sean's the next weekend and tried to tell him all about it, but I felt guilty about bothering him with the experience. I said that I felt he should pay half the expense, and he acted offended as if I had gotten very petty. But I wanted to punish him. It was the least he could do. He hadn't been supportive in any way. He wrote me out a check very slowly. We never discussed the abortion again.

"We made love again for the first time around four weeks later. In the act of penetration I suddenly and without thinking said, 'Please don't give me another baby.' He immediately pushed me away. I began to apologize and weep and wring my hands, but he wouldn't listen. He pushed me out of the bedroom and told me to get out. It was three A.M. I was trying to cling to him, to feel reassured, but he just wanted to get rid of me. He was horribly hurt by my remark, which I agree was thoughtless and stupid.

"It was the final kiss-off to our relationship. I took his car and drove to my mother's, and the next morning he came to get me but mostly to get his car. He said in the car coming back that he was prepared to overlook the whole thing, that all people had nights like that. He wanted to sweep it under the rug, the way he'd always done. He was saying, 'Let's pretend it never happened,' and I was willing to play the game of let's pretend. I felt comforted by it, that we could start over.

"We lived together another three years, but I didn't feel committed to him. I began to use him for my convenience and cared less and less about him. I must have been very bitchy to him both in private and in public, but more in public because I wanted to shame him to get rid of my anger. I'm not proud of the way I acted.

"We slept together in the same bed for all that time, but we never made love again. I never wanted to make love to him again. The feeling was gone. I actually felt repelled by him, and I'm sure he felt repelled by me. When another man came along, the decision was simple. Here was a man who wanted to love me, and there was a man who not only couldn't love me, but didn't. So fuck him.

"It wasn't until I had moved in with this other guy that Sean and I ever talked it out. I went to a psychologist with him a couple of times, and it was an important emotional breakthrough for both of us. All along, it turned out, he had wanted to help me but just didn't know how. There was a lot of hugging and tears and nose-blowing during those sessions, and we felt much closer then than we ever had before. We almost did pick up again, but I didn't want to really. I still didn't feel physically attracted to him. 'Do I care about him?' I would ask myself, then answer, 'Yes, but not as a lover.' If we'd started again on a whole new level, if he'd started dating me and I'd stayed at some other house, then it might have worked. But I didn't want any sexual pressure. I didn't want to feel I had to go to bed with him after all this agony. So we didn't get back together. I still love him, though. I really do.

"Then two weeks ago I was five days late with my period, and I started having those same physical symptoms. I called my doctor, and he said to have a menstrual extraction. This time the man I live with picked me up from the doctor's office, made me lie down at home and read a magazine while he fixed dinner—all the comfort and support I'd missed the first time. There was no question about this pregnancy. I really don't want the hassle. I don't want to be bothered with a baby, and that's the cold, hard truth. I'm simply not interested in bringing one up. Four years ago, yes, but not now. I don't even like babies. Keep them away from me. They are a drag."

Sean's story: "When Nancy first told me she was pregnant I felt . . . puzzled. I was not delighted to know I could father a child. More, it brought our relationship to a point of definition. I knew the decision whether or not to have an abortion had to be mutual. And part of the tendency on my part toward abortion lay in the fact that I was not convinced I wanted to live with her or marry her. I didn't want to be tied to Nancy, nor did I think it was fair to influence her decision. If she had decided not to have an abortion, then I would have had to prepare her for the fact that she might have to have that baby without me.

"Luckily she decided to have the abortion, and I felt enormously guilty that I didn't go with her to support her. Oh, she had a friend with her and someone to make her soup, but I just couldn't make myself go. Instead, I called her on the phone. It's something I've never forgiven myself for.

"I felt a great loss, but it was abstract and intellectual. I've managed to suppress the loss of the child both subconsciously and consciously. But there is always speculation in what it might have been. I still look at a blue-eyed, blond child and think it might have been mine.

"But the big loss was our relationship. Anything as dramatic as an abortion is going to change a relationship. For a while afterwards, everything was fine. But the first time we made love, she turned to me in the midst of it and said, 'Don't give me another baby.' I instantly went limp, and we had a terrific fight. I ended up sleeping in another bedroom. And in the last three years we lived together, we never made love again.

"It would have helped if we had talked about it. But we never did."

<hr>

Maria and Billy Carpenter have been married for four and a half years. Two years before their marriage, Maria had an illegal abortion, the horrors of which sent her into therapy. It almost terminated her relationship with Billy, a well-known musician. Maria felt that Billy let her down by not participating more in the abortion and by not supporting her afterwards. Billy, on the other hand, felt that Maria shut him out of the experience by not following his advice. More honest about their relationship, which is complicated by the fact that they are an interracial couple, Maria says their sex life suffered and that she became nonorgasmic for a period of time. Billy says their life went on relatively unscathed and that so far as he is concerned the abortion was no more than an appendectomy. If

170

Maria gets pregnant again, Billy feels she'd probably have another abortion. Maria does not think she could go through another abortion. It is unlikely their relationship could survive another unwanted pregnancy.

Maria's story: "I was a student at a music school in Greenwich Village when I started living with Billy and got pregnant. It was a time when abortions still weren't legal. We did not know what to do. We couldn't have the child. There was still that stigma of shotgun weddings, and my God, my parents were still supporting me. There was so much worry, not the least of which was that Billy was black. There was no thought about having the child. It was really that I had to have an abortion to function in my life—to continue in school—and to not let my parents know. There was a whole pressure about it. It wasn't like two married people sitting down and really thinking do we want to have this child.

"It was my own fault I got pregnant. I was using the diaphragm, but I miscounted and didn't use it for a while. It's a very strange thing. I think I was in a very spaced head then. It was probably a very masochistic thing. I decided I could go without protection for ten days after my period, which now I know I can't. I always wonder why I miscounted that month. In fact, the whole experience sent me into therapy.

"I really loved Billy then, but the abortion nearly did us in. It turned into a hate relationship for a while. It was really a traumatic experience. We were in love, and we were living together, but we did not know where to go.

"I was just so upset when I found out I was pregnant. I couldn't believe what was happening to me. I went to a couple of different gynecologists, running from one to another. When they confirmed I was pregnant, I freaked out. It was at lunchtime on my job, and I couldn't go back to work. It was the middle of August, and I was going home to my parents for Labor Day, and all I could think of was that I had to have this abortion now, before I went back to Detroit. Then I got so sick. I'm sure now it was all this emotional thing, but I had morning sickness, I couldn't eat. That added to the

171

pressure. I thought, My God, I can't go home like this. They'll know something's wrong with me. I got bloaty right away. It was really a scene.

"My sister and Billy arranged it all. I let myself be put in someone else's hands, much to my downfall. Billy came up with an expensive man on Park Avenue who was known to do a lot of showbiz people, but because he was a couple of hundred dollars more and we were in a poor time and my sister had to borrow money from the restaurant where she was waitressing and Billy borrowed money, we went to a guy in New Jersey. My sister got his name from the editor of *Screw* magazine. It was three hundred dollars instead of the five hundred for the guy on Park Avenue. She rented a car, and we drove out there. Billy didn't go. He was working three shows a night, six nights a week so he couldn't go.

"So my sister and I took off to do the whole thing. I was real scared going out in the car. I was scared I was going to be hurt—and all the stories I had heard. Everyone was giving me feedback: 'Be careful, be careful, the places are filthy, you get these infections.' It was all going through my mind. It was pretty awful. We should have split on the whole scene.

"We met him in the lobby of this disgusting motel in this real rundown neighborhood. He came in, and he was real cagey and we could even smell a little alcohol on his breath. But we still proceeded. I don't know where my sister and I were at that night. I think we were so desperate and we'd come this far and the thought of going home for Labor Day was looming for both of us.

"He drove us to this place. My sister tried to check out where he was taking us. He took us up to his office. We searched it out later and found that he had lost his license as a doctor because he'd been caught doing abortions and so now his practice was defunct. His office was decaying. It was dirty. It was slimy a bit. He asked us for the money right away. My sister saw a list in his hand. There were two other girls on it, one for two hundred dollars and another for four hundred. My sister was really pissed because she figured we could have gotten him down in price.

"The doctor was very calm and nice. He said it wouldn't hurt and would only take a minute. So we just kind of ignored the alcohol on his breath and his filthy office. So then he put me on the table, and he used the scrape thing and it was very painful. He gave me absolutely nothing, and it was so painful that I started to pass out. He tried to reassure us, and it worked. When he opened me up a ways he let my sister take a look, and he gave me a mirror so I could see, which was interesting because I'd never seen inside myself before, but when the pain began I just couldn't take it. I remember lying on the table and telling the guy to stop and feeling I was going to throw up. I'm sorry I'm crying now. I hope it doesn't mess up your tape.

"I think he panicked when he saw how painful it was for me, and he wasn't able to finish it. He said it would abort itself, that he'd scraped enough, that he'd loosened it enough so it would abort on its own. And then he did the stupidest thing. He took Kotex and stuffed it up me. By then I was so sick and so faint, but still I knew it was all wrong. I knew that you just didn't stuff Kotex up someone when they've just had an abortion and I knew I was going to start to bleed or hemorrhage. He gave me pain pills to take, and we left. My sister got me in the car. It was hard because every time I tried to stand or even sit I felt like I was going to throw up and pass out. He gave my sister a number to call him. I think he was concerned by then. I think he knew he'd butchered me.

"I lay down in the back seat of the car. I kept saying to my sister, 'It's all right because we're just going to go to a hospital.' At that point I didn't give a fuck if they wanted to arrest me for having partaken in something illegal. My body was telling me I was in big trouble. I went back to my apartment, took a pain pill, and waited for this so-called self-aborting thing to happen, but it didn't. A friend stayed with me that night—I don't remember where the hell Billy was that night; it's really weird that I don't remember. He usually came in around three or four, but I just don't remember him getting in. By early morning I started to bleed, and by nine-thirty it was bright red and heavy and I knew I was started to hemorrhage. My sister didn't dare call our local hospital because it was Catholic, so she called a guy at Judson Church and they were real supportive and told her to take me up to St. Luke's because they were the least shitty to women there. So we did. I was in a daze and the blood was gushing. They admitted me immediately and put me on an IV. I was there for three days. They gave me massive doses of penicillin because I had developed an incredible infection besides. The doctors were very upset. They had to stabilize me for a day before they could give me a D and C.

"When I woke up in the recovery room, I was so happy. It was over, I was in a hospital, and I knew I wasn't going to die.

"Billy never came to the hospital. It caused a real big trauma between us. He tuned out on it. He couldn't handle it. He was also real angry at me because if I'd listened to him and gone to his guy on Park Avenue this wouldn't have happened. That I'd listened to my sister instead. This has always been a problem. He's resented the power she had over me. He really had very bad vibes about this whole thing from the beginning because where we went in New Jersey is a Mafia town, and this doctor was connected to them.

"I went off to Detroit and came back and really freaked out. Billy got his own apartment, and it was break-up time for us. He hadn't been there for me, and I was really hurt that he hadn't. I was so hurt and angry at him. The abortion really severed us in a certain way. We were still sleeping together and it was okay, but it wasn't the same. But at that time nothing was the same for me. It was a terrible time. I can remember just sitting in my apartment on my sofa bed and just not wanting to move. I was aware that some terrible wave of nonfunctioning thing was coming over me and that I needed help. My sister was in therapy then, and she recommended it. My school had a program, and I started going. The abortion really was a catalyst that made me start dealing with a lot of shit. I was angry at Billy, I had a deep-rooted anger at my sister for always bossing me around and this time being wrong, and there were financial problems. My sister had borrowed money for the abortion and Billy wasn't paying her back, but was going out and buying furniture for his apartment.

"I never thought about the baby. I didn't want that baby. It's upsetting when you realize that you are taking away a life, it is upsetting on that level. And I tell all my friends that it really isn't that easy going through it. And I have had thoughts that God is a little child and that I took away a child's life and so I've hurt God. That really bothers me. Billy has two daughters by a previous marriage and I would have loved to have given him a son. I think about that sometimes. Was it the one and only little boy that maybe it would have been nice to have had? I think about how old he'd be now, and that bothers me. Even now sometimes.

"When Billy and I got back together, the sex didn't really pick up. I had no orgasms. No orgasms at all. But the sex gave me the support that I needed from him, so it was enough. I had faked orgasms with him up to that point, and that was the turning point. I confessed that to him and told him that from here on out we had to be honest. It was not one of our more passionate periods. We got married two years later, and now we've been married almost five years. It would be very painful now if I got pregnant. I couldn't go through another abortion and stick around. I'm too old for it. But we're just not ready yet.

"I feel I really did the right thing. I feel our circumstances—that child would have been so fucked up because I was so fucked up, Billy was so fucked up, our financial scene was so bad. Everything about our lives was so crazy and so unsettled and so unresolved that a child probably would have been so resented and so not treated well that he would have gotten the shit end of the stick. It would have been awful."

Billy's story: "I was afraid when I found out Maria was pregnant, because I felt that we were an interracial couple, we were not married, and we just couldn't have a child. Things haven't gotten any better really. It's just that we've gotten better. We've gotten used to ourselves. I don't view her as being blue, black, or different from me. But at that point she was very definitely white. I didn't know how I was going to deal with the abortion. I asked myself whether I was up to handling it. I was up for handling it if I had to because I really felt, well, I love her, and I wasn't going to not stand by her.

"What she did do, though, was to substitute her sister for me and to leave me out there by myself. She did it. She went and had an abortion from some quack that I didn't approve of, but she did it anyway. I didn't take her to the doctor because I thought that maybe I was overstepping my boundaries between her and her sister and her family and all that was happening between us. If she said, 'Look, this is the way I want to do it,' I didn't want to pressure her, to say, 'You

175

come with me.' I was in no position at that time to do that. If she had said, 'Yeah, let's do this together,' I would have taken her. I wanted to be part of the whole thing. I was very nervous. I was very concerned about her.

"I got drunk when she had the abortion. She did it in the daytime, I think. I can't remember. She went to New Jersey, and I took a job and went to work. I don't know if I came home that night. I may have blocked it out. I was in mental anguish and afraid. I've never been through that one before, and I hope I never am again. It threw me into a strange mental situation. I can't even remember what I was doing that night. I think I took a job. I must have. I played and played and played and then I can't remember. I might even have been with another woman.

"I saw her in the hospital but not very often. She wasn't in the hospital very long. I was touched when I saw her. I felt something inside, something strange. The funny thing about it was that she seemed very happy that she was there. What bothered me was that I felt that she was really a hypochondriac, and I wasn't brought up that way. I was taught to handle pain one way, and I learned how to handle a lot of pain that way. In Panama, there was like a village doctor, but people didn't get ill and they lived a long time. Then I met Maria, and it was this pill for that thing and that pill for this thing, and I'm thinking, What is she doing? When I saw her in the hospital, I was really sad because she was in the hospital and I was concerned and freaked out. But she was very happy and it was almost like she was where she wanted to be. My mind was sort of boggled. It looked like she wanted to be sick, so she was sick. It was like she was enjoying it.

"The loss of the baby didn't bother me at all. I didn't think about it. I was more concerned with her welfare rather than having a child at that time. If anything, it was like the child was not there, that we were not going to have a kid; that she was having an operation just to get cooled out. She could have been having her appendix out, and it wouldn't have made any difference to me at that time. I must have blocked it out, because of course it did matter. I love my children from my former marriage. I love children. But for us to have a child at that time was just so unlikely because we were not ready in any way, shape, or form. I was averaging around fifteen grand a year, playing any old job.

"When she got out, I had some resentment as to how the whole situation went down. I was not listened to. She had shunned me. She had put me down for her older sister, who had actually botched everything up. I never fell out of love with her, though.

"When we started making love again, it was no different. It was just one incident. If there had been trouble, if I had become impotent with Maria, for example, I'd be long gone. The sexual part of our lives is very important to me and to her. The first time we made love after the abortion, I gave it no thought at all.

"The abortion just wasn't that important in my life, and I don't play it up as being heavy, consciously anyway. I know that we'll have children when we're ready and when we can afford them. And it didn't affect our getting married. That was inevitable. If she got pregnant now, she'd probably have another abortion. I'm in a lot of debt, and we're just about breaking even. In a couple of years we'll be able to. We're not totally over the interracial thing yet, but it's totally minor. If two people stick together for a couple of years, the color doesn't really matter. It's how you relate to one another that counts."

6

Teenagers

No matter how sophisticated one fancies oneself, it is still shocking to see the ranks of teenagers filling the abortion clinics. Dressed in jeans and the latest T-shirts, their hair fashionably long and straight, their skin often still dotted with adolescent acne and their teeth gleaming with braces, the teenage girls in the clinics look more like ads for American youth than candidates for abortion. But almost one-third of the abortions performed annually in the United States are obtained by young women aged nineteen and under. According to Planned Parenthood, 325,000 teenagers had abortions in 1975, of whom half were eighteen and nineteen years old; 45 percent, fifteen to seventeen; and 5 percent fourteen and younger. In spite of wider use of contraception, the numbers continue to rise. Since 1973, the teenage abortion rate has risen by 60 percent.

The abortion rate is not as stunning, however, as the numbers of teenagers who become pregnant each year and either get married or go on to bear their children out of wedlock. Planned Parenthood estimates that 1,000,000 teenagers—one-tenth of all the young women in this age group—get pregnant each year, 30,000 of them less than fifteen years old. Faced with these numbers, what is surprising is that more teenagers do not have abortions but instead choose to have their babies. According to a 1974 study of pregnant teenagers, 28 percent were already married and went on to carry their pregnancies to term. Ten percent got married following conception, while 21 percent did not marry but had out-of-wedlock births. Fourteen percent had miscarriages, leaving the remaining 27 percent to seek out induced abortion. All in all, more than 600,000 teenagers give birth each year.

For those who choose to terminate their pregnancies, the decision and the procedure itself can be very difficult. Often the girls, especially those in the younger teens, have intercourse so sporadically that they do not practice any form of contraception and are stunned to find out they are pregnant. Still children themselves, they cannot comprehend that they are physically able to bear children of their own, and ignoring the clinical signs that signal pregnancy, they delay having an abortion until they are too far advanced for the simple first-trimester procedure.

There is great fear among pregnant teenagers that their parents will find out about it and react negatively. Those fears are not always unfounded. "The worst problem we have are the mothers," said one clinic staffer. "You'd think the end of the world had come when they bring in their daughters. But it isn't the fact that the daughter is pregnant that bothers them. It's the fact that she is sexually active. Maybe the mothers feel threatened. I don't know. What I do know is that time and again a mother will say, 'Okay, I'll forgive you this time, but if I ever catch you pregnant again, you've had it.' Then they turn to us and say she won't be needing birth control because she won't be having intercourse again. That's ridiculous and totally self-defeating." In many cases, the daughters return after their abortions without their mothers for contraceptive advice.

Pregnant teenagers, especially the younger ones, are often reluctant to have an abortion even though the pregnancy is unplanned and unwanted. At Harlem Hospital in New York, a doctor in the department of Obstetrics and Gynecology estimates that 50 percent of the pregnant teenagers she comes in contact with choose to carry their pregnancies to term. The problem is just as great in Ohio. "They seem to be getting younger and younger," says Betty Orr, a counselor at Preterm in Cleveland. "Thirteen is not unusual, and recently we had a twelve-year-old. The younger they are, the more they want to keep the baby. Most of them under sixteen are playing house. They picture the baby as a real live doll to play with. I ask them who is going to take care of the baby while they're in school? Where are they

179

going to get the money for its clothes? These are questions that have never occurred to them." At one Planned Parenthood clinic, a twelve-year-old girl finally decided on an abortion because it was football season and her pregnancy would interfere with her baton twirling.

Unrealistic though they may be, teenagers feel whatever they are feeling very strongly. Supersensitive and moralistic, teenage emotions swing widely and deeply in those formative years, and often it is the first time a teenager has felt these emotions at all. "Teenage love is felt deeply and is a highly sensitive area of the teenager's life," wrote abortion counselor Sharon Gedan in the *American Journal of Nursing*. "Feelings about children, although often romantic and unrealistic, are strong. Anger, jealousy and sadness are often new experiences. Because the teenager is unused to these feelings, she may be frightened or embarrassed about them and attempt to deny them."

The literal age of the pregnant teenager is also a major factor in how she approaches pregnancy and abortion. In a 1973 study entitled "The Adolescent Experience of Pregnancy and Abortion: A Developmental Analysis," psychologist Sherry Hatcher of the Department of Psychology at the University of Michigan breaks down the teenage years into the stages of early adolescence, middle adolescence, and late adolescence. Girls in early adolescence have little or no knowledge of birth control and often aren't even aware of the correlation between intercourse and pregnancy, Hatcher suggests. Upon learning she is pregnant, such a teenager is apt to express extensive denial, including disclaiming any responsibility on her part for her pregnancy. She cannot see herself as a mother nor can she see the fetus as a baby. As for the abortion, she accepts it for herself, but does not condone it for others.

By the time a teenager has reached middle adolescence, she does understand both conception and contraception but even so blames someone else for her pregnancy. Any figure can be the target, such as her boyfriend, but shc is more apt to cite authoritarian figures: her parents, who never told her about birth control, or the doctor who wouldn't. Older and therefore more responsible, such a teenager feels some guilt but externalizes it and gets rid of it by seeing her pregnancy and abortion as being forced on her by someone else.

The teenager in late adolescence has incorporated all these defenses and takes the blame on herself. Unlike her younger cohorts, she is not shocked by the fact of her pregnancy, as she fully understands how it came to pass. Often, in fact, the older teenager might even have become pregnant on purpose so as to consolidate a relationship or to force a marriage. As a recent study by Melvin Zelnik and John F. Kantner of the School of Hygiene and Public Health at Johns Hopkins University points out, fully 55 percent of single nineteen-year-old women in America today are sexually experienced, so it is reassuring to realize that at least they know what they are doing.

For it is the teenagers that cause the most frustration among clinic personnel and family-planning professionals. Ignorance abounds. In the same study, however, the authors point out that only 41 percent of unmarried teenage women between the ages of fifteen and nineteen know when in their menstrual cycles they are most likely to conceive. The reluctance of teenagers to contracept is also the cause of widespread professional frustration. Though 64 percent of the sexually active teenage respondents in the Zelnik-Kantner study reported that they had used contraception at the time of their last intercourse— an increase of 19 percent over a similar study five years ago—the numbers of teenagers who have never used contraception at all increased during the same period from 17 percent in 1971 to 26 percent in 1976. Whether the reluctance to practice contraception is from fear of the side effects of any given method, denial of ongoing sexual activity, difficulty in obtaining supplies, or just the divine right of teens, which doesn't allow for the possibility of anything unwanted happening to them, the result is still one million teenage pregnancies a year. At Planned Parenthood in San Francisco where teenage boys and girls are encouraged to attend Teen Scene birth-control clinics in the afternoons, fully 70 percent of the girls arriving at the clinic for the first time are there for pregnancy tests as well as birth-control advice. "We catch them too late," says Linda DuBrow, coordinator of surgical services at the clinic. "They are already sexually active and not using birth control."

As a result of contraceptive ignorance or reluctance, the numbers of repeat abortions among teenagers has risen dramatically. And the clinic personnel—especially the counselors, who see the same girls cycle themselves through the abortion procedure time and again, even after lengthy discussions and promises about birth control—may find this very depressing. As very few young women tell their parents about their pregnancies or their decision to abort, the counselor can easily become the mother surrogate and find herself deeply involved in the teenager's life. Sometimes a counselor's patience wears thin. "I have one kid here, seventeen, who's just had her third abortion," says Martha Mueller, a counselor with Planned Parenthood in Brooklyn. "I want to beat the shit out of her. I want to put her through the damn wall. 'What's the matter with you?' I say to her. Every time she thinks a relationship is going on the rocks, she gets pregnant. Then she has an abortion and starts up a new relationship. She swears every time she has an abortion she won't screw again. I tell her screwing isn't the problem, protection is. This time she's having an IUD inserted. I made her a deal. I told her she could try it out for a month, and if she didn't like it, we'd take it out. I can feel angry at a lot of my patients. I'm genuinely concerned about them. It's hard for me to understand why these kids or even older women have so little respect for themselves and instead keep putting themselves through abortion after abortion. It's such a case of low self-esteem. It's not their fault, they keep insisting. It's like saying no to the boy or man would be traumatic."

In the South, Mellonée Houston Willis, director of community affairs at the Atlanta Center for Reproductive Health, takes her teenage birth-control pitch into the black communities both inside and outside the city. Part of the problem, Willis insists, is the terminology well-intentioned city health workers use in trying to explain birth-control methods to teenage groups. "They use words like 'tubes,' 'ovaries,' 'sperm,' and 'sexually active,' " says Willis. "The kids don't know what she's talking about. When I talk to teenagers I use 'screw' or 'fuck' instead of 'sexually active.' I tell them when you're old enough to do that, you should learn how to do it correctly and reproduce when you're ready. So this little boy pipes up and says, 'I'm ready,' and I told him just because he has a penis or a dick is not enough. That doesn't make you a lover. Then I've got their attention."

But teenagers continue to get pregnant. For the younger ones, this can be doubly surprising. In the past hundred years, the age of menarche or the beginning of menstruation has dropped from age 16.5 in 1870 to 12.5 in 1968. Fertility, however, does not usually ensue for two and a half years after menstruation has begun. Those who are sexually active during those years and do not become pregnant gain a certain sense that it will never happen to them, and they are shocked when later their bodies deceive them. Often they do not recognize the symptoms of pregnancy, as their periods are still irregular. For older teenagers, pregnancy sometimes becomes a subconsciously or even consciously deliberate act. In a 1974 study, "The Resolution of Teenage First Pregnancies," fully 72 percent of the white teenagers and 32 percent of the blacks aged fifteen to nineteen interviewed said that they became pregnant to force a marriage. Other teenagers, especially those who were mistreated or came from foster homes, said they were looking for a source of love in a baby whether they had any affection for the father of the child or not. Another reason was the desire to set up their own household, while others felt that becoming pregnant and carrying the pregnancy to term made them feel more adult and mature. Loneliness was another factor in the pregnancy decision, and among lower-income teenagers the economic carrot of welfare payments to dependent children. For the student whose grades were poor, pregnancy provided a feeling of creative accomplishment, while for teenagers who were not as attractive as the others, pregnancy was a proof of fecundity and sexual desirability.

Though these reasons for becoming pregnant are all understandable, they are also all wrong. Children should not bear children. According to a 1976 compilation of statistics concerning teenagers published by the Alan Guttmacher Institute, young mothers between the ages of fifteen and nineteen are twice as likely to die from hemorrhage and miscarriage as are mothers in their early twenties, while the death rate from complications of pregnancy and birth is 60 percent higher among mothers under fifteen. Their offspring are no better off. Babies born to fifteen-year-old mothers are twice as likely to die as babies born to mothers between the ages of twenty and twenty-four. They are also more apt to be premature and of a low birth weight.

Aside from the physical hazards to both mother and child, there is the problem of the future life of both. Between one-half and two-thirds of all female school dropouts cite pregnancy and marriage as the reason for not finishing their high school education. Most don't get to finish the marriage, either. Brides aged seventeen and under are three times more likely to get divorced from their husbands than women who marry in their early twenties.

The interviews that follow are with teenagers who, for whatever reasons, chose not to continue their pregnancies. Some of them are articulate. Most are not. Some are damaged. Most are not. In the cases where the male partners let the girls down, one cannot help but wonder whether the lack of male support will affect their relationships with men in future life. The pregnancy and abortion experience has matured some of the teenagers and, indeed, was positive. To others, the abortion was meaningless. Only a few in the group I talked to have opted for birth control. With teenagers more than with any other group, it appears, abortion is considered a primary form of birth control. Except for the IUD, which is permanently in place, all other forms of birth control require constant monitoring and responsibility, and there is little that is constant during the teenage years. For these teenagers, perhaps, having an abortion shifts the responsibility of preventing and solving a problem to someone else; this is what they would rather do than taking the onus on themselves.

Victoria Melinquez, eighteen, has just had her pregnancy confirmed and is setting up a time for her abortion for the next morning at a Planned Parenthood clinic in Brooklyn. A high school senior and Medicaid patient, Victoria lives with her older sister, as her mother is dead and she doesn't know where her father is. Like many teenagers, Victoria is filled with misconceptions and fantasies about birth control and abortion.

*   *   *

"When they told me here they don't put me to sleep for the abortion, I say I am going to another place. I don't want to see what the doctor is going to do to me. The nurse said they stick a needle in the vagina and that they spray white stuff on the vagina and on my insides. I don't want to see nothing. I just want to sleep and let them wake me up when it's all over. They tell me if I get excited, something could go wrong and I'd have to go to the hospital and all this stuff about a cervix and vagina. Needles. I'd panic if I saw something like that.

"I never used birth control. I didn't know nothing about it. I thought birth control would hurt me. They didn't mention birth control in school. They talked about the uterus, ovaries, vaginas, but not no birth control. It would have been better not to get pregnant. My friend says she takes her friend's pills. Another says she takes her grandmother's pills. Bullshit. What would a grandmother need with birth-control pills? You can't believe nobody.

"My girlfriend says she's had twelve abortions. But I know you can only have two. This is going to be my first and last. I don't believe in it. They say abortions mess up your insides. I'm going to get me a big medical book if I can read it.

"I didn't even know I was pregnant. My sister looked at me and said, 'You're pregnant.' 'No, I ain't,' I said. But she made me come here to find out. She wasn't mad when I was. She said she'd excuse me the first time. But the second time she'd kick my ass in. My mother's dead. My father, I don't know where he is. My older sister died and my little sister is with a foster mother. My boyfriend, he told me he wanted me to have the baby. His mother said no, I shouldn't. My sister wanted me to have it and said she'd take care of it. Her boyfriend said yes, too. But she's already got one and that's bad enough. I told them straight, 'Get off my back. I want to finish school,' and here I am.

"I don't want a baby. I'm not ready for kids. I have to think about it. I probably never will have any after this abortion. If I hit a kid, I don't know my own strength. I hurt them. That's why I don't have a kid of my own.

"My boyfriend is twenty-one. I called him this morning, but no one answered. He said he didn't know if he had the time to come with me for the abortion. If he don't be at the house tomorrow before nine, I'm going to leave him a note saying don't bother to see me again. I'm going to be bold.

"I want to get it over with. I be feeling real sick. I eat a soda and a Whopper and feel like bringing it back up. It scares me. I've been eating and eating, and I've never done that. I've got to have an abortion before I get fat. Eating, eating, eating, and I don't even be hungry. I just be eating. What's wrong with me?

"It kills me that this abortion is going to be on Saturday. That means I won't be able to go out Saturday night. I'll just have to stay home and eat chicken soup."

———

Carlotta Thomas, seventeen, has just had her second pregnancy confirmed at an abortion clinic in Cincinnati, Ohio. She had her first abortion at the age of fourteen and will have this one next week. Carlotta's mother is on welfare, and though she said she'd take care of the baby, she did not oppose Carlotta's decision. Carlotta does not use birth control but relies on abortion instead. Having an abortion, Carlotta says, is easier than having a baby.

"This time is just like the first time. I feel sick, sick, sick all the time, and I just keep on vomiting. I can't eat at all, and all I want to do is sleep. I don't like it. When I found out I was pregnant, I was real upset. I didn't want to be pregnant.

"I told my mother about it, and she said, 'It's up to you, do whatever you think,' that I'd have to go through the pain. She didn't like the idea too good that I was pregnant. She fussed for a minute, but there was nothing she could do. She said she'd take care of the baby, but I didn't want her to.

"The first time I got pregnant I thought about the baby, and I felt bad about it for a minute. But if I'd had it, I didn't want to hear my parents' mouth saying all they had to do for me. They would have reminded me about it all the time, so I decided to come here. I told that boy the first time, but I also told him he had nothing to say about it. He wanted me to keep it because it made him feel like a big man. He was fifteen. He was my steady guy then, and he didn't know I had stopped taking the pills. They were making me sick, so I stopped. Then my aunt, she got a blood clot on the brain and had a stroke. That proved it to me, since I was having headaches. I knew I was bound to get pregnant because we were making it twice a week.

"Everybody's doing it. Some of the girls in my high school have two or three kids. I don't know who takes care of them. Welfare, I guess. My mother's on it, and I have two sisters and three brothers already. My mother didn't need another baby.

"On the first day of the month, my high school is empty. All the girls is home waiting for their checks. Maybe forty of them in the school have got babies. There are little girls walking around pregnant, around thirteen or fourteen years old. I'm disgusted. They don't take care of themselves at all. They don't even wear maternity clothes but just stuff their stomachs into their jeans. I don't know what's wrong with them. We have sex ed in school, but it just goes in one ear and out the other. I want to go to college. I don't want to be on welfare.

"This time the boy don't know about the baby. I don't want to hear his mouth. I'm the one who's going to have to suffer, not him. I knew he'd want to get married and I don't want to. My mother was sixteen when she had me, and I don't want to go through that. That's just too young.

"My mother didn't say nothing this time. I just told her I was coming on over here for an abortion. Maybe I'll tell the boy when I'm finished and maybe I won't. I'm fed up with sex now anyway. I just don't feel like being bothered."

Molly O'Hara, sixteen, has brought her teddy bear with her to the abortion clinic in San Francisco where she is just about to have her first abortion. One of six children from a Catholic family in Napa Valley, Molly tried but didn't dare tell her mother about her pregnancy or the abortion. She did tell her boyfriend, however, but he was not supportive and blamed her for getting pregnant. Molly says

187

she is going to go on birth-control pills after the abortion and hopes her mother won't find them. She also plans to start going to church again and to confess the abortion, which she considers to be a sin, but a necessary one in her case.

"It sort of bothers me that my boyfriend isn't here today, but I didn't know what it was going to be like here. If he came here, I think he would think it was a drag, just waiting around. He's kind of an impatient guy. I was disappointed in him at first that he wouldn't come. Then he called me and said he was sorry. He said that he would take me, and I told him no. I told him I don't want him to take me because I had already made plans. So he offered to pick me up afterwards, but I said no.

"I think it is going to change our relationship a little. Like he was telling me, it's your fault you're pregnant. You should have done something about it. It's not all my fault. He could have done something about it too. He just says it's up to the girl, and I don't like that at all.

"It's gonna be strange, I guess, seeing him again after this. I want to see him. I want to see what he has to say, 'cause I don't know what I'm gonna say. Once I go through this, I might feel differently about him. 'Cause I don't know what this thing's gonna be like. If it really bothers me, then I'll tell him. He knows that I feel hostile to him right now. He tries to do nice things, and I ignore them. I couldn't be nice back. He told me to call him at home after this thing tonight. I don't even know if I want to talk to him! I feel that he'll be worried, but he didn't have to say what he said in the first place.

"The abortion sort of bothers me, too. My friend says it's not a baby yet. It's not a baby until after fifteen weeks; then it starts to develop into a baby. She said it's just like tissue right now. It makes me feel a little better about it, but still . . . It does bother me. And I can't talk to my mother about this sort of thing. We're Catholic, and my dad especially is a strict Catholic. Abortion is just out of the question. I went to a parochial school till eighth grade, so I was taught that it's wrong to destroy a life. Every life has a right to live. So I have that on my mind too, but it's my decision. I couldn't take care of a baby right now, I don't think.

"I wish I could talk to my mom. This couple in high school, they just got pregnant, so I told my mom they had to get married. I wanted to talk to her about it, but I have to find a way to talk about myself by talking about other people. I wanted to see how she would react, so I told her about this other couple. She said, 'What else can they do? There's nothing else they can do about it but get married.' I wanted to say that I was doing something else, but I didn't because she would think it was terrible. She tells me, 'You can come to me and tell me anything,' but I know she wouldn't understand. I can talk to the lady at the clinic a lot easier.

"I'm going to get on the pill after this. I don't think my mother will find it. I have my own bedroom upstairs, and I have my own stuff there, so I don't think anyone will find it. See, we have six kids in our family. I'm second to the oldest, and there's four girls and two boys. We have a pretty large family; I don't know why they had so many kids, but we're Catholic.

"I haven't been to a confession in a while, and I think I might. Yeah, I really think I will. I think my conscience will feel better. Then I'll start going to church again. Lent's starting, Ash Wednesday was yesterday, so I should have gone to church yesterday. But I was feeling too ashamed."

Jennifer Hatchett, seventeen, is very nervous and is twisting a shredded Kleenex around her fingers. A pretty blonde, Jennifer is wearing a pink sweater with poodles on it. She is being counseled before her abortion at Preterm in Cleveland, Ohio, but cannot meet the eyes of the counselor. Jennifer's boyfriend left her as soon as she told him she was pregnant, and when she tried to call him again for advice, he hung up on her. Like many teenagers, Jennifer had called the clinic to set up a birth-control appointment, but when she arrived, she was already pregnant. The product of foster homes herself, Jennifer says she couldn't do that to another person.

"There's no way I'm going to have babies. I didn't want one anyway. I only slept with this guy once and there it was. I told the guy I thought I was pregnant, and he left. I called him on the phone and asked him what I should do, and he said he didn't believe in abortion. I still didn't know what to do. I talked to him again on the phone, and he hung up on me. I haven't heard from him since. I don't think there will be a reconciliation. I don't even care.

"My mother brought me today. My father doesn't know. He would be very upset at the pregnancy. He thinks of me as a little girl. 'Where are you going?' he always says. 'What time are you going to be home?' I'd feel better if I could talk to him. But I can't. He thinks my mother and I have gone shopping.

"My mother just sort of knew I was pregnant. She said, 'Come for a drive with me. Don't you have something to tell me?' She didn't yell or nothing. She just wanted to know if I'd called to get an appointment for an abortion. I had already called, but it was to get birth control. It was too late. I never got my period.

"I have no other choice. The abortion will be better than having the baby and then giving it up. I've been through foster homes myself, and I couldn't do that to another person.

"This is the first time I've ever been examined like that. I've never been to this kind of doctor before. I just lay there and tried to think of something else."

⸻

Molly O'Meara, sixteen, says she has just had her second abortion. Resting in the recovery room at a Planned Parenthood Clinic in Brooklyn, her freckles stand out sharply against her pale face. Molly speaks in a monotone and neither smiles nor frowns nor shows any emotion at all. An eleventh-grade student in high school, Molly has now had an IUD insertion but says if she gets pregnant again, she'll keep the child. The counselor told me later that this was Molly's fourth abortion, not her second. Molly's mother is chronically ill, and Molly doesn't have a father.

"My mother doesn't know I'm here. She's sick, and she's been sick for a long time. She didn't know about the first abortion either. I can't tell her because I wouldn't want to upset her. She'd have a fit. I don't think she'd allow me to have an abortion anyway. She'd make me have the baby and then give it up for adoption. If I went through the nine months I wouldn't want to give it up. That's how she had me. I don't have any father.

"But this abortion doesn't make me feel sad. I feel good. Really good. And very happy. There are no complications. And Medicaid pays for it.

"I had my first abortion when I was fifteen. I was on the pill then, but I stopped. I don't know why. I just plain stopped. The same guy did it both times. He doesn't want the baby either.

"Being Catholic doesn't bother me at all. But I don't confess it. I'm scared of what the priest would say. I wish I could tell my mother. But she'd be so angry. Maybe I'll tell her, but it would have to be a lot later on.

"She's never talked to me about sex at all. Not even the basic facts of life. We just don't talk about anything. Now they've put in an IUD. But if I get pregnant again, I'd keep this one. I don't know why. I just would. I've done this enough."

Connie Bridges, seventeen, is a junior at a Dayton, Ohio, high school. Overweight and pale, she is propped up on a sofa in an Ohio clinic having just had an abortion, her first. Like many teenagers, she got "caught" because she had intercourse very infrequently and therefore wasn't using birth control. Her boyfriend wanted to marry her, but she wanted to finish high school. She feels some guilt, but more relief.

"I didn't see any need for birth control because it was something I didn't do very often. The father is my steady fellow. We've been going together for seven months, but I only slept with him twice. He's my first. What a bummer.

"I felt confused and guilty when I found out I was pregnant. I guess I'm kind of old-fashioned. You're just not supposed to get pregnant if you're not married. When I told my boyfriend about it, he wanted to get married. But I wanted an abortion. I still have a year of high school and four years of college to get through.

"He was very good about it though. He said it was my decision. He's Catholic, so it was hard for him to adjust.

"I think I'll sort of miss being pregnant. As soon as I knew I was, I didn't want to do anything to hurt the baby. I did dumb things, like driving slower in the car. I had a passing thought about keeping the baby. But it was just for a minute.

"Now I'm glad it's over. I don't feel sad. If I sat down and brooded I would feel bad. I'll just ignore it instead. I'll think of it as just another experience, but one I don't want to do again. I really hope I won't think about it later because it will probably upset me a lot."

Karen Swan, nineteen, has terrible cramps and is lying on the floor of the recovery room in an Atlanta, Georgia, abortion clinic. It is her second abortion in two years. Mature and responsible, Karen does not blame anyone and says that she cannot afford a child right now, that it would not make her happy, and that it would be a mistake. She will not marry her boyfriend under these circumstances because the impetus for such a marriage is not clear. If anything, she would have the baby out of wedlock; having been involved with unwanted children, however, she does not feel it would be fair to the child or herself. Her only regret is that men cannot understand an abortion, and she wishes that just one man could get pregnant and go through what a woman has to go through.

"There was a real heavy scene at home when I was seventeen, so I quit school and went to work. Then I moved in with the manager of where I worked. At the end of a month I realized I wanted to go back to school, so I moved back home. I had found out I was still a baby. And I wanted to still be a baby. So when I found out I was having one of my own, the decision to have an abortion was easy.

"My mother and father cried. My father said, 'I never realized you were that stupid. I always thought you had better sense.' Now whether he meant not doing anything at all was better sense or using birth control, I don't know. He just thought I should have better

192

sense. My mother just cried. And they both thought abortion was the best thing. I thought it was the best thing too. I didn't care one way or the other about the guy. He was like ten years older than me, and like I said, I was such a baby that I didn't realize that he'd care at all.

"For a while after the first abortion I felt really bad. My sister was pregnant. She had her kid in March, and I had the abortion in February. And even while I was pregnant, it seemed that everybody was so happy for her and no one was happy for me. And I knew why. Because I wasn't happy for me either and I was really sick and even if I had been married and had a husband I don't think I could have gone through it that time. Maybe I was too young, but I was really sick. Just acutely sick. I couldn't go through a day without throwing up three or four times. I couldn't take that, you know. It's better this time, but it's probably because I'm older.

"Right now I can't afford a child. I have seen children who are not wanted. Three of them live with me. They are my older sister's kids. My parents adopted them because she didn't want them. She has no sense of responsibility and she just didn't want them, so she was going to put them in a home and they were going to be separated. You just can't find a place for three kids to go, so what else could my parents do?

"So you see, that's why I'm not having this baby. One of the things that messed up my sister was that she had a baby before the first of those three and she put it up for adoption. I think it's really more difficult to have a baby and give it away than to have an abortion. That's what really makes me mad about those people arguing against abortion, because I bet 50 or 60 percent of them never had babies at all or ever had to give them away.

"I'm having this abortion because I can't afford a child, I think I'm too young, I wouldn't be happy, and it would be a mistake. Me and Larry were talking about it. If he asked me to marry him, whether he loves me or not, I'm going to be thinking he's going to be marrying me because he thinks he should, whether or not that's his reason at all. There's no way I can prevent myself from thinking that. Abortion is more like a mutual agreement. Now I could choose to have a child on my own, which is what I would choose to do rather

193

than marry him, though I might marry him later, but I just think it's total confusion when you say, 'Oh, I'm pregnant' and so he asks you to marry him. You never know what the real reason is. You really don't. He didn't say anything about marriage because he knew I wanted the abortion. He agrees with me about it, but he let me say it first.

"I'm not telling my parents this time. I'm really ashamed. It was a stupid mistake. For another thing, they've got a lot of trouble right now. My mother wouldn't have had the money to give me right now, and she would have felt bad about that. I had to borrow the money from a friend's mother. I can see no use in telling her. I really want her to know because it's so terrible to think that this is a secret I'm going to have to keep for the rest of my whole entire life. Because if she ever found out I didn't tell her a thing like this, it's really going to be crushing. So she'll never find out. And I'll keep this secret, this terrible dark secret, all to myself.

"That's why I told her the first time, because I thought everyone's entitled to this one mistake and I really needed the security of them knowing what I was going through. She hasn't had an abortion, but she's had a baby so at least she can understand pain.

"I don't know whether it will work out with Larry. I could see him change as soon as I got pregnant. I told him, 'You just don't understand, you just can't understand.' I don't think any male can understand what it's like to be pregnant, what it's like to have an abortion, what it's like to go through the psychological part of it. They go through a certain amount of it, I know. Right now I am feeling I would like just one male to get pregnant so he can know what it feels like. How can they possibly know? That's why I get real frustrated when I talk to him, because I've been really sick. I've been avoiding seeing him because I don't like to go out when I'm sick and I'm not enjoyable. And he understands that, but he just doesn't understand what it's like to have an abortion. Although I know he doesn't understand because he's a guy and he's trying to understand, I just feel I don't want to be bothered with him. That's why I didn't want him to come today. I wanted to come with my friend who's been through this before, because she can really understand.

"Maybe it will work out with Larry if we just keep on talking. As

194

long as I keep explaining things and he keeps trying to understand, maybe."

━━━━━━━━

Regina Loomis, seventeen, has just had her first abortion at Planned Parenthood in San Francisco. A freshman in college, Regina is striking-looking, her hair meticulously coiled around her head, her turquoise and silver jewelry shining under her black velvet cloak. She claims to be a sixth-generation Californian and to come from a family who have decided not to bear another generation. Sexually active since she was thirteen, Regina has brought charges against the man who caused her pregnancy. Her story may be too bizarre to be taken seriously.

"All of my friends have had abortions. One in Hawaii had two abortions, and she was fourteen. About two years ago a friend of mine who was seventeen, she had an abortion. I just know so many people who have had abortions. My girlfriend in San Jose had two abortions, and when she got pregnant after the second abortion she decided to keep it. I kept telling her to use birth control. At my high school, no one knew anything about birth control. I took about five girls a month down to Planned Parenthood, and they were really thankful that I took them down. They didn't know anything. It's suburban, and their parents don't want to teach them anything. But I started going to the clinic when I was fourteen. That's when I went on the pill, when I was fourteen.

"At that time, there were laws. You had to be fifteen to get on the pill, so a lot of girls lied about their age. But I had a lot of problems with my pills. I got very, very sick. I gained fifty pounds in about three or four weeks, and I have stretch marks from it, too. Mentally I wasn't the same person. I was bloated all the time, and I had headaches and fainting spells, my heart would pound really hard, and a lot of other things. But my diaphragm was deteriorating because it was a year old. So I was going to get another one. There was just one time I didn't use it, and I got pregnant.

"I started having intercourse when I was thirteen, before I got on

195

my pills, but I guess I wasn't fertile then, because I never got pregnant. In our family it's hard for us to become fertile. Since my great-great-grandmother we've always had internal problems. But now I know I can.

"I kinda suspected I was pregnant because I wasn't feeling too well, and when they told me I was, I was a little upset but not too upset. I knew I was going to get rid of it, because I'm very strong on the feminist movement, an ardent feminist. I told the person because I had been going with him for a year and a half. He skipped town, so now I'm pressing charges for statutory rape and contributing to the delinquency of a minor. I told him that all I wanted him to do is pay the one hundred and fifty dollars and take me down to the clinic and watch the abortion. See the hell I had to go through. And he said sure. But he lied to me and left town instead. I went over to his house and told his parents, who got very mad at him. So he called me up and got mad at me for telling his parents. Well, that's too bad. I told his parents that my dad was gonna come after him with a shotgun, and that my mom was gonna press charges, and that we had already gone down to the DA.

"I'm mad at him because he said he would bring me down here and pay the money. I also feel that the male does get the female pregnant. It is the male's fault. That's the way I feel. He said it takes two, but I don't look at it that way.

"I said to myself a long time ago when I was twelve that if I ever became pregnant, I would have an abortion. I would be very, very mad, and I would never see that person again. So when he came over, before he left town, I kicked the hell out of him. I kicked him in the leg. He just stood there, 'cause he was afraid I was gonna hit him again.

"I won't ever sleep with him again. When I first met him, he was a very nice gentleman. But he's just gone downhill. When I was fourteen I really hated men, because that's when guys around seventeen, they're just beginning to experience sex. I don't have sex with people unless they have, well, unless they have money. Because if a man wants to take you to bed, and he won't pay for the bed, then he's not worth going to bed for. I rarely have sex as a result.

"The time I got pregnant, I had an orgasm. It was the first time.

196

I only go to bed with someone whose personality can turn me on. If I like the person I get physical pleasure, and I've found very few. Those are the only few I went to bed with. I've been in twelve schools in twelve years, in different environments all over California, so I've met quite a few people. I have friends all over the world. But only a few are worth going to bed with.

"The one who got me pregnant, the first date we had he gave me a rose, a single red rose. And he gave me this ring the third week after we began going out, and I had no sex with him at all. They don't owe me something after I have sex with them; they owe me something before. Sex isn't a thank you, it's kinda working for it. If they give me enough presents or appreciation, then I decide if I'm going to have sex with them. Or if I'm gonna get the presents out of them and then not have sex!

"I don't want to get married. If I do, I'll probably marry in my thirties. Right now I'm career-oriented. I want to become a CIA intelligence agent or FBI, and I was an applicant for Annapolis. I'm also a professional swimmer and runner.

"My mother, she's a very strong feminist, too. All our family is. And we're stopping the line right here, at this generation. My cousins on the other side and us were trained when we were very young not to have any children because the world is overpopulated. The world is growing bad. There's no food, the air is bad, there's a lot of radiation, and what good is it to bring up children when you can't even get a job in this world? I'm the oldest on both sides of the family, and I've wanted to get my tubes tied or get a hysterectomy since I was eight. But the doctors have always said I'm too young. But I've never changed my mind. Never.

"I live alone because in our family, when you reach a certain maturity level, mental-wise, you have to get out into the world and experience it. You have to fight for your life. We believe in doing it young so you're more successful. I don't let anyone know where I live because someone could always push his way into the door after a date, or lie and say, 'Why don't we go into your house and talk.' But you know what they really want. They just want to get on your couch, and those are just turkeys."

Wilhemina Curry, fifteen, epitomizes the frustration abortion clinic counselors face. A ninth-grade student, Wilhemina has just had her second abortion in three months at the Atlanta Center for Reproductive Health. She is still a little groggy from the anesthetic and giggles through much of the interview. She has learned nothing from the abortions and says that she will probably take the birth-control pills the clinic has prescribed for her. But just probably. She doesn't want to have another abortion, she says, because they make her throw up.

"I was going with this guy, you know. It wasn't meant to happen, but it just happened, you know. And I wasn't ready for it. I wasn't using any sort of birth control. I don't know why not. I just wasn't.

"We were screwing all the time, but I guess I just didn't think about getting pregnant. I wasn't feeling too happy when I found out about it. I didn't want a baby at the time. I'm too young and I wasn't really ready for it.

"My boyfriend, he didn't mean for it to happen, but he was happy for it when it did happen. He wanted to get married, but he's twenty-four and pretty old. I don't want to yet. He was pretty upset when I told him about the abortion. He kept asking me why I didn't want to have the baby. And I just kept telling him I wasn't ready for it. I had other plans at the time.

"He didn't want to come with me for the first abortion, but it didn't matter. We took right up again. I just don't know why I didn't think about birth control then. I don't think of abortion as birth control either. This time was the same thing. He still wants us to get married. He was even madder this time. I'll probably take birth-control pills now. Probably. I wouldn't want to have another abortion. I thought I was doing it for the best, and I feel sort of sorry for those babies.

"My mother wasn't mad at me when she found out. She was

198

disappointed, which made me sad in a way. But these abortions, they make me throw up. I wouldn't want to do that again."

═══════════

Missy Frank just celebrated her fifteenth birthday by taking a group of friends to McDonald's. What none of them knew was that she had had an abortion just two weeks before. Back at the clinic in Brooklyn now for a post-abortion checkup, Missy is more philosophic about the abortion than most girls her age. For a while she and her boyfriend played out the fantasy of getting married and even named the fetus Mark. But Missy thought ahead and decided that she had some growing up to do first. Missy now has a diaphragm, which she plans to use when she has sexual relations again. But right now, she says, she just wants to rest a while. With her hair pulled back in a ponytail and wearing a pink and white sweater decorated with a design of parrots, Missy keeps snapping her gum while waiting for her examination.

"I wasn't using any birth control. I didn't know about diaphragms, and I didn't want to take the pill. I had read about the side effects. So I was going on blind luck. I guess I wasn't so lucky.

"I only slept with him once. He lives a long way away. I kept putting off going to the clinic when I skipped my period. I guess I was scared of the whole examination. I'd never been to a gynecologist before.

"My mother and father never talked to me about sex. I wished they had. They don't know about this. Forget it. My father would be shocked if he knew I had slept with anybody. My older sister ran away from home at eighteen. He doesn't speak about her at all. He's very bitter. I was scared.

"My boyfriend and I considered having the baby. We thought about getting married. But we both wanted to finish school, and he wanted to go on to college to be a doctor. I didn't want to ruin that. A baby is a responsibility. You can't just have it, and that's that.

"Before the abortion I felt very depressed and sad. I couldn't eat or anything. I was very short-tempered. I kept thinking about what

199

it would look like. I wanted a boy. My boyfriend and I named him Mark. I thought I could go ahead and do it, but I want to make something of myself first.

"When I see people having babies now, I envy them. I don't want to ever have another abortion. It's a very frightening thing. The injection hurt a lot. But mostly I thought about the baby when they were doing it. I thought, I'm killing another human being, but then I'd remember that it wasn't even formed yet. I had two sides going in my mind against each other. But I'm glad for the most part I had the abortion.

"Where I live in Queens, having babies is almost a ritual for the kids in my high school. They all have their babies, and I see them wheeling them around, and they don't look so happy. It seems more a burden to them. I don't want to look like them. And it wouldn't be fair to the baby.

"It brought me and my boyfriend closer together. But I haven't slept with him again. My insides are okay now, so I can, but I don't want to. I just want to rest a while. A long while. And then I'm definitely going to use a diaphragm.

"I thought the abortion would be harder physically, but it turned out to be much harder emotionally than I thought. It was a strain. There were times I thought I'd never keep the appointment. In my mind I was playing all the time with little Mark. But I did come here. And I'm glad."

Chrissie Bridgeman, seventeen, had her first abortion two weeks ago, at the Special Care Center in Oakland, California. When she and her boyfriend were told at the clinic that Chrissie was pregnant, he at first denied having caused it, which made Chrissie very angry. Now he wants to break off their relationship, but Chrissie insists he still loves her. Her fantasies about her boyfriend do not include her sexual life, however, and Chrissie has now started on birth-control pills. She says the abortion has not changed her at all.

*   *   *

"This is the first time I've ever had a real steady boyfriend, and we had relations a lot. Really a lot. But I never used birth control. I don't know why. I guess because I just never went anywhere to get some. But I knew I could get pregnant. I was really paranoid about it. Sometimes he used a condom, or he would pull out before doing anything. But he could, what do you call it, come in you without even knowing that he did, but he didn't think he did. He swears he didn't come in me. He thought it was another guy.

"He was with me at the clinic when I found out I was pregnant. So right then and there he says, 'I'm never going to make love to you again.' That was his attitude, right in front of the counselor where she could hear. I felt horrible. I just looked at him because I couldn't say anything because the counselor was there. At least she told him he shouldn't take that attitude. He was saying he didn't know how it could have happened. Boy, I really hated him then.

"He finally admitted it was him, and he came with me for the abortion. I just wanted to get it done. There was no way I wanted the baby. No way. But I didn't think of it as a baby. I just didn't want to think about it that way.

"Afterwards our relationship was okay for a while, but he doesn't take me out much any more because he doesn't have any money. He said he wanted to break it off and that he wanted me to go out with some other guys. He still loves me, but he wants me to go out with other guys. He doesn't want me to sit home all the time. But I don't go out with other guys. I told him I didn't want to. I just want to go with him. I haven't had sex with him again because I just started on birth-control pills, and I have to wait three weeks before they work.

"I still feel the same way about him, even if he did say it wasn't his. I understand. And I haven't changed at all. The abortion didn't change me at all. There's no reason to tell my mother about it. She'd have a fit. She'll never know."

———————

June Mallory, eighteen, comes from a farm community in rural Georgia. She is obviously upset. Her long black hair is disheveled, and her eyes dart nervously around the counseling room at the Atlanta Center for Reproductive Health where she has returned because she has been bleeding since her abortion a month before. Single, June already has a twenty-month-old daughter, is on welfare, and can't find a job. She says she has felt terrible both physically and mentally ever since she had the abortion. Her current boyfriend was against her having it but had no intention of marrying her. June uses no birth control and has decided instead to give up sex. She is another candidate for a repeat abortion.

"I have some problems at home. My father drinks, like he's always been an alcoholic, and he and my mother got into a fuss because she's getting tired of it, so she went and stayed with my sister, her and my little girl, and I'm staying with a friend. I watch my little girl and everything during the day, but at night I take her back over because where I'm staying ain't nowhere for her to sleep 'cause I have to sleep on the couch myself.

"When I got pregnant the first time, I didn't have an abortion because I was too far along. At first I thought I was pregnant and then I thought I wasn't, so I went to the doctor, but I was too far along, so I went ahead and had her. She started kicking and everything, and I couldn't give her up. I stayed in a home for unwed mothers for about two weeks, but I couldn't stand it there and they wanted me to adopt her out, but I thought I couldn't give up my flesh and blood that easy. I'm real glad I had her. She means a lot to me.

"I started taking birth-control pills after I had her, but then I got side effects, and I had to stop taking them. I had spots before my eyes and stayed nervous all the time, had cramps in my stomach. When I found out I was pregnant again I thought, Oh, God, what am I going to do? I tried to hide it from my mother, but she could tell I was gaining weight, so she told me I better get somewhere and have an abortion. I was for it because I couldn't afford another kid right now. And I didn't care if my boyfriend cared at the time. He don't like to talk about the abortion. He said he thought I was doing something funny when I had it, killing a kid. He said he wanted to marry me, but he didn't have the money right now and couldn't afford it.

202

"I was real scared in that operating room back there, and when I woke up I felt sort of sad and sort of happy all at once. A lot of times I get to thinking about it, and it makes me upset and I get to crying. My life has been miserable since I had that abortion. I've stayed nervous and upset all the time. It goes through my head around eight every night. Everything goes through there. Sometimes I wish I didn't have the abortion, other times I wonder if I'm ever going to find a job, things like that. And then I just get to crying some more. But if I had had that baby, I don't know what in the world I would have done. I just feel guilty some of the time.

"I'm a Mormon, but I don't go to church no more. They don't believe in smoking, drinking coffee or taking birth-control pills or anything like that, like drinking tea. And I smoke and drink coffee and tea. I did go for a while when I was baptized, but I was raised a Baptist. It was my sister got me to be a Mormon. Now I'm a nothing. All those religions are making me feel guilty.

"And another thing that's making me feel guilty is my cousin. She's had two abortions and I talked to her Friday, and she said my other cousin had a book showing how the baby looked, and she said if I was to see the pictures I'd really be upset about it. Sometimes I think I killed this baby, and sometimes I don't. Think it's just best for me because I can't afford another kid right now.

"I try to talk to the girl I'm living with, and she says, 'Just quit talking about it,' and get it off my mind. But I can't get it off my mind. I just hold a grudge against myself for doing that, and that's all I can do right now.

"I got pregnant this time because I thought I was in love with this guy, and I still think I am. But I didn't think I would get pregnant. Everytime we'd have sex I'd go take a cold douche afterwards, but I got pregnant anyway. I've even made love to this guy again, like a fool. And it was different in a way. It hurt me real bad when I done it. I haven't made love to him again. I'm scared of having sex because I'm afraid I'm going to get pregnant again. I was thinking of having a loop put inside me, but I heard that's real painful. And I thought about having shots in the stomach at Grady Hospital, but there's a fifty-fifty chance that you could be sterile if you have that done, but

I may be doing that anyway. I'm just scared of sex altogether now. My boyfriend's scared too, but he wants to have sex anyway, and I won't.

"I been bleeding ever since I had that abortion, and I've had sharp pains in my stomach. Maybe I'm being punished. I promise that if I ever get pregnant again, I'll just keep the kid. But one kid's all I really want, I think. I'm thinking about going back to high school and finishing up, 'cause I quit in the tenth grade. I just feel so shamed I got pregnant that quick after my baby. After she was born, it was a long time before I had any sex. I got hung up on this one dude, and my friend she tells me I should date other people and just have sex with him but go to the movies or something with other people. But I'm just hung up on him.

"He's crazy. He works for his father, painting. He says if he ever gets straightened out, he wants to get married. But I don't want to get married. The way most people tell me is that marriage is just pure hell. Maybe in a few years we'd both change. But right now I'm not ready to settle down."

It has been a year since Noel Baker, eighteen, had an abortion at the Planned Parenthood clinic in San Francisco. Today she has returned with a girlfriend who is having her first abortion. Noel is very philosophic about her abortion which, she says, matured her. She and her boyfriend agreed on the abortion, and both of them told their parents about it. Since then, she and her boyfriend have broken up by mutual consent because they felt they were too young and they needed to meet new people. Noel now has a diaphragm but hasn't met any men she likes. Her abortion experience was a positive one, and Noel learned a lot about herself from it.

"We came from a small town, and things get around. Probably if I'd gotten birth control, we would have gone to the health center. But in the health center you see every other person in there that you know, and things get around. Kids talk. It crossed my mind that I could get pregnant, but I thought if I do, I do. I don't know. Just young, I guess.

"I wasn't shocked when I found out I was pregnant. At first, my period never came, so I thought, I'll wait, it'll come again. It didn't come, so I got the test at the health clinic, and it came out positive. It was strange, because I was sitting there waiting for the results, and one of my best friends walks in for a pregnancy test too. We didn't even know about each other. It was very strange. She came in with dark glasses and everything. Hers came out positive too, so she and I kind of experienced it at the same time.

"I was a little bit scared when I found out. I knew I had to make choices. The thought of being able to have a child was good. If you've been wondering, once you find out you can have a child you really think about it before you say, 'I'll have an abortion.' At least I did. I just started wondering what it would be like if I followed it through. But I think the nice things were overruled by the negative things, the facts.

"I didn't really think of it as a baby. I more or less thought of it as something that was going to be a baby, but not actually a baby. I didn't have any guilty feelings, like I was killing something.

"In classes that I had at school after the abortion, topics like birth control were brought up, and I would feel a little defensive, because I'd feel guilty and I didn't want to feel guilty. But I don't recall feeling guilty at the time of the abortion. I think I would have felt more guilty if I'd had a child. My boyfriend and I agreed on that; he's from a very strict Catholic family. We had a little bit of hassle there, 'cause we both told our parents. His mother thought I should have the child and give it up for adoption. When I settled on the abortion, she felt we should have the fetus baptized afterwards. Some strange thing like that. She was very upset. I think the thing that upset my boyfriend the most about it was upsetting his mother. But other than that, I don't think he felt bad about it.

"My mother's very liberal, and she thought the abortion was the thing to do. She told me it would be my choice, but she told me if it was hers that's what she would do. I've always been able to talk to her, so it was just another thing to talk to her about. I already knew her views on it, so I knew what she would say when I told her I was pregnant. I knew she wouldn't get hysterical or anything like that.

"After the abortion, my boyfriend and I broke up. We both agreed it was too serious, and we were too young. Now we're just friends, and I see him once in a while. Right after we broke up I slept with him again, but I don't think now I would. I had a diaphragm, and when I slept with him it felt more relaxed. Other times I kind of worried afterwards. It seems like I worried afterward and not beforehand, but with the diaphragm I didn't worry at all.

"I didn't resent my boyfriend. It wasn't so much the abortion that made us break up but what the abortion made us see. I think we just felt we were very young and needed to break away for a while and meet new people. He was two years older, so he was nineteen and I was seventeen.

"I have no boyfriend now. I haven't really met any men I like, who interest me other than as friends. I guess I made a choice to slow down, to do what I want for a while. In a way the experience made me feel older. Because when my friends and I read something now about abortion or discuss it, I listen to their views and they sound ignorant to me. They have no idea of what happens to you when you find out you're pregnant and you're only seventeen.

"I don't know if I'd ever have another one. When I brought my friend here today, I thought, What would I do if it happened again? And I really couldn't say. I'd probably have another abortion, but I think it might bother me more. I think I'd feel guilty about having two abortions and only being eighteen years old. I'd think, What is wrong with you? One—well, everyone can understand that."

7

Parents

It is difficult to fathom what is going through the minds of the mothers who accompany their daughters to abortion clinics. The mothers try to appear calm and supportive while their daughters twist and squirm uncomfortably beside them on the couches in the waiting rooms. It is not until the daughters' names are called and they vanish behind the interior doors that the strain begins to show clearly on the mothers' faces. There is fear on those faces, and sadness and shame.

In their generation, which was not so long ago, premarital sex was a taboo; those girls who indulged in it were called "fast" or "bad" girls, and they were definitely not included among the God-fearing respected members of the community. The fact of their daughters' pregnancy brings these mothers face to face with the values imbued in them by their own parents. And many of the mothers in the waiting rooms blame themselves for having failed to impress those same values, however outdated, on their own daughters. Oh, they know that times have changed. They've read innumerable articles about the rise in teenage sexual activity and the ever-increasing number of teenage abortions and cases of venereal disease, and they've watched the daughters of their friends and relatives become part of the statistics concerning teenagers. But proof of the trend in one's own immediate family is nonetheless shocking. It is not someone else's daughter. It is one's own.

Permissiveness and the general breakdown of the family structure have been blamed for the rise in teenage sexual activity. With the divorce rate now running at one out of every two marriages in America, there is a sharp increase in the number of single-parent households, where supervision of children is reduced. As more and more women eschew home life altogether for careers outside, many of these households become in fact zero-parent households, where no one is in charge. According to Zelnik and Kantner's study on "Sexual and Contraceptive Experience of Young Unmarried Women in the United States, 1976 and 1971," it is these homes that become the arenas for teenage sex. Girls under the age of thirteen tend to have their initial sexual experiences in their own homes; at thirteen, first experiences tend to be in the home of a friend or relative, while from fourteen on, the home of the partner is the most likely trysting spot. If "home" is not available, black teenagers are more likely to go to a motel or hotel, while teenage whites seek out automobiles, or, in their words, "the great outdoors." With this highly mobile younger generation, it is no wonder that the stern public-service words that issue from many of the nation's television sets—"It is ten P.M. Do you know where your children are?"—strike chords of anxiety in the listening parents.

Anxious or not, most parents are still reluctant to discuss sex and birth control with their children. Whether hampered by embarrassment, by lack of knowledge themselves, or by the fear that even talking about it might be taken as an implicit indication of approval of premarital sex, parents remain mum. In a study of over 400 adolescents who came to Planned Parenthood in New York during a six-week period in 1974 for contraceptive information, pregnancy tests, or abortions, the communication level between them and their parents turned out to be incredibly low. Although 90 percent of these teenagers still lived at home with their parents, fewer than 30 percent of them had told their parents that they were going to Planned Parenthood. In a more specific breakdown of ages, one out of every four teenage girls under the age of sixteen reported she had no one to talk to about the need for family planning; among eighteen-year-olds, only 17 percent had turned to their parents for advice while the vast majority (72 percent) had discussed it only with their boyfriends.

208

There is a distinct correlation between the parents' attitude toward sexuality and contraception and the teenagers' willingness to contracept, the study goes on to point out. When asked whether they thought their parents would approve of their visit to the clinic to secure birth-control information, fully 62 percent of the teenagers who said yes reported having used some form of contraception in the past. In contrast, the teenagers who thought their parents would react negatively to the visit or who were unsure about their parents' reactions (56 percent and 69 percent respectively) had never used contraception in the past. "Thus," the study concludes, "adolescents who expected a positive reaction from their parents were not only more likely to discuss their family-planning needs with their parents, but also were more likely to actually use contraceptive methods in the past."

More and more teenagers are turning for advice to the family-planning clinics that have sprung up around the country, resulting in a rise in teenage enrollment from 453,000 in 1971 to 1,100,000 in 1975. Schools and other social services have also stepped up their sex-education programs, but these, especially in schools, are the subjects of constant controversy. "The entire situation is a very sensitive matter," said Mary Ann Benson, director of the Huntington, Long Island, chapter of Planned Parenthood. "We try to keep a low profile because we've found that there seems to be resistance to sex education in the schools. Many people believe that sex education is the responsibility of the parents. But somehow that's just not working out."

In fact, many parents leave sex education to the school, a position educators do not necessarily want to be put in. "Either their mothers won't tell them about birth control or they're given totally technical advice—a simple lecture on what fits where," says Joan McMenamin, headmistress of a private girls' school in New York. "The church has lost contact with the families. Parents are terrified of alienating their children. And no one is saying sex is a commitment. Instead they are all laying it off on the schools. We try to give the girls factual information here, but I shy away from the morality of it. That simply does not belong in our province. Instead I keep *Love and Sex in Plain Language* in the library. Twelve copies disappear a year, and I tell the librarian just to replace them with no questions asked." At a secondary school in Fairfax County, Virginia, the school's principal and indeed the county school superintendent in 1976 prevented the editors of the school newspaper from printing an article on contraceptive habits among the sexually active students, prompting the young editors to bring a First Amendment suit against the school officials. The issue also prompted an editorial in the *Washington Post,* which decried the lack of willingness of parents, school, and churches to assume any responsibility for the education of young people in sex and birth control. "That neglect helps explain the depressing statistics on pregnancy and VD," the editorial read. "It also helps explain the impetus among school-newspaper editors to fill an informational vacuum created by the neglect of adults." In 1976, the American School Health Association reported that only six states and the District of Columbia required the teaching of some form of sex education in schools—and that many of the programs precluded any mention of contraception.

When a teenage daughter becomes pregnant, the subject of sex can no longer be avoided. In some families, the crisis can draw the family closer together. "My experience is that by and large parents are supportive," says a minister at Clergy Consultation Service. "Sometimes facing an unwanted pregnancy together results in a family confronting basic issues of their lives for the first time." In many clinics, the mother is counseled along with the daughter, or separately if she prefers. Abortion counselor Sharon Gedan believes strongly in family counseling and urges the parents to discuss their feelings about their daughter's pregnancy, to question themselves if they are judgmental toward her behavior, and to exorcise any self-blame if it exists. And surely self-blame does exist. Over and over in my discussions with various mothers, they would say, as if to themselves, 'What did I do wrong?' The answer is 'Probably nothing.'

The fact that a daughter is pregnant is devastating to many parents. Burying their heads in the sand, some parents practice the age-old trick of hoping it will all go away; obviously it doesn't. This group of parents presents a great problem to clinic and hospital staffs, who want to catch any pregnancy in its earliest weeks so as to minimize the risks in abortion. "The mothers are really our biggest

210

problem," says a gynecologist at Harlem Hospital. "Even when these girls tell their mothers they are pregnant, the mother says, 'No, you're not, you're not.' It's the typical psychological denial of what they don't want to know. As long as the mother denies it, the action is delayed and neglected. That's why so many of these girls go beyond the safe time for the suction method and end up having saline abortions."

Other parents accept the pregnancy and abortion but refuse to accept the fact that their daughter is sexually active. Instead of dealing with her problems maturely and encouraging her to use contraception, they pretend this is a one-time accident. In contrast, Dr. Lonnie Myers, midwestern chairman of Sex Education Counselors and Therapists, believes that parents should start talking about contraception to their children when they are as young as four years old. "We insist on the absolute integrity of our children's development, yet we distort matters of sex," says Myers. "Most sex is recreational, but we continue to tell kids it's something mommies and daddies do only when they love each other and want a baby. That's lying!"

For young women under twenty-one in some states, eighteen in others, there is a mounting confusion as to whether parental consent is required before a minor can have an abortion. Although the U.S. Supreme Court ruled in a case brought in Missouri that the need for blanket parental consent is unconstitutional toward minors, the court left ambiguous just what degree of adult consent would be acceptable. As a result, current state legislatures are expected to pass modified parental consent requirements or modified consent notification criteria that would slow down, if not preclude, abortion on demand for teenagers. Such a move has prompted great fear among family-planning professionals that the time lost in girls' gathering up the courage to tell their families and the time then spent in coming to a decision will delay the abortion until the second trimester, or raise the numbers of children born to unwed mothers.

All of this is of little concern to the mothers who wait restlessly in clinics across the country. Many of them are nervous about the procedure and uncertain about their feelings toward their daughters, so the abortion appears to be upsetting them far more than it is their

211

daughters. Still other mothers are proud of the way their daughters have handled an unwanted pregnancy. To the one potential grandfather I chanced upon during a train ride, the aborting of his first grandchild has left a deep hurt. To him, it was the loss of his immortality.

━━━━━━━

Isabelle Anderson is very upset. Her hands tremble, and she wipes her nose again and again, while tears stream uncontrollably down her face. She is in the waiting room of an abortion clinic in Ohio while her seventeen-year-old daughter is having an abortion. She seems close to collapse and gratefully accepts a tranquilizer from a concerned woman who is also waiting for her own daughter.

"I found out about the guy. I found out all about him, things my daughter doesn't know. He's been in the pen, and he's married to another woman who is six months pregnant. My best friend told me all about him. She told me about my daughter, too. Can you believe my daughter told her she was pregnant before she told me?

"When I found out she was pregnant, it was like the bottom fell out of everything. I never had a child of my own. We adopted her when she was eight. Everyone warned me she'd only bring trouble and sorrow, and that was the first thing I thought of when I found out about her condition. I feel very tearful.

"How could she make it with someone she had only known for a month? I asked her, 'Did he give you drinks or cigarettes?' She only wanted to know whether I was going to give her a beating, and I said, 'No, but you deserve one.'

"I'm so scared my husband will find out. We told him we were going shopping and had to get an early start. Then I turned the clocks up an hour all over the house so we'd have plenty of time to get here without his knowing. I was so scared when he woke up and asked me what time it was, but he believed me.

"She was scheduled first for next week, but we moved the appointment up to today because my nerves can't stand it. I have colitis, and

212

I got a bad attack. I got angry with everybody that this thing happened. Will she be able to have another baby? I cleaned the whole house, washed loads of clothes, dug up the whole garden waiting to come here today. This is my first day of vacation. Oh, I'm so nervous. Will it hurt her insides?

"She asked the boy for the money for the abortion, and he said, 'Oh, boy, here goes another stretch in the pen,' and hung up on her. I called him, too, to ask for the money, even though I've never met him, but his father answered and I just hung up. I've been saving up for a long time for a vacation or for her to go to college, so I paid for it.

"He's twenty-four, so he knew what he was doing. I think she needs someone caring for her so much. But he's not so neat and clean as her other friends. I couldn't imagine her sleeping with him.

"She told me she was thinking of running away when she found out she was pregnant. 'Don't worry,' she said, 'I'll get out of your hair.' But I said to her, 'What will that prove?' Do you know she could have this abortion without my consent? That's too young, too young.

"I hope she'll learn a lesson, but I don't know. Some girls yearn for sex. Maybe psychiatry can solve that problem. She always asked why I didn't get her a sister. But that won't solve her problem if it's men she needs.

"I'm not ashamed. I'm more hurt. They say everybody does it these days, but everybody isn't her. I doubt I'll ever trust her again. I tried to make a big joke of it when she went out on a date the other night. 'No babies tonight,' I said when she ran out the door.

"Fifty percent of her tenth-grade class are the same way. Some had their babies. They couldn't even fit in their desks at summer school, they were so fat. It's terrible. What's the matter with them? I just can't understand it.

"I waited eight years for her. She was the baby I lost when we were first married. So many people think so much of her, I'd hate for them to find out about this. They'd think the less of her, for sure. I lent the money to my girlfriend's daughter to have an abortion, and a month later she was pregnant again. There's nothing you can do.

213

"My husband always said I let her go out too early. Oh, the ceiling would blow off in our town if he knew. These kids can really get you. They think it all comes so easy."

———————

Wynona Curry, forty-three, is waiting for her fifteen-year-old daughter, who is having an abortion this morning in Atlanta. It is the daughter's second abortion in three months. Wynona, the mother of five children, is shocked but warmly supportive of her daughter. A laid-off cleaning woman, Wynona is on welfare and would have supported the child but couldn't afford it. Though she thinks abortion as well as premarital sex is a sin, she would rather see her daughter finish school before she gets married and has children. Wynona got birth-control pills for her daughter after the first abortion, but evidently, Wynona says, the girl didn't take them.

"When I found out she was pregnant the first time it hurt me so bad I thought I was going to lose my mind. I don't know. I don't know what went through my mind. Just everything. It just upset me so bad. I guess I'm lucky when you think I got five children and she be the only one what got pregnant.

"I think that she might just be trying to act older than she is, to be more like bigger kids or her three sisters. But I don't know. I just don't know. Maybe it was a bad example that somebody set before her, like some of her friends.

"She has some of those pills, but evidently she must not have been taking them. After her first abortion, I got her those pills from here and I gave them to her so this wouldn't happen again. But it did.

"Her friends, sometimes I hear them talking and they talk like it is murder having an abortion or taking something so you don't get pregnant, so maybe that's why she didn't take them. I told her it's murder to have an abortion but it's not murder to take the pills, but that's what they saying anyhow. It's just a sin if that's the way they feel about it. I heard her cousins once talking to her about it. This one cousin, she feel like it was just murder, and she felt it was like a sin to take something. Well, it's a sin to even have intercourse if

214

you're not married. I'm not a Baptist. I'm Christian.

"I was brought up to believe that intercourse was a sin before you are married, and I believed it and I still do. So according to the Bible she has sinned. I think you are supposed to be married. That's the way I feel about it. And I told her that, but I guess she didn't pay no mind. We are church-going people and I take her there every Sunday. But I didn't talk to the preacher about it. Only her sisters and her brother and my mother know. And they didn't say anything about it. But they never going to tell me what they say to each other.

"She didn't want to have the baby. And I tell you the truth. After that first shock when I first heard about this, I wasn't too particular about her having the baby. Because really and truly I am not even able to support another child in the family. At first I thought she should go and get married if she was to continue having babies. Then I changed my mind because she is still in school and I think she should get her education first. Then if she is going to continue this way, she should just go ahead and get married.

"I don't think she's a bad girl. It's just these older people that she be with. They hold some kind of influence with her. I'm not going to treat her any different. I am going to treat her just like I always have. I'm not going to keep a closer eye on her. You can't see everything a child do. You have to get out and work and everything. And it don't do you no good to watch them anyway, because whatever they going to do, they do.

"I still love her. I don't feel no different or nothing. I don't believe in treating her right or wrong. Because anybody can make a mistake. But it upsets you though, because some people make more of it than that. It upsets you. The first time it happen it shocks you worse than it do the second time, though you don't appreciate it neither time. But it happened. I don't feel any different taking her to church now, no more than when she was a baby. I pray for her constantly just like I do for all my kids, and so far I've been lucky because I've got four girls and one boy and all of them is older than she is and this is the first time I've had any trouble. Nothing like this ever happened in the family.

"We were brought up real strict. If we all had done something like this my daddy would have been cussing and telling us he was going to burn us up. He was real strict about dating. See, we couldn't go out like these kids today. If you try to keep them in now, they going to find some way to get out. I wouldn't try to hem them in anyway. It wouldn't profit me anything to try and stop her from going out. They learn more when they going out. They can experience more, and that's good until it goes bad. I think a child should be exposed to something, but still you don't want something like this to happen. We are none of us made out of iron, you know."

================

Mildred Sawyer's circumstances are the stuff of soap operas. Sitting pale and tense in Grady Hospital in Atlanta where she has brought her seventeen-year-old daughter for an abortion, she alternates between tears and anger. Her daughter, who ran away and got married at sixteen, had a baby and was deserted, has returned home. Mildred takes care of the baby, insisting her daughter complete her high school education. Instead, the daughter got pregnant again and dropped out of school. Her boyfriend refuses to acknowledge his part in the pregnancy, a fact that caused Mildred's husband such distraction that he had an accident and has been forced into early retirement. Mildred's love and concern for her daughter has been stretched to the breaking point. "We are worn out with her life," she says. Mildred, fifty, has four children and cannot understand why one turned out to be such a "complete failure."

"She had just turned seventeen when we found out she was pregnant. She started getting sick and simply refused to go to school. She skipped twenty days of school, and every day the counselor would call asking where she was. I didn't know what to do. My daughter just kept telling me one lie after another until she began to get fat, and then of course, we knew she was pregnant.

"We were real shocked and mortified. We've always been very family proud, sort of old South, you could say. My husband had a good government job and was planning to retire next year with enough retirement pay so we could live real well. Then all this happened, and suddenly I had a baby to raise and a daughter who's

216

pregnant again. Her husband left her flat without a cent, without nothing. What else can I do but take care of the baby and hope that after this abortion she'll go out to work and get on her feet again? If she's ever been on them.

"For a while my husband and I blamed each other for her life. Then we came to the conclusion that some children just have it within them to rebel against discipline. Their peers have more influence on them than their parents. And from the crowd she was running with, I knew there was going to be trouble. But we did everything we could. We have three boys who turned out real fine, and one of them is a paratrooper. Now how can you have a kid like that and one who's a complete failure? Now she admits she was hard-headed and stubborn, but who knows if she'll change. We are worn out with her life.

"Though he loves the boys, my husband felt her life was more of a tragedy. He thought she was tops. It is a great disappointment to know she chose this way of life. I feel her life is tragic. She just has nothing of her own. I want to get this abortion over with as soon as possible so we can try to begin again.

"I had thought that my husband and I could make our plans after our kids were raised, but we've been sidetracked. At times I feel animosity and bad things about her. But I try to get them out of my mind. I can't let her know I even think these things or she'd go back into that life. She says she's learned her lesson, but time will tell.

"When we found out she was pregnant with no husband at seventeen, I felt so ashamed I even skipped church. I thought no one would accept us. Then we began to hear about this daughter and that daughter, and we realized we were not alone. There are some children who just won't ever learn. What went wrong? I ask myself that time and again. I remember when she was sixteen, before she ran away, she told me she wasn't going to church any more and that I couldn't make her. My reaction was that I'm bound to give to any child what I think she needs in her life. But I obviously couldn't give that to her. Sometimes I feel that I never want to see her again.

"The thing that has comforted me and brought me through all this is prayer. And my husband agrees. But our lives now are worse than they've ever been. When we found out she was pregnant, we called

217

the boy on the phone to ask him to help pay for the abortion, but he said he wouldn't help. He said we'd have to bring a court case against him to prove it was his fault. It's made my husband sick. A while ago he fell off a ladder and cracked a vertebra in his back. He said he was thinking about that boy who wouldn't pay and he was so distracted he had the accident.

"That was three months ago and he's been out of work ever since. Now he's got lung congestion and heart problems because of the stress and strain he's been under. Instead of us finishing our plan for the rest of our life, he's got to take early retirement, which doesn't give us enough money to live on, and him being so sick and all. Our daughter has really wrecked our life. And if she jumps out of the frying pan into the fire again, well, the next time she's going to jump alone."

Marlene Campbell, forty, twists her hands nervously in her lap as she sits on a wooden bench in Harlem Hospital in New York waiting for her fifteen-year-old daughter to have her post-abortion checkup. Her voice is low and bitter as she discusses her daughter, and she is reluctant to speak about the abortion at all. Her daughter, on the other hand, is all smiles and is more concerned with her bubble gum than her abortion. Dressed in skin-tight jeans and a tiny knitted top, the daughter keeps dancing to an inaudible rock song.

"It's disgusting to talk about it. Just disgusting. It doesn't make you feel any better to talk about it. Forget it. Just forget it.

"Before the abortion I was upset. Real upset. But not now. I didn't get mad at her. I was just surprised. But she shouldn't have. These kids grow up too fast. She started too young. She got her period when she was nine or ten. She started too young.

"I took her to the doctor, but I knew she was pregnant. She like to eat and run and go, so I knew something was wrong when she was just lying around sleeping. I imagine she knew too, but she didn't want to admit it. The doctor said she was too young to have a baby. At that point she was six weeks pregnant. I had all sorts of feelings

218

at that particular time. All sorts of bad thoughts I just don't want to describe.

"The main thing is that it don't happen again. These kids just don't know what they're doing. Now they've given her some sort of birth device thing, but she better not need it.

"I always had a curfew on her but she didn't feel like following it. I didn't pressure her then, but now I will. I have ways to keep her home. I don't want to beat her, but if I have to, I will. Maybe I'll punch her every once in a while. Maybe that will be enough."

———————

Mark Rothberg, fifty-eight, is an amiable, gregarious life-insurance salesman in Danbury, Connecticut. The only time his face loses its relaxed jocularity is when he discusses his daughter-in-law's recent abortion. It would have been his first grandchild. But he is determined that his son and daughter-in-law will never know how much it has hurt him. He thinks abortion is a form of genocide against Jews.

"My son was in medical school in England because he couldn't get into a good medical school here. My daughter-in-law was getting her master's in sociology in England at the same time, so they thought it would be a good time to start a family. They were visiting us here a few weeks ago, and she told me she was having a baby. We were delighted. It was our first grandchild. My wife and I both felt a quiet, exuberant joy.

"Then suddenly he was accepted at medical school here. And she decided to stay in England to finish up her master's before joining him. Rather than face the complicated mess, they decided it was not the time to have a child. And she had an abortion.

"When they told us about the abortion just two weeks after they'd told us she was having a baby, it was crushing. I felt a deep chagrin. Being Jewish, and moving more toward Orthodox than not, I felt it was not something that is done. And my conservatism, family wise, is ingrained.

219

"I have such awareness of this girl's strength, I felt no deprecation toward her. But it was hard for us, hard.

"We didn't cry. My wife and I talked and talked about it. We tried not to judge her for what she had done. She was right not to tell us before the fact, because she wouldn't have accepted our dictum. And I couldn't have handled being part of the decision.

"It's a special thing, you know, a grandchild. It's continuity. And if you have a strong family, which we do, then it's the first dividend.

"It's more than a loss of family continuity, too. Jews are being screwed out of existence. Who uses birth control? Who gets all these abortions? We're being physically wiped out. Now there's one less. But even more, we lost our option for personal continuity. I feel dreadful."

========

Jessica Kroner, fifty-one, is a vibrantly attractive woman who, after twenty-five years of marriage, divorced her husband and entered the social and political chaos of the sixties with the same energy as her then teenage children. More of a friend to her children than the traditional mother, Jessica insists they call her by her first name. When her daughter, Karen, had her first abortion at fifteen, Jessica was very supportive and indeed pleased to be able to help her. Jessica was equally pleased, when Karen had another abortion last year, that she was mature enough to handle it on her own and to tell her only after the fact. Jessica lives in Philadelphia where she is active in politics.

"Karen was about fourteen when the whole world started going to pieces, my own included. What a year that was. Within twenty-four hours, all three of my children came to me with shocking stories. One son was arrested on a pot charge, and when I went down to the police station he was brought out in handcuffs. It's an incredible experience to see your son in handcuffs. My other son announced he had venereal disease. And Karen came to me to confess she was pregnant. In fact all these crises suited my temperament. The point was to get all the problems lined up and get them all over with. But I told them, 'Next week don't feel you know me that well.' I needed a rest.

"When Karen told me, 'I think I may be whatever,' I said, 'We'll get an appointment.' I was not terribly surprised. From the age of eight she was twelve going on forty-two. We'd talked a lot about birth control. I told her although I didn't condone arbitrary sexual activity, I'd be remiss in not telling her what birth control was available. I told her what clinic to go to, but that I was definitely not saying go ahead and make love to everybody.

"When she told me she was pregnant, it never crossed my mind she might want to have the baby. Instantly in my mind it was all business as far as I was concerned. I felt deep distress for her for maybe fifteen seconds, then decided to get on with it.

"I had to be tough for her and on her. She was scared to death to have the abortion. We made an appointment at the hospital, then made up a story for her father that she had some trouble with her female parts. There was no point telling him about the abortion. He didn't want to know. He never asked one question.

"I didn't spend one cent of his money for the abortion, either. I get two thousand dollars a year from my grandmother's estate, and I felt it was a luxury to be able to do this for Karen. I didn't want to use his dough without telling him.

"I knew it had to be done right then. It's not like waiting for an appendix to kick up again. Karen turned herself over to me and let me help her, which made me very grateful. She hated me at that point, and had since she was nine. To have a flamboyant parent in charge of your world is very tough, but I think it's got to be more positive than negative.

"I knew that the whole time she was hating me, I was still the best friend she had. She knew I would always support her, and there are not that many bunches of people like that around. I was so glad she did and could talk to me.

"I took her to the hospital. I had no thought of the fetus as a grandchild. I just wanted to get my child through it, and she pro-

221

tested all the way. It was her birthday, and she was determined not to have the abortion in the hospital on that day. But I succeeded, and I've never mentioned it to anyone. It's totally her business. I never even asked her who the father was. It made no difference. I saw it as just solving a problem.

"I talked to her about birth control after the abortion, but I felt I couldn't make any headway. What a time that was. I put my younger son on the road to thumb his way out to Ken Kesey's farm in California and was convinced I was never going to see him again except in a pine coffin. I got arrested in Washington in the May Day sweep, and I could never get the tear gas out of my clothes. The sixties were an incomprehensible time for all of us. I said to my kids, 'I know you're all in a dark forest, but I want you to know, so am I.'

"Karen was a product of the sixties, too. There were drugs, the new morality, and her particular vulnerabilities. I wonder how she would have fared with a different mother or father. But I do think the strength I gave her made a difference. I don't think I failed her where it counts. But to be as bizarre as I was at that time was highly objectionable and distasteful to her. But that's the way I am. At least now we can be good friends.

"With her second abortion, she didn't tell me until afterwards. She and the boy had dinner with me the night before the abortion. She was very quiet, and I wondered what was going on. She told me a week later, which I thought was just great. It was an enormous step for her to carry it off without me.

"I wasn't angry with her the second time. It was just the feeling my God, that's so stupid, but use-it-and-don't-do-it-again department. I haven't talked to her about birth control this time. She's twenty-two and has had two abortions. Are you kidding?

"But she is coming along. When she had the first abortion, she said to me, 'I recognize it as murder, and I'm willing to do it.' Boy, I was impressed with that. Really impressed.

"I hope she won't do it to herself again. But she's still so desperately vulnerable to being hugged. I try to hug her all the time, but I guess it's not enough."

222

Jessie Lomax, forty-four, was shocked when her thirteen-year-old daughter came to her three years ago to confess she was pregnant. Though it was not uncommon for high school students in the town in Iowa in which they lived to get pregnant, the Lomaxes never thought it would happen to their daughter. They signed the papers for her abortion, as parental consent was then required, and haven't discussed it since. Jessie does not know if her daughter uses any kind of birth control now.

"I was shocked—not that she was pregnant, but that she was having sex. And I was disappointed that she was. All our children know that we don't approve of that sort of thing, but so many girls are doing it nowadays and so many do get pregnant. I guess we shouldn't have been so upset. We often sat down with her and her sisters and brothers and discussed sex, and they knew we didn't approve of it. So we never thought it would happen to her.

"We were proud of her, though—that she had the abortion all arranged. She just needed our consent, which we gave. We felt she was too young to get married. And she hasn't had any seemingly bad results. She's still getting straight A's in school and still going with the same boy whom she's planning to marry.

"We sat down and said that abortion was the best thing. But we said that she was smarter than this, in that she was jeopardizing her future. We told her we didn't want it to happen again.

"The boy is very nice. He comes from a Catholic family, but a nice one. He's going to be a doctor. He was quite upset about her getting pregnant, and he came over and talked a little bit about it to us. But we said it was over and done with, and we didn't want to bring it up again. I told her I'd pay for the abortion, but I didn't want her doing sex again. I don't know whether she's using birth control or not now. I guess you might call it a kind of mental block. I don't think the less of her for it. After all, the two of them handled the whole thing quite maturely. I guess they're all older than we think."

223

8

Women Looking Back

Even before abortion was legalized in 1973, there were abortion undergrounds and sympathetic doctors who would defy the law. But for women thirty, forty, and fifty years ago, the risks and shame of terminating an unwanted pregnancy were almost beyond imagination. Family structure was much tighter in the thirties and forties, and pregnancy in a single woman brought real repercussions of disgrace and scandal not only for her but also for all her family. For a married woman, abortion was supposedly unheard of, and it had to be an extreme case for any panel of doctors to give consent for a therapeutic abortion. The threat of physical damage and death was very real in illegal abortions. And yet women persisted in their fight to control their reproductive lives.

It was also extremely difficult to secure contraception; in many states, contraceptive devices were available only by prescription and only to married women. There was no sex education in the schools and little or no discussion of sex at home. For young women growing up fifty years ago, there was no one even to talk to about sex because women then had not learned to talk to each other. Virginity was a quality not only to be admired but to be demanded by the wedding-night husband, whose own sex life was of course never questioned.

So it took a tremendous amount of courage for a woman to rid herself of an unwanted pregnancy. For those with money and connections, doctors could be found to perform the back-room operations, although many of these proved to be quacks. Even luckier women could travel to England, where abortions were safer and condoned, if not legal. Those less fortunate suffered horribly at the hands of unskilled abortionists, who often left women with a damaged uterus and a barren future.

It would be a disservice to women undergoing abortion now not to listen to the women who had abortions then. Women's bodies are not new. Abortion is not new. What *is* new is the sense of decency and dignity the law now provides for women who do not wish to continue a pregnancy. Their reasons are not new either, though in the following interviews one is circumstantial and was brought about by World War II. The rest of the women were caught in a failing marriage, between marriages, or just before marriage. It is only now, in one case fifty-five years after the fact, that these women feel they can talk about their abortion experiences. Their shame, fear, and relief have long since faded, and they envy the women today who can opt openly for abortion and not skulk and hide as they did. These are not people speaking from the feminist front, Catholic activists, or the sexually liberated. These are simply women.

Mica Brody, fifty-two, is a Hungarian who fled from there in 1957. She and her husband have two daughters born in 1946 and 1947 in Budapest. When Mica became pregnant again during the Russian occupation of Hungary, the instability of the time led her to have an illegal abortion. It cost $10,000 in gold. Twenty-eight years after the abortion, Mica is still bitter about it. Her third pregnancy, after she came to America, ended in a stillbirth. She now works as a lab technician in an abortion clinic, where she worries that American women are too soft.

"In the late forties Hungary was overrun by the Russians. There had been so much loss of population from the bombings during the war that abortion was then completely illegal and punished by life imprisonment in Siberia for the patient, and capital punishment or a lifetime imprisonment in Siberia for the doctor. It was a matter of life and death on both parts, imposed entirely by the Russians.

"My husband was a prominent lawyer in Budapest at the time, and his father was a Supreme Court judge until the Russians imprisoned him. All our land was confiscated, and they wouldn't even give us ration tickets for food. We had to buy all our food on the black market, which carried a ten-year imprisonment sentence if we were caught. Every time we went shopping, there was the chance that one of us might not come back. The only currency then was diamonds and gold, and with the inflation rate that was only good from night to morning. I remember taking a suitcase full of money to the market to buy two pounds of salt. In normal times, that amount of money was enough to buy a house.

"We had two children already. I was still nursing the little one, and I thought that while I was nursing I couldn't get pregnant. But I did. There was no way we could raise a third child under those conditions. Even so, I was so happy when I found out I was pregnant. We had two girls, and I so much wanted a boy. Because my periods are irregular, I was three months pregnant before I actually knew it. My husband started nosing around for someone to perform the abortion and finally found a man. It cost us ten thousand dollars in gold, which he had gotten as pay from his clients. We had already sold our piano, my fur coat, and the family jewelry for food.

"We went at night to the sixth floor of an apartment house quite far away from us. There were three other couples there. Because other people lived both under and over this man, he kept some sort of electrical equipment running which made a noise like scraping a wall so no one would hear us if we screamed. He had no anesthetic, no codeine, no nothing. He told me to make a fist, but not to make a sound. If I got sick afterwards, I was not to call him.

"It hurt very much. Very much. I didn't quite faint, but I was on the verge of not being able to stand it. I knew I had to make it. I had seen a country go down in flames, so I wasn't going to die there. It took plain sheer heroic will power. Afterwards I had to walk down

226

five flights of stairs and walk three blocks to catch the bus, because he didn't want anyone to see us outside his building. The bus ride took an hour. Then I had to walk ten blocks to another bus stop, and finally I got home around four A.M. The will power. When I see these girls here complaining that they hurt a little, or it's too cold or too hot, oh, if they could experience a little bit of what I went through. They are very soft. God help them when something happens in this country.

"I blocked out everything about the abortion. It was just another thing we had to do. We never talked about it then or now. The baby was just another victim of war. It left a scar on both of us. We knew when the baby would have been born, but we just tucked it away and tried to forget it. We had no choice to dig ourselves into an emotional state. It was survive or die.

"I got pregnant once again. I was thirty-two or thirty-three when we came here. My husband finally got a job as a lab technician, and when he filled out the papers for a loan for our house, he had to sign a clause that said I would not have another baby. I was pregnant at the time, but he signed it anyway. The baby was born dead.

"If I hadn't had the abortion, maybe the baby would have been all right. There was blame. Maybe it was the Good Lord's punishment. I don't know. After that, I decided I'd never go through it again. The pills came out, and I said, 'This is it.'

"The abortion had to be done. That was all. I never judge anyone who has an abortion here. And I never judged myself. But it was very hard. Three years after my abortion, it became legal in Hungary. Oh, the resentment.

"There was my religion, also. I consider myself a good Catholic, and like a good Catholic, I confessed my abortion to my priest. I was excommunicated. My religion was terribly important to me. I was raised in a nun's school for ten years. I felt worse about being excommunicated than about the abortion itself.

"I'm back in the church now that I'm here in America, and I feel much better. Both our girls got married in the church. And it's all behind us. Way behind us. I've never told them about the abortion. I've never told anyone."

227

Ruby Sherman, now fifty-seven, had an illegal abortion thirty-five years ago when she was first married. She never got over her resentment at having to have the abortion and divorced her husband twenty-three years and two children later. Ashamed of the abortion, she did not admit having it to anyone until two years ago, when she told her children, both of whom were then in their twenties. Like many women who have had disturbing experiences with abortion, Ruby works part-time for an abortion clinic.

"I had a diaphragm but wasn't using it when I got pregnant. I didn't think we were going to have intercourse. We had gone to bed and to sleep when my husband woke me up in the middle of the night. I said no, but he said it was the right time of the month. I thought he must be right. He was wrong.

"After I had missed two periods, I told my gynecologist I didn't want to be pregnant and he found me an abortionist in Columbus, Ohio. He gave me an address to go to at night.

"I never knew his name or saw his face. It was covered with a surgical mask. There were no nameplates on the door, either. I don't even know whether it was his office or not. My husband waited in the other room. He had a delicate stomach.

"I was pretty brave. It was like going to the dentist. You don't know what to expect. I didn't know at all what I was getting into. I didn't know I'd be feeling menstrual cramps, which I did. There was no follow-up and no medication like Ergotrate then, which helps contract the uterus, or an antibiotic to prevent infection. But then I knew the abortion wasn't going to be a big social whirl.

"I was very glad I'd had a professional person to do it. I wanted to live and not be sterile afterwards. The price wasn't too bad, either. Only two hundred dollars.

"But I didn't feel good about it. I was very angry with my husband. He should have taken some responsibility for it. There were other times when I was bone-tired at midnight and he would wake me up. Sometimes I thought it was a dream. After the abortion I was

228

fearful of sex, and I got even more angry when I found myself being made love to in the middle of the night. He said he had to have it or he couldn't sleep or function. Women can go without sex and men can't, he said. I began getting more firm about these nocturnal visits. I didn't like being taken advantage of. And he finally started using rubbers. Men always seem to know when the time of the month is safe. What do they know?

"I never told my family or friends about the abortion. I didn't even like the word. I never said it. Whenever I had a physical or even when I was pregnant with my son, who is now thirty, I never told the doctor I'd had an abortion. It was an unmentionable, like intercourse.

"I felt that I had been put through something that was an unnecessary experience for me, and that my husband was responsible. I began doubting he was right on a lot of other things. He was years older than I, and I'd always looked up to him. From that point I began doing things on my own.

"Our marriage was unsteady to begin with. And the abortion didn't help. Our marriage didn't blossom into love the way he said it would.

"Our first child after the abortion was unplanned. He had come home on leave from World War II and I was in the WACs. We slept together the first night, and that was it. I was not delighted, but we had been married five years by then and I was not about to have another abortion.

"Then I had a miscarriage which made me feel bad even though that baby wasn't planned either. I wondered what that child would have been. It was much more upsetting than the abortion. I had felt the stirrings when the fetus was four and a half months. I tried not to lose it, but I did. I didn't hold that against him at all. I must have lifted something heavy.

"Looking back, the abortion was a positive experience. I didn't want children then. I was immature in the ways of life. Mostly I'm glad I no longer have my husband. I didn't admit for the longest time that I'd had an abortion. It took me thirty years to say the word and admit it. I decided my children had the right to know. I told them two years ago. They were surprised, but it didn't really matter. I wanted them to know me better, to know all of me. It's just one more thing about Mom that they know. My son is thirty now and my daughter is twenty-seven."

It has been forty years since Elsa Ruppert, now sixty-two, had an illegal abortion in New York. Like many women of that era, Elsa preferred to have an abortion than create a family scandal, even though she was engaged to marry the father at the time. Motivated by guilt afterwards, she and her husband went on to have a child immediately after their marriage. When her mother and aunt visited her in the hospital, they counted the days on their fingers to make sure they had no cause for shame. Elsa and her husband divorced sixteen years later.

"I had a very good job at a magazine in 1938, and one of my greatest coups was hiring Joseph. I was six months older than he, but it didn't make any difference. We fell very much in love and shortly found our way to bed. He was a virgin, but I was not. I had been lucky up to then. There was no such thing as birth control in those days. To get a diaphragm you had to be married and to have a prescription from your doctor.

"I felt quite shattered when I found out I was pregnant. I kept looking for that reassuring little red spot, and it never appeared. I went to my gynecologist, and he confirmed the pregnancy. Joseph and I never had one feeling about the baby. We knew we were going to marry and would presumably have children, so all we thought about then were our families. His father was a strict Roman Catholic and a great romantic, and his mother was early Victorian. I had made a huge point of not taking any financial assistance from my father after I graduated from college, and I was not about to admit to him that I had made any mistake about anything. It would have been awful to have that child.

"The doctor said we could disguise it by getting married right away, but it would have created many raised eyebrows. The date was all set for our wedding, which was five months away, and we just felt

230

it was more sensible and considerate to our families to have the abortion. So I did. My gynecologist sent us off to a doctor, and even now I have trouble driving by the 72nd Street entrance to the West Side Highway in New York where his office was.

"He was a very nice man. The office was clean and neat. They gave me an anesthetic, the nurse held my hand, and when I woke up, that was that. I had no physical reaction. There was no pain. But it turned out to be an emotional shock. We were both overcome by guilt. It seemed a betrayal of our love that we had destroyed something that we'd created. I couldn't get it out of my mind. But then Joseph always told me I wouldn't be happy if I weren't guilty.

"Because of the abortion, we had a baby just as soon as we were married, though we couldn't afford it at all at the time. It was the guilt that caused us to have that baby so soon. Then, of course, we felt fine, because if we had had the first one, then we wouldn't have had our son, whom we loved enormously. I had experienced great pain during intercourse after the abortion, but I never let on to Joseph because I thought it would hurt him to know he was causing me pain. Perhaps it was psychological. I don't know. But after I had our first son, the pain went away.

"Eighteen months later we had another son by accident. The doctors had discovered I had an ovarian cyst which had to be removed, and they suggested they remove it and the baby when I found out I was pregnant. But I didn't want to have another abortion, even though this time it would have been therapeutic. Instead I went ahead and had him, and then had the cyst removed. And I'm so grateful I did. He was killed in a car accident when he was twenty-four. I'm so glad I had him for all those years. You don't try to find reasons for a child dying, because there aren't any.

"Joseph and I loved our children so much that I tried forever and a day to have more, but I just never could. We created two wonderful kids and the one that was gone. I remember going to a gypsy fortuneteller with him one night and she looked at our palms and said to Joseph that he was going to have three children. Then she read my palm and said, 'You have had one child and then two more.' When Joseph got remarried he had another child, and the prophecy was fulfilled.

231

"I don't regret having my abortion at all. I can remember when I had my first son my aunt and my mother sat there and counted out the days from our marriage—280 days—and both of them said, 'Thank God.' I'm very small and showed right away when I was pregnant, and they were terrified the family was going to be shamed.

"If anything, the abortion brought Joseph and me closer together. I didn't resent our families for causing us to have the abortion, but then I've always been very low on resentment. And we did have a nifty wedding."

Theresa Wainwright, now sixty-four, had two abortions in 1937 and 1939. Married and divorced twice, then widowed by her third husband, Theresa's abortions occurred between her first and second husbands. Neither of the abortions took, and both had to be done over, one in London, the other in New York. Theresa does not regret the abortions, only the secrecy surrounding them. No woman, she thinks, should have to go through what she did. An earthy, tough woman, Theresa lives alone now in Nantucket, Massachusetts.

"I was around twenty-five and divorced in 1937 with a baby and a lover, natch. I was living then with a man I knew I didn't want to marry. And if anyone had found out I was pregnant, I might have lost hold of my son, who was then two. There would have been a terrific scandal and a lot of trouble about it.

"All my family was still alive then, my parents and my four brothers and sisters. So my only thrust was to find an abortionist and get on with it. The man I was living with found one, and off I went to an apartment on the West Side in New York and had the job done. He was a medical man, I believe, and all he did was abortions. It was a six-room apartment, and each room had various beds with stirrups in them. There were six of us going through at a time. It was an assembly line. You paid your three hundred dollars cash as you walked in, the nurse took you in and shaved you, and then he dashed through to abort you and move on to the next.

"I was relieved that it was going to be done. I wasn't particularly apprehensive about it. But I should have been. This particular doctor had the charming habit of not approving of abortion, so he didn't administer any anesthetic. The pain was excruciating, the kind that makes you throw up, the sweat-on-the-upper-lip type. But I didn't make a sound. It was my upbringing, you see. I couldn't let it show.

"Afterwards I felt woolly, shook up but definitely relieved. I had no moral feeling about it at all. Just the physical shock of the operation.

"A month later I failed to menstruate, and I was panic-stricken that it hadn't worked. My father invited me to England for a stay, and off I went with my son and a nurse. My sister came over from Paris and told me that I was an idiot. Either I was pregnant again or else the doctor in New York hadn't gotten it out.

"She came up with the name of a very famous English surgeon, and off I went to a nursing home. I told my father I was having female troubles, and he decided to believe it. He must have known. He couldn't have been such a jackass. The doctor told me to say it was a miscarriage to the staff at the nursing home, which I did. Unlike the first abortion, this time I had Sodium Pentothal, and when I woke up I was in a paneled room with a fire going. What luxury. He couldn't understand what had happened in New York, and thought perhaps I was having twins and that only one had been removed. I asked whether the fetus was maimed, and he said, 'No, not at all.'

"He gave me the name of a doctor in New York to get a diaphragm from, and I stayed in the nursing home for a week. I was now doubly relieved, though it was shattering to have to be so sneaky. My father was either very polite or dumb, but he never let on. All I could think of was losing my son, which would have been far more traumatic than just having an abortion.

"When I got back to New York I removed my lover from the scene. Our relationship had just plain worn itself out. Then husband number two came along. We were sort of vaguely engaged, and suddenly, because I was too lazy to wear the diaphragm, I was pregnant again. We could have gotten married then, I suppose, but we didn't. Instead I went off to have another abortion.

"This time it was a Park Avenue doctor. Because I was more

ambivalent about this baby, being fonder of the father, I waited till I was over two months pregnant. The doctor turned out to be the most unpleasant man I had ever met. He examined me on the table, told me I was indeed pregnant, and to come back the next morning with five hundred dollars. There I was still in the stirrups and suddenly he began groping around again, and it was definitely not medicinal. That bastard was making a pass at me. I sat bolt upright and said, 'Cut it out,' and he mumbled something and stopped.

"I came back the next morning, the nurse shaved me, and they put me on the table. The doctor put the mask for the gas over my face, then said the machine wasn't working and he was going to have to do it with no anesthesia. All I could remember was the last pain I'd been through, but I decided I wasn't going to give in to that son of a bitch. And I didn't. The pain almost sent me out of my head, but I never made a sound. When I was resting in that little pen they always have by these rooms, I overheard the nurse saying that there was nothing the matter with the machine at all. He was just punishing me for not giving in to him.

"I was more upset about losing that baby than the one before. I thought both before and after the abortion that maybe I should have married the father. That's why I was so pokey about getting the abortion. The guy was very nice, and I thought maybe I was wrong by not marrying him. Maybe he wasn't so much of a bum.

"When it came time for my period, nothing happened again. I went to my doctor, who was very stuffy and wouldn't help me at all. Then I went to my gynecologist, who said that under the laws of the city there wasn't anything he could do, but if I had the slightest complication, any bleeding at all, to call him immediately. Nothing happened until I began to panic that the baby was going to show. I held my stomach in until it ached. I went five months. All I could think was Oh, Christ, what will I do? Then one day I went to have lunch with my other sister and suddenly felt very peculiar. I went into the bathroom and found I was pouring blood. I didn't want her to know what was going on, so I stuffed some towels in my underpants, told her I wasn't feeling well and made it home. I called my gynecologist, who came right over and drove me to the hospital.

Thank God they were still making house calls in those days and could motor around the city.

"He told me to tell the nurses I was having a miscarriage and not to discuss it any further. And he gave me a D and C. But I suffered a horrible postpartum depression that time. Right by my bed was a sign that had to do with live babies, like whether you wanted to reserve the circumcision room. Then the nurse came in and asked me whether I wanted to have a funeral. Evidently I had conceived twins again. I felt horrid. It made me realize without a doubt that I had killed something. And the nurses were so sympathetic it just made it all worse. On the one hand, I had wanted those babies because I felt sorry for my son. I don't think only children are as happy as ones with siblings, and looking back, I feel my son and I might have been happier. On the other hand, I was relieved. It was a very difficult ambivalence to come to grips with.

"There was also the consequence of abortion that I'd lost something that had been friendly and comforting to me for all those months, for at least a little while. It was a difficult time. I went on to marry the father after all, but we never could conceive any other children. The abortions may have messed up my insides. I don't know. The fact that we remained childless was disappointing, but it wasn't that bad.

"I don't think guilt kept me from getting pregnant or the feeling that I was being punished. Having left the Catholic church at the age of sixteen, I totally dispensed with even the idea of godlike punishment, and I never felt that the hand of God had anything to do with it, because I didn't honor the fact that there was a god, let alone his hand. And besides, my husband only wanted a child for prestige, to prove his worth as a male and to keep on the family name. I finally realized the marriage wasn't going to work and considered myself lucky not to have burdened myself with any more children. 'You're lucky, lady, get out,' I said to myself.

"I married again and lived for the next eighteen years on a yacht, so there was obviously no way to have a baby. My son was then fourteen years old and it would have been ridiculous. My husband and I never even discussed children.

235

"Sometimes I wonder now what it would be like now to have a set of forty-year-old twins, but the fantasies don't fill me with sadness. I have no wishful thoughts. My abortions were two difficult experiences made far more traumatic because I had to hide them. No girl should have to go through that. But then we really didn't know anything in those days. We weren't as knowledgeable about sex. Sex life just wasn't discussed. And abortion was unthinkable.

"I knew I'd been pretty foolish, but I never wept about it to myself or anybody else. It was my own damn fault. I admit, it's a tough attitude, but then I always was a tough little bird. My son has been going through family therapy now with his second wife and his stepchildren—they are all supposed to sit around and cry. I was appalled that he would do that. I couldn't. Nobody's going to make me cry. It just isn't the way I was brought up. I can remember fox hunting one day and my horse falling on top of me. Everyone was very concerned for the horse and checked him carefully. I then finished the hunt and didn't find out till later that I had fractured a vertebra in my back. But that was my attitude then and now—you just pick yourself up and get right back on the horse."

It has been fifty years since Virginia Martin had an abortion. Twenty-three at the time and an editor on a fashion magazine, Virginia had been married for three years to a theatrical producer, but they had never made love. A chance meeting with a Hungarian diplomat ended up with Virginia pregnant and searching for an abortionist. It took her six months to find one. Haunted by dreams of a giant fetus afterwards, Virginia annulled her marriage and ran around New York, going to bed with many men. Married and divorced again twice, Virginia has become a spokesperson for abortion. Now seventy-three, Virginia is a journalist and lives alone in Boston.

"It was during the Depression, when I was in my late twenties and early thirties that I was an editor. I was very much the girl about town and had a great deal of attention. I was delighted by men. I was married at the time, but it was a child's marriage. We were enormously fond of each other, but certain things didn't work. There was something wrong between his organ and mine. Mine just wouldn't take his without the greatest pain. And we were so young, only twenty and twenty-two at the time.

"I went to a party and met a stranger, a Hungarian diplomat who got a fix on me. He invited me up to his flat for a chat, but I knew it was wrong. I'd been brought up in the European sense, and my parents had always told me that men just wanted one thing. But how was I to know?

"In his hotel room, it became obvious he wanted to do more than chat. He was using no protection at the time, and I knew nothing about birth control. I did demur a little, but he was already on top of me and calmed me down by saying, 'I'm known for my great facility for pulling out just before I come,' so I said, 'Okay, let's go.' It was very exciting. He got hot and I got hotter and his extraordinary facility for getting out in time foundered.

"I went quickly to the bathroom and sprayed myself, but I knew soon I was obviously getting pregnant. My breasts grew larger. I had no monthly. It was horridly real. I was going to have a baby by a man I hardly knew.

"My friends took me from one abortionist to the other on the West Side, but they all had the primeval smells that come from doctor's closets. And everything was dirty. I just couldn't do it.

"Finally, after months of searching, my friends took me to a place in Gramercy Park that was at least clean. There were four despondent girls lined up on one side of the room, and four men on the other side. I joined the girls' line. Everyone looked disturbed and unhappy.

"When it was finally my turn, I was taken into a room with a bed and all the necessities. I had such a combination of feelings—of fear, of wondering why I was there in the first place, and a confusion of what was happening.

"The doctor came in and put what I assumed was a great bunch of forks inside me. Then he approached me with a huge long tong that looked like a puller a butcher uses to tug a chicken leg this way or that. The nurse gave me an anesthetic and told me to count to a hundred. I counted all the way up and the last thing I remember is asking her to hold my hand. The rest I did not feel or know.

"Fortunately I didn't feel the fetus coming out. I was so dumb I didn't even realize I was six months pregnant. But when I finally came to, I asked what it was. They said it was an 8½-pound boy. It was a beautiful fetus, they said, which made me feel better.

"They put me in a room for twenty minutes or so, but then I had to leave, there was such a crowd. I was weak and trembling both physically and emotionally. I knew something wrong had been done, not surgically but emotionally. How could I have gotten myself in this situation?

"I paid them three hundred dollars in cash. Later I sent a letter to the gent who did it telling him about it, and he sent me back the money by return mail. It had never occurred to me to tell him about it before the abortion. It was all my fault. Or at least I felt it was. It had been a hot moment. He was hot. I was hot. But it was wrong, just wrong.

"I was very hardy in those days, and I was back at work in two days. I told my parents I had a slight fever which was why I had missed work.

"But I felt things shouldn't be like that. I began to have hallucinations of a huge fetus growing into a man. He might have grown into an extraordinary human being, but I wouldn't have known how to bring him up alone, and how could I have explained him to any future man. He would have had a miserable life. And besides, though his father was a very sensitive lover, he was ugly.

"Nothing about it really proves anything. After that, I took a shield with me wherever I went. My marriage was annulled, and I ran wild. I slept with everyone I wanted and who wanted me. Damn it, I loved men and loved what they did to me, except make babies.

"All I wanted to do was close the chapter. It was finally erased because I discovered I wasn't the only one who had had an abortion. I started by pointing the finger at myself, but the more I talked to friends, the more I discovered it was a common experience. Suddenly I found myself recommending the same doctor.

"I married twice again and had a boy with my last husband, whom I loved deeply. I never related this baby to the one I'd lost because I didn't want to. And I never told my husband about the other baby. He was just not the sort of man who would want to know.

"The point was I couldn't bear to have the body of someone I didn't like inside myself. In speeches now I say it's the crime of the unwanted child that counts, not the unwanted fetus. If every Right-to-Lifer kept an unwanted child for a year, then I would have respect for them. But when a child comes from nothing and goes to nowhere, that's the crime."

Sarah Atkinson, now seventy-five, was twenty years old when she married Sidney Wigglesworth, whose family owned a textile company in Massachusetts. In the first three years of their marriage, Sarah got pregnant three times and miscarried twice. When she became pregnant for the fourth time, her marriage had dissolved to the point that she was determined to have an abortion. It was 1926, and abortions were extremely difficult to come by. But Sarah persevered, then divorced Sidney and married another man with whom she was deeply in love. Again she became pregnant but miscarried. The second time she became pregnant she suffered a partial miscarriage, and doctors in New York decided to complete a therapeutic abortion. Now widowed and in poor health, Sarah lives by herself in New York.

"Two days before Sidney and I got married, he confessed to me that he was going around with a mill girl at his factory and had no intention of giving her up. I was shocked but it never occurred to me not to marry him. I was dumb, naïve—definitely not with it. And I had no one to talk to. My mother had been ill since the birth of my little sister, and no one had ever told me the facts of life. Her nurse had to explain to me what had happened to me when I first got the curse.

"So we married and went off to a fishing camp in the Maine woods for two months. In the fall, I discovered I was pregnant, but by spring I had started flowing and had a placenta previous. I went to bed for two months and at eight months pregnant delivered a perfectly beautiful boy who weighed only four pounds. He only lived twenty-four hours. The hospitals then didn't even have incubators.

239

God, how upset I was. I had sewed for him, made curtains and cushions and padding for the baby scales.

"We went back to the Maine woods again the next summer, and sure enough, I came home pregnant again. I had left college in my junior year to marry him, and by the time my class was graduating, I had been married, lost one baby, and was pregnant again. This time I went to a big specialist in Providence. I hated him. He told me I couldn't dance, couldn't ski, couldn't drive. Sidney's family sent us to Florida for the winter, where I was practically bedridden and got fatter than a pig. I had my son Alan on the first of July. And by September I was pregnant again. I miscarried again at six months. There I was at the age of twenty-three, having been pregnant three times in three years, with two dead babies and only one to show for it.

"I knew then I was never going to stand the course with this man. He'd gone to bed with me three times, and three times I'd gotten pregnant. Meanwhile he was making love to every other girl in town. A year and a half later, I was pregnant again, even though I had had such little contact with Sidney. I had a Catholic doctor, so no one would give me any birth-control devices. There was no such thing in the 1920's unless you were very wealthy and could go to Europe and have pessaries fitted.

"I was determined not to have this baby. I went home to Boston and told my mother that we had to get two doctors to sign releases saying I needed to have an abortion for my health's sake. You would have thought I'd told her that I was going to marry a big black nigger in Africa, or that I'd turned into a lesbian, though she wouldn't have known what one was.

"I also needed Sidney's signature, which of course he wouldn't give me. I'm sure his mother was influencing him not to sign, but finally he did when I was already four months gone. But I was determined to do this thing decently and respectably. I also persuaded the two most prestigious doctors in town to sign the forms by telling them I was getting a divorce from Sidney and had no intention of having another child. My father took me to the hospital, where they put me out just like a regular operation. Nobody said anything to me at all. They were all very decent. And I never asked whether it was a baby girl or boy. I just put it out of my mind. I can be very tough when I'm driven.

"His family gave him ten thousand dollars a year, and he gave me a measly three hundred a month for food, supplies, presents, nurse girls for Alan, the cook. Even in those days the money wasn't enough to live the way we were supposed to be living, and I couldn't get one more cent out of that bastard. I wasn't even allowed to call him at the mill. God, you have no idea how much I hated him. And I sure in hell was not going to have that child. I had the abortion to hurt him primarily. But I don't think it did at all. We were married in 1922 and divorced in 1929.

"Of course it's easier now. But I don't think people are much happier. I feel sorriest for the sixties kids. They honestly thought they could change things, and they couldn't. The pill and not worrying about getting pregnant has made the biggest change, and for the best. Most girls were nice girls in my day. I was a virgin when I married Sidney. If we could have had just a sexual relationship, I never would have married him. I was terrified of marriage, pregnancy, our families, and sex. We would have just had an affair, and then his true colors would have come out and I would have walked away. That's of course what I did, but I did it the wrong way.

"I got pregnant twice with my next husband. Oh, how I wanted to have his baby, but the first time I began to bleed and the doctors decided to give me a D and C. Unfortunately the doctor had been drinking the night before and his hand slipped during the operation and perforated my womb right into the intestine. They had to perform a colostomy to save me from dying from peritonitis. Just think, peritonitis at thirty-one and just married. I was in the hospital for three and a half months and had a nervous breakdown. I just couldn't stop crying. I had an open colostomy for fifteen months and then had to go back to the hospital to have it closed up.

"The last time I got pregnant was on a freighter that sailed down the East Coast through the Panama Canal to California. The doctors had sent me on the cruise to recuperate from my last ordeal. And by the time I got to California I was two and a half months pregnant. I nearly died with joy when I found out I was pregnant again. And George was just as excited. I remember his making love to me very

241

tenderly the night we found out. In the middle of the night I woke up and felt very peculiar. I turned on the light and found I was lying in a pool of blood and was hemorrhaging. The doctor carried me to the hospital, where they discovered I had a very rare condition called a split ovum, which is like having twins. What happens is you miscarry part of the split ovum and what is left usually doesn't come out right. I was in the hospital ten days and then recuperated in Palm Springs.

"To get home, George chartered a Tri-Motor Pacer, which took twenty-four hours to cross the country. The doctor in California had doctors meet the plane at every stop. When we landed in New York, I was rushed to the Harkness Pavilion, where the doctors decided to take the baby away. They kept giving me tests and the rabbits kept dying, but after dickering and bickering they decided to take it away anyway, and so they did. George said that I had almost died twice trying to have his babies and that I was far more important to him than having his baby was. So I got fitted for a diaphragm and never got pregnant again.

"Do you wonder now why I'm tired and don't want to live to be eighty-five? I'm tired, and I think I have a right to be. I hurt so much. Why can't someone discover how to cure arthritis?"

9

Abortion: Where It's Going

There is little doubt that the public has accepted the need for abortion. In the 1976 presidential campaign, for example, opinion polls showed a bare 1 percent of the public considered abortion a national election issue. Yet in spite of the accepting climate and the proliferation of abortion clinics, there are still many women in need of abortions who can't get them.

According to a report published in *Family Planning Perspectives,* a magazine put out bimonthly by Planned Parenthood, as many as 770,000 women were unable to obtain abortions in 1975. The problem lies in the clustering of abortion services; the farther a woman gets from metropolitan centers, the less likely she is to find an abortion clinic. Only 5 percent of all abortions performed in 1974 were done in small towns and rural areas. More than 50 percent were performed in eleven major metropolitan areas across the country. This concentration naturally excludes the poor, the very young, and rural residents who cannot afford to travel hundreds of miles to find abortion facilities. Local hospitals could have picked up much of the slack, but a 1976 Supreme Court decision upheld a "conscience clause," which stated that private hospitals were not compelled to offer abortion services. Only one in five public hospitals in 1975 were providing abortions, three years after the Supreme Court decision that declared restrictive state anti-abortion laws unconstitutional. Even after legalization, abortion has remained more readily available to middle-class women than to the poor, who are more apt to turn to public hospitals for all their medical needs.

The result is an ongoing practice of illegal abortions performed primarily in rural areas that do not have abortion facilities. Though the numbers of deaths from illegal abortion have fallen dramatically since 1973, the fact that there are any at all is discouraging. Again, those who suffer are the poor and older women, whose risk factor in any abortion, legal or illegal, is greatly increased. Blacks and other nonwhites also have a much higher degree of mortality from illegal abortions, more than ten times higher than the ratio for whites. Though money and travel time to existing clinics are partially responsible for the continuance of illegal abortions, ignorance is thought to be the greatest cause. "Some women simply don't know abortions are now legal," says Dr. Charles Flowers, head of obstetrics at University Hospital in Birmingham, Alabama. It is thought that women enduring illegal abortions still abound, but the exact number of such abortions will never be known. "We only catch the ones who develop complications," said a Montgomery, Alabama, obstetrician. "I'm sure there are many we never see."

In light of actions taken in the early summer of 1977 by the Supreme Court and Congress, however, it appears that poor women are going to suffer even more in the future. In a stunning reversal for the pro-choice forces, the Supreme Court in June 1977 upheld the right of individual states to deny public funding for elective abortions among the poor. As upwards of fifteen states already had laws, policies, or administrative regulations on their books to restrict their share of Medicaid payments, several, including Connecticut, Missouri, Pennsylvania, and New Jersey, moved instantly to halt any state financing of elective abortions for the poor. Already woefully inadequate in providing abortion services, public hospitals were also let off the hook in terms of having to provide abortion services, and advised they could indeed decide not to permit any elective abortions at all.

In August a further blow was dealt pro-choice advocates when the Supreme Court upheld an earlier Congressional amendment banning federal funds for abortions for the poor, except where the mother's life is at stake. And Joseph Califano, head of the Department of Health, Education and Welfare, the government agency that allocates such funds, promptly ordered the federal government's share of Medicaid abortion funds cut off. Defending the Court's—and Califano's—actions, President Carter conceded that such removal of federal funds for abortion could discriminate against the poor, but insisted that "there are many things in life that are not fair, that wealthy people can afford and poor people can't." The federal government, Mr. Carter went on, should not "take action to try to make these opportunities exactly equal, particularly where there is a moral factor involved." Morality for the poor appears to be an appropriate legislative issue, while the better-off can buy their own.

As the issue of federal funding for abortions is tacked onto the annual appropriations bill of HEW, the question comes up again every year. And even while the Supreme Court was handing down its decisions on the 1977 bill, Congress was embroiled—and dead-locked—on its abortion stand for 1978. Though the stated issue was money, the debate was personal, primarily because the fiscal facts just didn't add up. In 1975, some 300,000 women (one-third of them under nineteen) had abortions at government expense, at a cost of $50 million. Though $50 million is not a sum to be dismissed lightly, the projections for public funds being spent on those same women if they had their babies were even more staggering. In another report issued by the Department of Health, Education and Welfare last year, the agency estimated that if all the women who had utilized public funds for abortion instead carried their pregnancies to term, the ensuing cost to taxpayers for prenatal care, birth, and then public assistance would amount to $500 million annually, a tenfold increase over the cost of abortion. In terms of safety, and going to the other extreme in assuming that all these same women would seek out illegal or self-induced abortion instead, HEW projected 250 deaths and 25,000 injuries a year from such abortions. There was no question that Medicaid funds could be used to clean up after such botched illegal abortions. The no-no was to pay for safe legal abortions in the first place.

The repercussions were immediate. According to the Morbidity and Mortality Weekly Report issued by the Center of Disease Control, five women with septic conditions following illegal abortions were admitted to a South Texas hospital in the two months following the cut-off of federal Medicaid abortion funds. One, a twenty-seven-year-old woman of Hispanic descent, died on September 27, 1977. The women had approached her doctor twice complaining of pain linked to pregnancy, and when he advised her that Medicaid no longer paid for abortions, she went to Mexico for an abortion instead. On September 26, she was hospitalized with a temperature of 101.8, blood pressure of 110/80 and a pulse of 110. "Her uterus was markedly tender," the report states dispassionately, "and was not easily examined because of abdominal guarding." On September 27, the young woman underwent a hysterectomy "to remove the focus of infection." Her condition continued to deteriorate, however, and on October 3, she died. In a editorial note, the weekely report states that this was the first confirmed illegal-abortion–related death since funds were cut off, but that the Center of Disease Control had launched a study of other possible illegal abortion deaths in the states that had withdrawn their abortion funds as well as in those which were continuing them.

As of this writing (November 1977) Congress is still hopelessly deadlocked in its stand on funding abortions for the poor, though there is little doubt that such funds will continue to be cut off. The squabble is now merely contained in what few instances the government will pay for abortions. The Hyde Amendment (proposed by Representative Henry J. Hyde, Republican of Illinois) passed the House of Representatives in June 1977; it curtails all Medicaid funds for elective abortions sought by poverty-level women regardless of their health or safety. The all-male Senate showed more conscience two weeks later: though it passed the anti-Medicaid abortion bill, it excepted cases where the pregnancy was caused by rape or incest. In a last-ditch stand, Edward W. Brooke, Republican of Massachusetts, managed to add his amendment to the Senate bill. It included the term "medically necessary" and would permit abortions for psychological as well as physical reasons. The House rejected it as not strict enough. Five months later, Congress was no closer to agreement on the language of abortion, and the Senate-House conferees were considering giving up and letting a new group try to work it out. Equally polarized by the question of abortion, the study group appointed by the Carter administration to investigate alternatives to abortion was

246

disbanded by its chief in November 1977. Abortion is "an option, uniquely, which is exercised between conception and live birth," wrote Connie Downey, chief of the U.S. Abortion Panel, in an intergovernmental report. "As such, the literal alternatives to it are suicide, motherhood, and, some would add, madness."

Politically then, abortion remains an insoluble problem, with compromises from either side being totally unacceptable to the other. In the all-or-nothing atmosphere that has always surrounded the politics and rhetoric of abortion, both sides continue to feel they have lost. The anti-abortion forces want just that: no abortions for anyone, anytime, anywhere. The pro-choice camp is just as adamant, supporting abortion on demand for anyone, regardless of age or financial position. Far from being settled, the abortion issue just won't go away. While the access of poor women to elective abortion has been jeopardized for the time being, court cases, Capitol Hill debates, and zealots on both sides continue to treat a woman's reproductive life as a political football.

Free abortions for the poor is not the only issue under attack; also being threatened are abortions for every woman. The anti-abortion camp is very adept at practicing legislative harassment, sometimes taking it to the level of the absurd.

On state levels, anti-abortion groups are continually proposing riders on bills, such as the requirement that death certificates be issued for aborted fetuses, or that the aborted fetus be buried. There are also bills being introduced in their own right, such as a consent requirement between the patient and the clinic that includes the clinic's obligation to show the woman pictures of the stages of fetal development.

In more subtle ways, anti-abortion groups have succeeded in having their beliefs written into legislation that just peripherally touches on abortion. In California's recent "right to die" statute, which allows terminally ill patients to refuse extraordinary measures to prolong their lives, anti-abortion protagonists managed to have a clause inserted which negated that right to pregnant women. Even such institutions as the March of Dimes have come under their attack. The National Right to Life Committee decided last year to boycott the March of Dimes because it endorses amniocentesis, and

247

thereby possible abortion of handicapped or damaged fetuses.

Impossible and improbable regulations concerning abortion clinics are proposed constantly, such as extra doctors on call at all times, including a pediatrician in second-trimester abortion procedures. In California, the Health Department proposed a regulation that called for an increase in the size of the sink drains. When asked why such an expense should be incurred by the clinics, the reply was, so that the aborted fetuses wouldn't stop up the drains. The clinic personnel had to explain the obvious—that the fetal tissue was not flushed away, but sent to a laboratory for analysis.

There has also been a movement to change the Constitution itself. By the summer of 1977, there were thirty-six bills before Congress that would either reword the Constitution to guarantee the right to life of every human being from the moment of fertilization or return to the states the authority to regulate abortion. Other anti-abortion protagonists prefer to go beyond a constitutional amendment to the rewriting of the entire Constitution. To date, nine states have passed a resolution calling for a constitutional convention which could, if twenty-five more states pass it, convene the first group of constitutional conventioneers since the U.S. Constitution was adopted in 1787. Such a resolution has also been introduced in thirteen other states, and pledges to introduce it have been made in eleven more. A highly controversial subject, the "Con-Con" resolution would put the Constitution itself into the hands of as-yet-unknown authors who would presumably add that all-important phrase—"from the moment of fertilization." "Do we feel threatened? We feel very threatened, especially when we realize how much money is on the other side," says Deborah Jacobs, at the National Abortion Rights Action League (NARAL) in Washington, D.C. "One group—the National Committee for a Human-Life Amendment—raised over $900,000 in fourteen months. Different states pass different bizarre laws every week, and we go crazy trying to keep track of all of them."

The anti-abortion movement hasn't missed a beat on the street, either. The annual Right to Life march in Washington, D.C., on the anniversary of the Supreme Court decision drew some 35,000 marchers in 1977, and sporadic vigilante raids on abortion facilities around the country continue. In a recent rally in Georgia, a small community hospital that was just about to offer the first second-trimester abortion services in the state was panicked into withdrawing its plans after an impassioned rally staged by members of the Right to Life movement and local residents. Free-standing clinics are also frequent targets of anti-abortion proponents. At the National Right to Life convention in 1976, detailed minute-by-minute orders on the take-over of a specific abortion clinic were distributed on mimeographed sheets. Participants were advised to meet at the clinic at 8:00 A.M. and to park on side streets so that the staffs of the clinic would not be alerted by an overfull parking lot. Women participating in the sit-in were instructed to meet on a street corner next to the clinic, while husbands and boyfriends who would picket during the demonstration were to meet in the parking lot next to the toy store across the street.

The detail of the attack continued to the finest point. The entrance to the rooms where the abortions are performed were to be blocked by the Right-to-Lifers' bodies. If the clinic staff caught on quickly and locked the doors before all the demonstrators could get inside, the late-comers were instructed to sit outside the elevators to block them. On the assumption that the clinic would call the police, the instruction sheet went on to point out that the press would, it was hoped, arrive at the same time, so the takeover would get the best possible media coverage. Meanwhile, the demonstrators were supposed to continue singing the songs on the work sheet ("You've Got Her Whole Life in Your Hands" and "Where Have All the Children Gone"), and if the police decided to carry off the demonstrators, "those who remain will have been shown how to lay down in a relaxing position with muscles at ease in anticipation of being carried out." Nothing was left to chance. One instruction on the three single-spaced pages was all in capital letters: "USE THE TOILET BE-FORE YOU COME."

Attacks on abortion are still highly centered in the Catholic church. On New Year's Day in 1977, Pope Paul VI not only called abortion a threat to world peace but branded women who have abortions killers who "freely and consciously murder the fruit of their womb," and in August of the same year, the National Conference of Catholic Bishops announced a new offensive to ban all abor-

tions and family-planning programs. Although a poll conducted by
American Catholic bishops found that 90 percent of the people
questioned favored abortion at least under some circumstances, the
Catholic hierarchy remains rigid in its stance. Many Catholics, however, tend to feel that their reproductive organs belong more to
themselves than to the church, a decision that often brings with it
an overload of guilt. For example, some Catholic women who have
undergone abortions ask to have the fetuses baptized. Others who are
regular churchgoers choose not to confess the fact that they've had
an abortion, either out of shame or out of anger that the church
considers it a sin.

There is a growing movement within the church, however, to resist
the dictates of the hierarchy. Groups like Catholics for a Free Choice
and Catholic Alternatives have become actively involved in counseling Catholic women who are troubled by both reaching the decision
to abort and dealing with the guilt afterwards. Contrary to church
dogma, various groups are also leading teenage discussion groups on
sexuality and distributing birth-control devices. "The issue of abortion is going to force the Catholic church to capitulate on religious
liberty and will eventually be the legitimation of the church in the
United States," says Joe O'Rourke, a former Jesuit priest and a
Catholic activist. "Right now, the only hold-outs are the bishops.
Ninety percent of the Catholics in the pews are not against abortion.
The key problem is much deeper, which is why the bishops are
fighting so hard. At issue is the maintenance of their authority:
abortion, celibacy, and women as priests. The bishops are paid to
take care of the crotches for the rest of society."

One "pew" Catholic turned her abortion experience around to
start a one-woman campaign within the church. Ten years ago the
woman, who is a lawyer, had an abortion and subsequently confessed
it to her priest. He reacted by excommunicating her, and for five
years she was consumed by guilt. Then one morning she woke up and
decided that she was right and the church was wrong. Immediately
she began to make the round of confessional booths, confessing her
abortion to priest after priest, then telling them many good Catholics
have abortions in good faith and should not be driven from the
church as a result. "She is not alone," says O'Rourke. "Abortion is

returning Catholics to their own church. They get concerned, rebel, and then turn back toward the church rather than away from it. As a result, the priests are easing up like mad. It goes straight up the hierarchy to just below the bishops, where it stops dead. There isn't much talk about it, however, because the new attitude is still useless politically."

In the clinics, the reaction to the boom in abortions is taking different directions. Members of the Feminist Women's Health Center in Los Angeles, for example, are concerned that some women who choose to remain child-free, whether by use of birth control or by abortion, are depriving themselves of part of their experience as women. Political, societal, and economic pressures, these feminists believe, are working on women, especially poor women, to make them decide against ever having children. There are as-yet-unknown ramifications to this childless course many women are taking. "It's not at the time of making the decision not to have children that it's hard," says Carol Downer, a director of the health center. "It's the total effect, the years of not having a child, not just this time. I've heard women say, 'Now let's see, my child would have been three now,' and they keep thinking about this potential child that doesn't exist. And every year the child gets older it's another year the woman didn't have it. If the societal disapproval of women who have babies in spite of their family and economic situations doesn't let up, then there's going to be a lot of bitterness."

Downer and her group are considering setting up birth clinics, in addition to their regular clinics, to support women who choose to continue their pregnancies. They also plan to work on public attitudes toward single parenting and to lobby for day care and increased federal aid for children, which would raise the standard of living above the poverty level. "Having children is a tremendous experience," Downer continues. "There is an association with true innocence. And there is the role of yourself as being a pretty nice person. If a child has survived for six months, you know that woman has gotten up in the night when she didn't feel like it. She has had to break out of that selfish thing that all of us are in. That means a lot to her character." Downer admits that her views are not popular with other feminists and indeed were received very negatively at a feminist health conference. But she has persisted. "All of us are so used to the line from the pro-natalist people that they don't care anything about the feminine experience and just want to control our behavior, that we've kind of thrown out the baby with the bath water. Women ought to be able to have that baby if they want to have a baby. There are some of us who are looking around now that we have abortion and for the most part it has ceased to be a problem and asking instead—what are our real problems?"

Other clinics are trying to slow down the rush to abortion. Instead of offering pregnancy testing and abortion all in the same day, certain clinics are suggesting the women wait for anywhere from two days to a week after their pregnancy tests before they come in for an abortion. The passage of time, the clinics think, will give the woman more opportunity to reach a firm decision about her pregnancy, and more importantly, to make the decision outside the atmosphere of the clinic. "Women seem sort of pressed in the abortion facilities to decide for abortion on the spot," says Frances Kissling, director of the National Abortion Council, who is in favor of the time lapse. "When some facilities reported that there seemed to be a post-abortion syndrome of regret or guilt, they reassessed what they were doing and put in a certain interval of time. This is a new field, so there is a constant learning process going on."

New directions in counseling are also being studied. At Yale, Michael Bracken has developed a model counseling program in which the counselor puts hard questions to the woman, such as working through all the alternatives to pregnancy including adoption, looking in depth into the meaning of having an abortion and the meaning of having a baby—questions that are more apt to raise anxiety in the woman than to lower it. "This technique raises stress in making the decision, but we argue that it forms an emotional inoculation," says Bracken. "By making the decision a little more stressful you're preventing a great deal of more serious distress in making the wrong decision. We force them to think through the issues. I think it will move people around so that some women who previously might have aborted will deliver, and some women who previously might have delivered will abort. This is the kind of counseling we want, to challenge women to think more about what they

252

are doing. It's stressful rather than supportive counseling."

Bracken's theory of decision counseling, as he calls it, is bound to raise all sorts of hackles on counselors who still see their roles as protecting and soothing their patients rather than challenging them, but Bracken bases his theory on his work in pregnancy rather than just on abortion. "It's the first model for women who are pregnant. That's the point," says Bracken. "In a study we did for the Kennedy Foundation, which compared a group of women who were preparing to deliver with a group of women who were preparing to abort, we found the decision-making was lousy—on both sides."

In the darker moments at abortion clinics around the country, there are some counselors who think their counseling has very little, if any, effect. In Atlanta, one counselor shook her head in frustration at the end of the day. "I'm not sure counseling helps at all," she said. "It's all just part of the procedure that the women have to go through. They say what they think the counselor wants to hear just to get on with the routine. And if they have regrets or guilt later, how do you catch them?" In Ohio, another counselor also voiced her uncertainty. "Abortion is very emotional for everyone," she said. "The women think, Let's just get it over with fast. They don't open up in counseling like they should, because obviously they wouldn't be in the clinic for an abortion if they hadn't made up their minds before they got here. They don't want to open up their decision-making again just before the fact. So the trouble doesn't come out till afterwards and they just keep it all in. Post-abortion counseling doesn't do any good either, because if the woman has any regrets, admitting it will feed her guilt feelings even more, and that doesn't serve anyone. Abortion is an age-old problem. Legality puts the decision right back on your own shoulders. And many women can't handle it."

To others, it seems pointless to ask questions at all, even to sociologists and theoreticians who are trying to compile statistics and trends. Many women who have had more than one abortion don't admit it, for example, and make sure their abortions are performed at different clinics or under different names. Moral attitudes toward abortion are also difficult to tabulate. "Attitudes and behavior often conflict," says Jerry Cahn, senior program research analyst at

Planned Parenthood in New York. "Twice I've seen women wearing Right to Life buttons having abortions. They can talk until they are blue in the face about how they'll never have one and that others should never have one, but when I've asked them how they are dealing with the fact that they're having an abortion, their answers are very simple: 'I can't afford to have a kid now.' "

Teenagers are difficult to pin down on their feelings about the morality of abortion. "If anything we have underestimated the ability of the young person, who knows exactly what it is that everybody wants to hear," Cahn continues. "Teenagers are short-term thinkers, so all they can really do is pronounce a lot of societal values that have nothing to do with their own concepts. That really says a) let's stop our study of teenagers, and b) we are co-opting young people's intelligence and creative capacity at a super-young age."

The conflicts and doubts that exist within the professionals of the abortion world are multiplied a thousandfold in the women who sit in the waiting rooms of the abortion clinics, shredding Kleenexes or chain-smoking while their pregnancy tests are being processed. Their minds churn with the list of advantages they foresee if the tests come back positive: "Yes, indeed, I have proved my fertility." "Now Sam [or Joe or Harry] will never leave me." "I will have a baby to love who will love me." "Now my parents will be forced to realize I am grown up." Meanwhile the negative realities are churning at the same speed: "Do I really want to drop out of school and lose a chance at the future?" "Just what about Sam [or Joe or Harry] for the rest of my life?" "How can I cope with another child when I've already got three at home?" "What if Sam [or Joe or Harry] bugs out and leaves me alone with a child; do I have the strength, the money, and the selflessness to go ahead and have this child for the rest of my life?" And some ask the question none of us can collectively answer: "Just when does life begin?"

For myself, I know the answer to that one. When I became pregnant five years ago, there was no doubt that life was right there, in my womb. Left undisturbed, that blob of cells would have grown into a baby. The process was beginning, and I chose to end it. Making a mental list of the pros and cons of continuing my pregnancy was easy; the cons far outweighed the pros. But I was totally unprepared for my mounting ambivalence as the time for the abortion came closer, an ambivalence that turned into grief and guilt for a period after the abortion was over. The little ghost haunted me for about six months before it disappeared, and after it was gone, I even missed it a bit. But as my children grow and take up more and more of my time and energy, I am increasingly sure that the addition of another child for me would have been negative rather than positive. Though the abortion and what it eventually made my husband and me see about where our lives were going drove our marriage almost to the breaking point, having a fourth child would most certainly have driven me, if not our marriage, past that point.

I wonder what would have made the abortion easier for me to handle. I already had a week's time lapse between the confirmation of my pregnancy and the abortion itself, so the additional time put more stress on me rather than less. In terms of counseling before the abortion, the process I went through was merely a matter of having the procedure explained to me and being told about different sorts of birth control. When the counselor asked my group if any of us had any problems we wanted to discuss, every head shook no. Had she persisted, I most certainly would have broken down and fled the clinic. And that would have been the wrong decision. What if my husband and I had been counseled together and had gone through the abortion together? I don't think we would have. His grief, though unspoken at the time, was so extreme—much more so than mine—that it would have come out during counseling. I would probably have weighed his against mine and opted to continue the pregnancy. And that still would have been the wrong decision.

There are no neat answers to the question of abortion, and perhaps there never will be. Men and women will continue to seek out the sexual side of love, to share in intimacy and comfort, regardless of the consequences. While birth control has drastically shifted the odds in the prevention of unwanted pregnancies, accidents will happen. One out of every three married couples practicing birth control over a five-year period have unwanted pregnancies, for example. But the brunt of the accident always falls on the woman. The overemotional debate about abortion is blown way out of proportion in people's minds—and in the policy-making bodies of this country.

255

The proper debate should concern support systems for the caring and raising of the children we have, and should perhaps result in making it more possible for women who honestly wish to continue their pregnancies to be able to do so. Conception takes place in a second. Pregnancy takes nine months to complete. Child-rearing takes the rest of a woman's life.

It is a matter of biological fate that it is the woman's body that conceives, her body that undergoes great physical and emotional stress during pregnancy, and her societal role to continue the nurturing after birth. It is women who suffer from nausea, fatigue, and fluid retention during pregnancy, and from anemia that can become so severe that some women have to have transfusions. It is women behind the wheels of nursery school car pools, women whose legs children cling to in the welfare offices, women who sit for hours in pediatric clinics around the country, waiting for their children's names to be called.

And it is women who shoulder the blame when it all goes wrong. Working mothers are fingered as one of the reasons for the dissolution of the American family, when, for the great majority, these women are not only supplementing the family income but in many cases being the sole support. But the rise in teenage sexuality, venereal disease, and pregnancy is blamed on just such women; instead of fighting back, most women accept that blame. Even unwanted pregnancies are blamed on the women. "She" is always the one who was not using birth control, or whose body couldn't tolerate the pill or the IUD, or whose diaphragm ripped or was dislodged. And it is she who endures the punishment of shared sex by either bearing an unwanted child or seeking out abortion. Pregnancy, be it wanted or unwanted, is always "her" problem.

There is, of course, no alternative to the physiological differences between men and women, and who would want it? The joys of a wanted pregnancy and child are multifold and satisfying beyond all other experiences in our life. The shock of an unwanted pregnancy and all that it forbodes provokes an emotion equally extreme on the other side. The words "You're pregnant" can never be received with indifference. With those words, regardless of whether they provoke happiness or despair, a woman becomes instantly isolated in her individuality, in her health, in her present, and in her future. Her life is forever altered.

Who is to say what she should or should not do? Each of us, having heard those words, has to make her decision and then act on it with the best of whatever faith she can conjure up. Abortion, be it legal or illegal, paid for or not, is here to stay. It is not up to men to tell women what to do under these circumstances. Nor is it up to women to tell each other what to do. Solving the dilemma of an unwanted pregnancy is probably the single most important decision an individual will ever have to make.

And regardless of whether she chooses to continue her pregnancy or to terminate it through abortion, it is her decision alone. So it falls to all of us to support that decision with grace, safety, and understanding—and to live with it, and each other, as best we can.

257

Index

ABOUT THE AUTHOR

LINDA BIRD FRANCKE was born in 1939 in New York City. She attended the Spence School and Miss Porter's and was graduated from Bradford Junior College, Bradford, Massachusetts, in 1958. An advertising copywriter from 1960–1967, first at Young and Rubicam, Inc., and then at Ogilvy and Mather, Inc., she was the recipient of a Cannes Film Festival award in 1969 for a commercial she created. In 1968 she became a contributing editor to *New York* magazine. During the next four years she wrote free-lance pieces for *McCall's, Ms., Harper's Bazaar, The New York Times* and *Institutional Investor*. Her work has been included in several anthologies, including *New York Spy* (1967), *Running Against the Machine* (1969), and *The Power Game* (1970). In 1972 she joined *Newsweek,* where she became a general editor in the Life/Style department. Four years later she left to write this book. At present she is living in Sagaponack, New York, with her three children and is at work on her second book, which is about fathers and daughters.